Myths & Hitches

1

MISCONCEPTIONS, FALLACIES & FALSE BELIEFS

about

Kings, Emperors & Dictators
Founding Fathers
US Presidents & British PMs
Queens, Grand Dames & Heroines
Explorers, Discoverers & Pioneers

Don M. Ferry

DEDICATION

To my wife Olivia, our children Gia, Rica, Dondi, Bill and Manley, and all our grandchildren, and to those friends and associates who have supported us in this endeavor.

ACKNOWLEDGMENT

The author is highly indebted to his wife Olivia A. Ferry for editing portions of this work, and to his son Dondi A. Ferry for his contributions to the cover design of the book.

TABLE OF CONTENTS

4

PREFACE

This is the first volume in the series entitled *Myths & Hitches*, a comprehensive collection of misconceptions and fallacies culled from popular lore. Arrayed in its pages are more than 300 items of information in several genres, from *kings, emperors and dictators* to *founding fathers, American presidents and British prime ministers*, and from *queens, grand dames and heroines* to *explorers, discoverers and pioneers*. What they convey may seem ordinary, but only in the sense that most everything in this world is ordinary. In fact, they are a cut above common trivia, owing to a feature that makes them uniquely engaging: each is a pseudo-fact, a lie dressed up as a truth (or vice versa), a belief that's flawed to the gills. People love trivia because they entertain, and trivia debunked can do no less—like a pratfall, which signifies nothing except that it's amusing. A pratfall deflates the pompousness of human behavior, while a fallacy exposed deflates the pomposity of human knowledge.

Many profess to debunk for a higher purpose: to enhance education and promote general literacy by eliminating errors and fallacies from the vast reservoir of popular information. It's an ideal, of course, but in raising the bar, it turns what should be a fun-filled exercise into something truly demanding and, at times, hardly feasible. Very often, the lie to be excised may have already become entrenched as myth, a myth even more wholesome and beguiling than the truth. What, for instance, would the historian achieve by embarrassing Shakespeare in his grave with the finding that Cleopatra's death was not caused by the bite of an asp? Would literature be any poorer if Alexander Dumas' *The Man in the Iron Mask* were renamed *The Man in the Black Velvet Mask* to honor a small detail in the novel's underlying real-life story? And to what extent would Spain's Catholic history be tarnished by the knowledge that her national hero El Cid bore an Arabic nickname and for a whole decade actually fought on the side of the Moors?

We share in the ideal, too, but only where, by exposing the untruth, we are able to ferret out the corresponding truth. When we fail, as we often do, we can only take comfort in Von Goethe's words: "It is easier to perceive error than to find truth, for the former lies on the surface and is easily seen, while the latter lies in the depth, where few are willing to search for it." Sadly, even the few who do decide to search 'in the depth' find out soon enough that truth has many faces, that "what is true by lamplight is not always true by sunlight." For truth may vary as to place: the ancient Roman writer Suetonius often failed to agree with his Greek counterpart Plutarch on significant details, making the study of Greco-Roman history thoroughly confusing to one who is not a pupil of either. Truth may also vary as to time, a phenomenon that that archetype of reference books, the Encyclopedia Britannica, makes evident whenever it launches a new edition to update or revise an earlier one. In a sense, the 'untruths' presented in this book are just versions of the truth, which means that, unless we are sure of our grounds, we should not impose the ideal by banishing them from popular lore as falsehoods.

Still, while we aim primarily to entertain, we hope to leave the message that the inability or difficulty of finding the truth is no license to falsify it. Information, essential or not, deserves to be reported accurately or not at all, and the historian, journalist, screenwriter, artist and blogger who care enough for what they do must keep that trust. The way information is handled in a society impacts ultimately on that society's respect for truth as a value on which all other values must rest.

Don M. Ferry

N.B.: The above has been lifted essentially from the preface of a similarly themed book, *Untruths and Nothing But* (Infinity Publishing, 2009), by the author. The contents of that book have been greatly expanded, reorganized and carried over into this volume of *Myths & Hitches* as well as into three other volumes of the series (*Myths & Hitches 1, 3* and *4)*, all available in eBook format. Please refer to the end of each volume for a detailed list of the topics covered. —DMF

Kings,
Emperors
&
Dictators

I

Roman Scandals

On Nero and the Roman Empire

"Do I live for the people, or do the
people live for me?"

•

Nero

1. Persecution Complex

Myth! Nero was the first and the worst Roman persecutor of Christians.

Movies and textbooks conspire to portray Nero as the first and the worst persecutor of Christians. The earliest sources of this satirized image of the emperor are the apocryphal and inaccurate reports made many centuries after the fact by the ancient historians Tacitus, Suetonius and Cassius Dio.

Nero may have been one in a long line of Roman oppressors that drove early Christianity to near extinction, but he was definitely not the first and the worst. Some decades before Nero, there was Saul of Tarsus, a Roman citizen of Jewish descent, who acquired a reputation for his relentless pursuit and imprisonment of early Christian worshipers in 33-34 AD. Saul would later convert to Christianity, and as the apostle St. Paul would become, through missionary work, a veritable founding father of the religion. In any case, when Nero came into power in 54 AD, the Christians in Rome were still too few to arouse attention, much less genocidal intentions on the part of anyone. St. Paul had just arrived in the city, and full-scale proselytizing for his cause would not start until after Nero's dethronement fourteen years later. Modern historians believe that, before his final decline into corruption and unmitigated violence, the tyrant had been a benign ruler, attuned with the masses and with the knowledge that he would not benefit from wiping out a fledgling religion. Accounts that accuse him of executing St. Paul and St. Peter fed on mere rumors or on each other, and only gained ground more than three hundred years after traces of Nero's influence had disappeared.

What may well be the worst persecution of Christians by the Romans occurred just before the Empire faded away in the early fourth century. With Nero dead and a mere 100 years before Constantine I became the first Christian emperor of Rome, the Augustus Diocletian destroyed churches and books and tortured and executed the clergy and the faithful. Diocletian, one of the few emperors who actually ruled well, was not motivated by prejudice but by a strong sense of duty to preserve the unity of the state. Unfortunately, his action was abetted by the undue prodding of the

9

Caesar Galerius, a fanatical follower of conservative Roman paganism.

Fortunately, though, much of Diocletian's depredations occurred far from Rome—in the eastern part of the Empire, particularly Egypt, Palestine and the Danubian regions. Ironically, too, the persecutions strengthened the church by causing the faith of the martyrs to blaze forth in the face of the threat of annihilation to their religion.

2. Days of the Living Dead

Myth! To escape persecution by Nero's men, Christians and their families dug catacombs and hid in them.

Catacombs predated the Christians and the Romans, and could be found all over the Mediterranean world as well as in Egypt, Syria and Tunisia. The famous ones at Rome, discovered in 1578, represent the early Christian type and account for the coinage of the word 'catacomb'.

It is not true, nevertheless, that there were these underground vaults in Rome at the time of Nero, or that Christians used them during the age of persecution primarily as hiding places. The Christians began the Roman diggings only in AD 100, which was several decades after Nero, and their purpose was not to conceal living or dead persons but for burial utilizing economy of space and expense. Workmen excavated long subterranean passages at various levels and the dead were laid in superimposed crypts along the sides of these galleries. The only features to suggest that the catacombs might also have been employed as safe shelter for religious fugitives and refugees are the devious passages that characterize some of them. But these were apparently only incidental, as the real objective was to accommodate the unique burial practices of the early Christians following Syrian and Etruscan traditions.

Those who believe the catacombs were devoted to a clandestine use maintain it was the Christian asylum seekers who did the frescoes, relief and other art works that flourished in these places. Actually, professional artists were commissioned for the task and the results were deliberately kept near the tombs or on the walls as part of the homage to the dead.

---

3. Beastly Behavior

Myth! Nero built amphitheaters to host the spectacles of Christians being sacrificed to wild beasts or pitted against trained Roman gladiators.

It was reported that 5,000 men, women and children suspected of professing the Christian faith were sacrificed over one 30-day period alone. But modern researchers say ancient historians were prone to either exaggerate or invent, and in the case of the much-vilified Nero, they invented.

Nero's atrocious treatment of Christians appears far-fetched in light of the finding that the emperor was allergic to the spectacle of violent death and had little tolerance for bloody sports. He built a wooden amphitheater in A.D. 57, but he also ruled that no gladiators, not even condemned criminals, were to be killed in any of the games presented there. The events were initially fencing matches that were hardly fatal, and it was only later that Nero would bow to public preference for the competitions to be fought to the death. Nero was basically against capital punishment as well as the unjust treatment of slaves, and even when nearing the end of his reign, he was generally lenient to his enemies, pardoning many plotters against his rule.

There was never any ancient Roman spectacle of Christians being devoured by lions at the time of Nero or of any other emperor. Roman amphitheaters—including the Colosseum, which became operative only twelve years after Nero's death—were devoted mainly to contests, oftentimes between gladiators or between gladiators and beasts. While Christians and Jews could have been tortured in these places when they were not otherwise used for sports, it was probably not by putting them without any means of defense at the mercy of wild animals.

A Hollywood misconception (evident in the 2000 Oscar winner *Gladiator*) matches hapless Christians and slaves against Roman warriors in gladiator fights at the Colosseum, but in reality this was also uncommon. Gladiator fights used to be held at Roman

11

funerals to commemorate the dead, and rarely on a broad scale until the first century BC, when they would be staged at various holiday celebrations using mostly prisoners of war, convicted criminals, and volunteers who wanted the prestige. Later, the events would achieve unprecedented popularity as a form of public entertainment and, necessarily, of private enterprise. As the latter, gladiator sports bred professional combatants, many of the superstar types, as well as a community of agents, handlers, financiers (called *lanistae*), referees, trainers and doctors. But to protect their investments if not their lives, participants rarely fought to the death, and (shades of professional wrestling!) contests were often orchestrated to spill only enough blood to appease the crowds.

The myth of Christians being martyred for the sake of sports was started by Pope Benedict XIV, who declared the Colosseum to be holy ground consecrated to the blood of Christians spilled there. Benedict's true intention was to stop the pilferage that had become rampant and was costing the great structure its fine marble seating, statues and masonry. The ploy succeeded, but so did the legend of Romans relishing the sight of Christians being murdered in the Colosseum.

4. Fiddling with Fire

Myth! During the great fire that ravaged Rome, Nero climbed to the top of a tower and played the fiddle while watching the flames.

The great fire had raged for ninety days, after which Nero expanded his palace and built his own colossal Domus Aurea on the ashes—hence, the belief that he had set the blaze because he wanted to rebuild Rome on a more magnificent scale.

The 1951 movie blockbuster *Quo Vadis* (following the cue of Cecil B. DeMille's 1932 *Sign of the Cross*) rekindles the fallacy of Nero as the fire starter obsessed with the idea of creating a new Rome. The MGM adaptation of Henryk Sienkiewicz' novel conveniently ignores even the findings of historians, such as Tacitus, who wrote that the fire in AD 61 could not have been Nero's handiwork since the emperor was then at his villa in

12

Antium 30 miles away. According to Tacitus, Nero was seen rushing back to find the city in flames, weeping at the sight, and starting to command the firemen about. After several days of the blaze, the overworked Nero retired to the roof of his pavilion to play a lute called a *fidicula* (the fiddle, with which it has been confused, would not be invented until the 16th century). Later, he opened shelters for the homeless, reduced the price of corn, and had food brought in from the provinces.

Nero may have unjustly laid the blame for the conflagration on the Christians to divert attention away from him. But because this group wanted to cleanse the city of its paganism, there is as much, if not stronger, reason for saying they had a hand in burning Rome down.

---

5. The Winter before the Fall

Myth! The great Roman Empire fell from east to west in AD 476.

One of the most advertised events in history is the fall of the Roman Empire, said to be in AD 476, or 408 years after Nero's death. But on closer analysis it wasn't really that spectacular and it didn't happen all on that date.

What fell in AD 476 was only that part of the Empire pertaining to the West. After Diocletian politically divided the dominion between East and West in 285, it had been reunified under one emperor off and on until 395, when the division became permanent with Theodosius' death. The fall of the West in 476 had no impact on the East, which continued in all its Byzantine glory. On this date, the Roman emperor may have gone for good, but definitely not the Empire.

AD 476 as a milestone in the history of the Roman Empire is not any more noteworthy than three earlier dates: (1) AD 270, which saw the temporary collapse—political, social and economic—of the Empire as the troubled rule of Claudius II ended (although it was restored with the emergence of the emperor Diocletian in 284); (2) AD 395, the year the Empire was permanently divided into West and East at the end of Theodosius' reign; and (3) AD 455, when the emperor Valentinian III died (his

13

factotum Roman general Aetius died the year before), signaling the end of imperial authority as it was known in the West. AD 455 is sometimes considered as the true date of the Fall, but like AD 476 and the rest, it merely culminated in a diminution of the Roman Empire and not in its complete disintegration.

AD 476 stands out in history books as the year the barbarian Odoacer deposed Romulus Augustulus, Rome's last emperor of the West. But its real significance lies in the fact that it marked the dividing line between the ancient and medieval periods of history.

---

6. Phantom Empire

Myth! The Holy Roman Empire was traditionally ruled from Rome as a cohesive political unit embracing most of Christian Europe.

It was the French writer Voltaire who once described the popularly vaunted successor to the Roman Empire of Nero and the Caesars as "neither holy, nor Roman, nor an empire." Its sovereign was usually the German king, whose dominion was secular and essentially limited to the German lands. It was called holy only because of its alliance with the pope, which was originally strong but soon degenerated into a long rivalry for the leadership of Christian Europe beginning in the mid-11th century.

For much of its history the Empire did not include Rome within its borders. The word Roman was a reference to the old Roman imperial title that Pope Leo III conferred for the first time in 800 on Charlemagne, king of the Franks. After the Carolingian line died out, the title was borne by successive dynasties of German kings almost continuously from the mid-10th century until its abolition at the turn of the 19th century.

As to the Empire, it may have existed once, but after the Thirty Years War devastated Germany in the period 1618-48, what remained was a loose collection of semi-independent states under the nominal authority of the emperor.

The first known use of the term 'Holy Roman Empire' was in 1254, although the terms 'holy empire' and 'Roman empire' had occurred previously. The head was sometimes called Roman Emperor, at other times *imperator augustus*, but never Holy

14

Roman Emperor. The full form was merely a convention adopted by later historians and was never officially used, whether by Charlemagne, who started it all, or by Francis II, who abandoned the office in 1806.

7. They ate Horses, didn't They?

Myth! The Romans called the formerly hostile Northern tribes barbarians because of their animal beliefs, low morals, destructive tendencies and crude behavior.

Etymologists state that even in Nero's time, the word 'barbarian' had no unsavory connotation, and merely meant anyone who wasn't Roman or had not been assimilated into Roman society.

The Romans were more advanced than the barbarians only because of an earlier head start and a stronger antecedent—Greek culture. While the barbarians were admittedly weak in art, philosophy and the sciences, the Romans probably would not have fared much better without their Greek heritage.

The Vandals, despite what their name connotes today, were not the uncouth savages who wanted to see Rome destroyed. The Goths and the Franks were able to co-exist with the Romans under Gratian and Theodosius I, and some, like the Visigoths, even agreed to help defend the empire from the Huns. The Roman army in time came to be made up mainly of barbarian forces, with a barbarian, Stilicho, as head of the armed forces of Emperor Honorius.

Except for the Huns, a small minority that proved incorrigible, the Romans had a high regard for the barbarians both before and after the fall of the Empire. In his *De Germania*, Tacitus praised the barbarians for their appreciation of personal freedom, independence of spirit and love of their land, as well as the respect they gave their women. It was only the Renaissance humanists who, shocked at the awesome beating that Greco-Roman art got from the sacking of Rome, painted all barbarians as savages. An acute artistic sense dimmed the capacity of these sophisticates for understanding that wanton destruction of property in ancient

15

times, whether by cultured forces or by lowly races, was just an ordinary act of war.

8. City on the Edge of Forever

Myth! Rome earned its nickname 'The Eternal City' for being the oldest capital city in the world.

The epithet 'The Eternal City', epitomizing the ageless splendor of Rome, encourages the thinking that it is the oldest capital city in the world. But as Rome is not even the oldest *inhabited* capital city on the planet, the theory falls flat on its face.

Rome had already been around more than 800 years when Nero rose to power. Tradition traces Rome to as far back as 753 BC, which makes it more than 2,700 years old. Still, there is Damascus, Syria, which was already flourishing a couple of thousand years before Rome was founded. Damascus is mentioned in the Old Testament in connection with Abraham (*Gen.* 14:15, 15:2), but it seems to be even older than that. The Jewish historian Josephus, relying on Hebrew lore, attributed its founding to Uz, the son of Aram and the great-grandson of Noah. Assyrians, Macedonians, Romans, Arabs, Mongols, Turks, the British, the French, and finally modern Syrians have controlled Damascus at some time or other through its long history.

But while Damascus, which was founded sometime between 3000 and 2500 BC, is the oldest inhabited capital city in the world, it is not the oldest *continuously inhabited* city in existence. That is yet another distinction for which Damascus cannot qualify in light of evidence that it has been abandoned several times in the past due to turbulence and upheavals. The oldest continuously occupied city on earth is Istanbul, Turkey, which used to be Constantinople and before that, Byzantium, founded by the Greeks in 667 BC.

The oldest capital city—without the adjectival limitations and in the sense of being the center of a wider civilized area—is several millenniums older than Damascus. It is one of the world's first true cities, which were all in the Middle East and included Ur of the Chaldees in Mesopotamia. Ur was founded approximately between 4000 BC and 3500 BC, and probably during this period

16

Thebes and Memphis, at various times the capital cities of ancient Egypt, were also established. Our honoree, the most ancient of the group, is Jericho, located fourteen miles from Jerusalem in Jordanian territory now occupied by Israel. Jericho was a Biblical city that became famous when the men of Joshua brought down its walls with God's help. Recent excavations have proved that the site, existing 825 feet below sea level, consisted of at least twenty successive layers, each indicating a different period of settlement. The earliest of these—a mound near modern Jericho called Tell es-Sultan, built on an oasis on the desert's edge—has been dated to approximately 12,000 years ago.

9. Naying in a Hoarse Voice

Myth! Caligula appointed his horse Incitatus consul and co-regent of Rome, regularly bringing the animal into his quarters to dine with him.

Most historians agree this story about one of the most hated figures in history is myth. There is no reliable evidence to support it as fact and, more importantly, the logic is suspect. They point out that no Roman politician in his right mind would have tolerated such an insult to the Roman state and government. Although Caligula might have been depraved (an accusation that was also leveled against his nephew Nero), Shenkman says several major biographies of the despot published in the last fifty years have concluded that he wasn't mad. He might also have been self-centered and arrogant, but he was "capable of rational decisions, capable of statesmanlike acts."

Many of the adverse reports about Caligula, including those on Incitatus, were provided by Suetonius, an ancient historian who was better suited to gossip writing. But it was actually later historians who gave false credence to the wonder horse, since Suetonius himself had acknowledged that the story was mere rumor. The pseudo-types among them would carry the gossip to the limits, saying that Caligula's successor Claudius continued to accord Incitatus honor by maintaining the animal in his ivory manger with a golden drinking goblet for partaking of wine.

17

"In modern times," a wit points out in reference to the popular Western star Roy Rogers, "the highest tribute an owner paid to a horse was to have it stuffed after it died."

10. Bloody Mama

Myth! Nero had his mother assassinated on learning that she was plotting against him.

Apparently, she had been more than your typical monster mom. Described by ancient and modern sources as "ruthless, ambitious, violent and domineering," Agrippina had become an Empress and the most powerful woman in the Roman Empire through incestuous dealings and murderous intrigue. Her critics claim she had her own uncle-husband, the emperor Claudius, and his son and heir Britannicus poisoned, and that Nero had every reason to feel he would be next.

That Nero had his mother killed remains no more than an assumption, however. Ancient historians notorious for their anti-Nero sentiments have thoroughly muddled up the circumstances surrounding Agrippina's death, which some insist was really suicide. Wikipedia notes that all surviving stories of Agrippina's death "contradict themselves, each other and are generally fantastical." Tacitus, Suetonius and Cassius Dio give widely differing versions of her fate, although each seems to agree that Nero deeply resented his mother for unduly interfering with his clandestine affair with a married woman named Poppaea Sabina. But modern historians, finding this motive too petty to justify murder, have posited the wholly unproven theory that what really pushed Nero to the brink was Agrippina's plot to have Gaius Rubellius Plautus, his maternal second cousin, replace him on the throne.

Obviously, in a scenario where evidence is grossly wanting and there are too many suspects that have motive, means and opportunity, the person with the most odious reputation is bound to be the fall guy.

II

Cut Out To Be Somebody

On Julius and the Caesars

"If you must break
the law, do it to seize power: in all
other cases observe it."

•

Julius Caesar

1. Unnatural Born Roman

Myth! Julius Caesar earned his name from being born by caesarean section.

The popular history of the Caesars began with Julius, which is why this character is generally regarded as the first of the line. Pliny the Elder wrote that Julius was called Caesar from being born by caesarean section, implying that no person named Caesar preceded the great Roman general. The Britannica quashes the suggestion, maintaining that the name Caesar had been in existence long before the general's birth. One of Caesar's ancestors was Lucius Julius Caesar, a one-time consul of Rome, while another, possibly an uncle, was Sextus Caesar, a consul in 91 BC. Historians more credible than Pliny say the name Julius Caesar was taken from *Julii Caesares*, the title of the *gens*, or clan, to which the dictator belonged. Gaius, his father's name, was added to distinguish Julius from certain ancestors and relations in the same *gens*. In some ancient documents our hero is called Gaius Julius rather than Julius Caesar, although his oft-used nickname is Caesar—pronounced *kaiser*, like the German title.

While this tells us the adjectival 'caesarean' more probably derives from 'Caesar' than the other way around, die-hard Pliny followers insist it is an older term that comes from *lex caesarea*, the title of an edict issued by the legendary Roman king Numa Pompilius six hundred years before Caesar. The Pompilian law directed that the belly be cut open of a woman dying during the last few weeks of pregnancy, not so much to save the child as to allow separate burial for mother and infant. In turn, *lex caesarea* may have been rooted in the Latin *caesus*, the past participle of *caedere*, to cut. The trouble with this view, however, is that Numa's edict was codified originally as the *lex regia* and did not acquire the title *lex caesarea* until well into Caesar's time. This was when every Roman quack was already calling the surgical technique a caesarean in the belief that it was the general's unprecedented mode of birth.

Actually, very little is known about the circumstances under which Caesar was brought into the world. Pliny as the first to report 'officially' on the matter apparently glossed over the fact that the first caesarean section on record was done much later than

Caesar's known birth date. Because the procedure was crude and seldom tried on living women, it is believed that, had Caesar's mother gone through the ordeal, she would not have lived as she did many more years afterwards.

2. After July Comes August

Myth! Julius Caesar lent his name to the succession of emperors that ruled Rome and the West.

'Caesar' rings most familiar when it is used as a synonym for 'despot' or 'emperor'. Which is odd, since Caesar himself was never an emperor, whether in Shakespeare's mind or in real life. He was a mere general and one of several that were kept in commission to protect Rome from the barbarians. Although he could have been emperor, he refused the crown when it was offered him and was assassinated before he could change his mind. Rome itself was not an empire, remaining formally a republic during Caesar's day and for some time after he had quit the scene.

The Roman Empire emerged only seventeen years later, when Julius' successor Octavius ascended the throne as the first Roman emperor. Octavius went on to become the greatest as well, taking the name Caesar Augustus; 'Caesar' was by virtue of his being the adopted son of Julius under the latter's will, and 'Augustus', meaning "the revered one," was the honorific the Roman Senate conferred upon him for his excellence in governance and the Roman peace he created. From then on, 'Caesar' and 'Augustus' were imperial titles offered to all succeeding Roman rulers, with a few declining the second title in the belief they would not be as deserving as the original holder. 'Caesar', a unanimous choice, became official when Diocletian ordained that it should be the title of the Emperor of the West. Russia, Germany and the Islamic world maintained the Caesarean tradition in the modern age by calling their rulers *czar* (or *tsar*), *kaiser* and *qaysar,* respectively.

21

3. Latin 101 ca 47 BC

Myth! After handily defeating his enemies at Zela, Caesar stood on a promontory and shouted, Veni, vidi, vici—"I came, I saw, I conquered."

The big-sounding four-letter words—*veni, vidi, vici*—would be bigger still if they had really been shouted by Caesar from a hill as a final flourish to his magnificent victory at Zela in northeastern Anatolia in 47 BC. This particular account of how the expression came about may be the most often told, but it is the least reliable of the four known versions of the incident.

Plutarch's version—the second—asserts that Caesar sent the words back from Zela to Rome as soon as he had put to rout the forces of Pharnaces, king of the Cimmerian Bosporus, to conclude the Pontic campaign. Yet another version—the third—was supplied by the ever helpful Suetonius, who wrote in *Lives of the Caesars* that Julius had the words inscribed in Latin for display at the victory procession held in his honor upon his return to Rome. As the campaign lasted only 5 days, Suetonius surmised: "This referred not to the events of the war…but to the speed with which it had been won."

The fourth version is Sir Thomas North's interpretation of Plutarch; it may well be the newest, yet appears to be the most credible. It states that the general wrote a letter to his friend Amicius some time after the event, and in it used only the three words *Veni, vidi, vici* to describe the 'suddenness' of his victory at Zela.

4. Caesar's Place was no Caesar's Palace

Myth! Julius Caesar invented Caesar salad and the Caesar cipher.

Julius Caesar has a supposed connection with two famous inventions, the Caesar cipher and Caesar salad, which accounts for their names. Any such connection can only be coincidental, however, since Caesar was not around when both items came into being. The first invention preceded the general while the second turned up many centuries later.

Julius Caesar would have been surprised in his grave if the famous salad had been named after him, as he never saw a serving of it in his whole life. It was Caesar (or Cesar) Cardini, a restaurateur of Tijuana, Mexico, who launched the salad in Caesar's Place, one of his restaurants in the city, in celebration of the July fourth weekend of 1924. Casually called Caesar's salad, Cardini's blend of romaine lettuce, grated cheese, croutons and anchovies, with a dressing made from olive oil, lemon juice, garlic and coddled eggs, caught on with the tourists, mostly the Hollywood crowd. It was later brought over to Romanoff's and the other great restaurants across the border to become their specialty.

Though used extensively by Caesar in both military and civilian matters, the Caesar cipher, which employs simple letter substitution, originated with the Greeks long before Caesar's time. It had first appeared in one of the earliest works on military science, *On the Defense of Fortified Places* by Aeneas the Tactician, and, as Julius Caesar himself would attest in his *Gallic Wars*, was only subsequently applied to Roman military strategy. Obviously, it came by its name because of Caesar's penchant for using it even in routine matters. According to Suetonius, the general foisted the cipher on Cicero and others, writing to them in a form in which the plaintext letters were replaced by letters standing three places further down the alphabet. To this day, any cipher alphabet consisting of a similarly transposed sequence is called a Caesar alphabet.

5. A Roman Head with no Heir?

Myth! Julius Caesar died without siring a son.

Mainstream history doesn't say much about Caesar having a son. The Britannica asserts that he only had a daughter, who, to seal a bargain her father had made, married his great rival Pompey. Finding Caesar to be one prolific sire would not at all be remarkable, however. According to the Britannica, Caesar's sexual promiscuity "was out of the ordinary, even by Greek and Roman standards...There is no doubt of Caesar's heterosexual affairs,

23

many of them with married women. Probably Caesar looked upon these as trivial recreations."

Others believe the greatness of the man may have overshadowed the fact that Caesar left sons, in fact three of them. One was illegitimate, the second adopted, and the third putative. Caesar never acknowledged the first, Caesarion, although Cleopatra was able to win Antony's support in publicly proclaiming the boy as her son by the Roman general. Octavius captured and executed Caesarion shortly after he became Ptolemy XV Caesar when Cleopatra died. Ironically, Octavius himself was Ptolemy's adoptive brother, having been made Caesar's son and sole heir and officially named Gaius Julius Caesar Augustus under the late Caesar's will.

The third son was the unlikely Brutus, one of those who spilled Caesar's blood on the senate floor. Most historians are of the opinion that assassin and victim were just good friends, some saying Brutus was a former enemy whom Caesar had pardoned and afterwards befriended. But a minority that includes Plutarch claims Brutus was really Caesar's illegitimate son by a well-born lady named Servilia, with whom he had an affair lasting some twenty years.

---

6. Triangle with an Angle

Myth! Julius Caesar was a member of the First Roman Triumvirate.

A triumvirate, generally speaking, is a trio of power holders, and in this sense calling the alliance of Julius Caesar, Pompey and Crassus in 59 BC the 'first triumvirate' may not be all that improper. The system, uniquely Roman at the time, worked similarly as the *troika*, which figured prominently in Soviet politics during the Cold War after the death of Stalin. The word 'triumvirate' is basically Latin, however, while *troika* is Russian, a reference to any vehicle drawn by three horses abreast.

Caesar was consul and *pontifex maximus*, the highest and most powerful in the Roman hierarchy. But for stability of tenure he had to rely on Crassus, who had the connections, and Pompey, who had the soldiers' vote. Caesar united these two rivals in his

24

support, voluntarily sharing powers with them and giving them political and financial concessions.

However, the three commanders were never really installed as a Triumvirate, as this term became officially understood in ancient Rome. The office of Triumvir would not be created until sixteen years after the Caesar-Pompey-Crassus alliance—in 43 BC, to be exact, when political necessity called for the institution of the first and only Triumvirate in Roman history. Octavius rallied together Mark Antony and Lepidus, both with their armies, and all three had themselves appointed to a five-year tenure as 'Triumvirs for settling the Constitution'.

After crushing Lepidus in 36 BC, Octavius rendered the title a misnomer by continuing officially as Triumvir in the West with Antony in the East. Later, the two, despite being brothers-in-law, would have a falling out over political and personal matters. Eventually, the Triumvirate disintegrated when Octavius defeated Antony in the Battle of Actium in 31 BC, leaving the former the master of Rome and future emperor.

7. Killing Time in the Capitol

Myth! Brutus stabbed Caesar, bringing him down at the base of Pompey's statue inside the Capitol.

We are told that Caesar was in the Capitol, trading political views with his lackeys (mainly on whether he should assume the emperorship that had been promised him), when some mavericks attacked and brought him down lifeless at the base of Pompey's statue. Later in a speech before an agitated crowd, Brutus admitted to the murder, but not without qualifying it as a justifiable act intended to vindicate democracy.

We can't really be certain that what Brutus confessed was the truth, given that, as an autopsy revealed, only one of Caesar's many wounds was fatal and it was probably not Brutus who inflicted the killer blow. Surviving the first wound, which was just below his throat, Caesar was able to hit back at his assailant with a stylus. The rest of the wounds were on his chest, back and arms— twenty-three thrusts all told, one of them managing to reach the

25

heart. Brutus made a weak stab, apparently more as a token of sympathy for the conspirators than as a hostile act against Caesar.

Still, whoever killed Caesar didn't do it in the Capitol, as we have been led to believe. Some accounts, including Shakespeare's fictional version, place the scene of the crime in the Senate House, which was separate from the Capitol in Roman times. But even this is only partly correct; according to historical researchers, there was no Senate House on the day of the assassination since the old one had burned down in political rioting many years before. More likely, Caesar was slain in a meeting hall—some say it was the Pompeian Assembly Room—of the Campus Martius, which the senators used for their sessions. Caesar, who was seating himself on the chair-of-state when stabbed, finally succumbed at the base of Pompey's statue—'a touch of irony dictated by history, not literature'.

8. You too, you Brute?

Myth! Caesar said, *Et tu Brute?*, on seeing Brutus about to stab him.

The phrase has been a polite way of saying "You traitor!" ever since Shakespeare reported it as the dying utterance of a half-disbelieving Caesar addressed to his old friend—and possible son—Brutus.

But some historians accuse the Bard of taking liberties with the death scene in his play *Julius Caesar* for the purpose of dramatizing the tragic ending of 'the greatest Roman of them all'. They claim Shakespeare, having no clue on what Caesar really said, felt compelled to lift the line *Et tu, Brute* from one of his other plays, *The True Tragedy of Richard Duke of York*, published four years earlier.

With no real proof of what Caesar said when he gave up the ghost, two views have emerged in addition to Shakespeare's own. According to the first, Caesar may have actually confirmed he was Brutus' father by greeting his attacker with the words *Kai su, teknon*, Greek for "You too, my son." It was well known that Caesar had a habit of speaking Greek to family members and intimates, most especially to Brutus.

26

The second view maintains that Caesar died without speaking a word, a possibility that to the cynics makes better sense. As Suetonius wrote, "Caesar did not utter a sound after Casca's blow had drawn a groan from him"—and Casca struck first, the dagger wounding his throat.

9. The Day his Number Came Up

Myth! To signal his invasion of Italy, Caesar forded a river with his troops and on the opposite bank proclaimed, "The die is now cast, I have crossed the Rubicon!"

As Caesar was fond of ceremony, it was rather typical of the man to do what tradition says he did to signal his decision to invade Italy, where Pompey and the Roman senate held sway. To this day, we consider that symbolic act a defining moment in history, one that heralded the era of the Roman Caesars and the Golden Age of Rome.

But ancient Roman historians like to have their say, too, contributing unfamiliar details that change the picture significantly. Suetonius, for one, writes that Caesar and his troops were coming up on the banks of the Rubicon when they halted to rest. Shortly afterwards, a person playing upon a pipe to the shepherds and soldiers around him snatched a trumpet from one of them, ran to the river with it, and sounding off with a piercing blast, crossed to the other side. Whereupon Cesar exclaimed: "Let us go whither the omens of the gods and the iniquity of our enemies call us. The die is now cast."

Suetonius suggests the whole thing transpired before, not after, Caesar had crossed the Rubicon. As soon as Caesar uttered the words *Alea est jacta*, Latin for "The die is now cast," he proceeded to wade across the water, an act tantamount to a declaration of war against the Roman senate and the loyalist general Pompey. Others deem the point unimportant in light of the suspicion that the reported crossing in 49 BC did not actually happen. Plutarch noted that even before his time, 'crossing the Rubicon' was a mere metaphor signifying one's decision to commit to a dangerous course from which retreat was no longer possible.

Geographers add that the Rubicon, equivalent to one of three modern watercourses—Pisciatello, Fiumicino and Uso—could not have been more than a small stream forming the boundary between Italy proper and Cisalpine Gaul, the province allotted to Julius Caesar. It would have been entirely out of character for the ambitious general to choose a mere rivulet as the center prop for his dramatic entry into Rome.

10. Guilty by Suspicion

Myth! Shakespeare's line, "Caesar's wife must be above suspicion," cautions the wife of a public official against unseemly behavior that could compromise his career.

Unaware of the works of Caesar's ancient publicists, many are quick to assume that Shakespeare scripted every wise saying attributable to Caesar in various media. In particular, users have elevated the line, "Caesar's wife must be above suspicion," almost to the level of an idiom without realizing it was the real Caesar, not Shakespeare, who made the remark to reveal his reason for divorcing his wife Pompeia. It would have been inappropriate for Shakespeare's character to utter the line because the play is set during the time when the general's wife is no longer Pompeia but Calpurnia.

However, only those publicists seem to have an inkling of Caesar's exact words, an indication that these may have been no more than part of the gossip of the times. Both Suetonius and the Greek writer Plutarch agree that they were heard at the trial of Publius Clodius, a profligate young noble who was indicted for causing a scandal in Caesar's house. Clodius had attended a celebration there of the rites, for women only, of *Bona Dea*, allegedly to conduct a love tryst with Pompeia. When asked to testify, Caesar admitted he knew nothing of the clandestine affair but had divorced Pompeia anyway because of the suspicion cast on her. According to Suetonius, Caesar said, "My family should be free not only from guilt but even from suspicion." Plutarch had it somewhat differently: "Because I (Caesar) thought that my wife should not even come under suspicion."

28

As tenuous as its roots may be, the line has given rise to the expression 'like Caesar's wife', which describes a very strict standard requiring one, particularly a public official, to be innocent in fact and even more importantly in reputation. A clear conscience is not enough to be 'above suspicion'; his character must also be unsullied by rumor, defamation or false accusation. Rather a tough order from one whose own indiscretions led to his untimely end.

11. Bang the War Drums Softly

Myth! Lambasting the warmongers in his midst, Caesar said, "Patriotism is a double-edged sword."

"Beware the leader who bangs the drums of war in order to whip the citizenry into a patriotic fervor, for patriotism is indeed a double-edged sword. It both emboldens the blood, just as it narrows the mind. And when the drums of war have reached a fever pitch and the blood boils with hate and the mind has closed, the leader will have no need in seizing the rights of the citizenry. Rather, the citizenry, infused with fear and blinded by patriotism, will offer up all of their rights unto the leader and gladly so." The general's closing words allegedly were, "How do I know? For this is what I have done. And I am Caesar"—a self-serving assertion obviously to convince that the entire quote is truly Caesar's.

But researchers can't find the original in any historical record, old or modern—and the idea that it could turn up like some artifact in an obscure cave or ruin in Pompeii would be ludicrous at this point. Others suggest it might be a reconstructive piece that Shakespeare did in his lesser moments, but there is no single clue in the Bard's history and known works that this is so.

The speech would have made better sense if it had been spoken not *by* Caesar but *to* Caesar by one of his enemies—and these include Pompeii, Crassus, Cicero, Brutus and the latter's co-conspirators, any of whom carried enough of a grudge against the warmongering despot to warrant the lofty rhetoric. Still, the text, with its modernistic idioms and untimely metaphors, would have been out of place in Caesar's biographies or in Shakespeare's writings.

The line has no known antecedents prior to September 2001, the date that al-Qaeda made famous with its shameless attacks on New York's Twin Towers. Immediately after the debacle, the words began to appear on the Internet, and a year later, or on September 29, 2002, the singer and actress Barbra Streisand repeated the line in a speech she delivered at a Democratic Congressional Campaign Committee meeting. On the same day, Paul Conrad followed suit with a political cartoon based on the quote.

Presumably both Streisand and Conrad relied on a website for their source without knowing that it was a false quote. But the hoaxer's message, which the two were evidently trying to propagate, was all too real—to warn President Bush and his Republican administration against responding prematurely to the 9/11/01 terrorist attack by entering into an armed conflict in Iraq.

---

12. Tripping in Africa

Myth! On arriving at Adrumetum to review his troops, Caesar tripped and fell, but with great presence of mind kissed the soil and exclaimed, "Thus do I take possession of thee, O Africa."

A falling bust of Caesar would have shattered helplessly with little hope of being pieced together. But the real thing was made of sterner stuff—wit, self-confidence and audacity combined.

The trouble with the story, however, is that it is also told of Scipio the Younger (185-129 BC), the Roman general who burned Carthage, as well as of Scipio the Older (237-183 BC), the general who defeated Hannibal at Zama in 202 BC. The locale occasionally shifts to Britain, where Caesar becomes William the Conqueror, who supposedly exclaimed when he fell on his face, "I have taken *seisin* (possession) of this land with both my hands."

In all versions, our protagonist puts up the pretense that the misstep is intentional to hide his embarrassment and to forestall the bad omen that it indicated.

III

Lion Heart Or Lying Heart?

On Richard I and King John

"Mine honor is my life; both
grow in one; take honor from me,
and my life is done."

•

Richard I

1. Trading Places

Myth! During the Third Crusade, Saladin was the cruel Saracen who massacred Christian settlements, and Richard was the chivalrous knight whose courage was rivaled only by his compassion for his enemies.

Western schools, abetted by Hollywood, have drawn contrasting portraits of Richard I the Lion-Heart (1157-99) and the Moslem champion Saladin. Unfortunately, the results don't equate with reality—unless one portrait is switched with the other!

Richard's popular image is a throwback from the days when troubadours touted his legendary exploits far and wide to make him their greatest hero in the age of chivalry. That has been made even bigger in adventure literature, such as Sir Walter Scott's *Ivanhoe* and *The Talisman*. Scott and other writers based the essence of Richard's character on his mythic reputation as a dashing warrior who, barely out of his teens, began leading his peripatetic army into the fiercest of battles and winning vast domains and fiefdoms in England, France and the Middle East.

What Scott apparently omitted—because history was not too frank about it—is that, while Richard was brave in battle, he was also "cruel, haughty, and vindictive," displaying this attitude to all his perceived enemies in England and abroad. To boot, he had a terrible temper that provoked rapacious behavior among his followers and major revolts in his kingdom. At his crowning, Richard, an anti-Semite, issued a public notice forbidding any Jew from attending the ceremony. When some Jews appeared anyway to present gifts to the new king, Richard's courtiers initiated a massacre that rates as one of the first holocausts on record.

Richard's dossier stands out for a singularly cruel act perpetrated during the Crusades, that of having 2,500 Moslem hostages, mostly women and children, beheaded before the walls of Acre because the leaders of the city delayed its surrender. When Saladin showed his resentment, Richard gave his sister Joan in marriage to Saladin's brother al-Adil and signed a peace treaty with him. Later, on learning that Saladin was faced with a revolt in the East, he rejected the pact and promptly took Darum, advancing to within 12 miles of Jerusalem.

Richard excelled Saladin in generalship, engineering and inspiring valor on the field, but he had none of Saladin's moderation, patience and justice. Saladin's appearance as a chivalrous warrior in Scott's *The Talisman* was not meant to be satirical, for in real life, the Moslem champion was gentle to his servants, merciful to his enemies, and faithful to his word. Historians regard as authentic the stories proving he had more Christian virtues than his Christian counterpart. In one of these accounts, the two were in the midst of battle when Saladin saw Richard unmounted and sent him a charger; and in another, Saladin learned that Richard got sick, and sent him pears and peaches and his own physician.

2. Looking for Richard

Myth! Richard was the epitome of English manhood.

Richard was essentially *not* English, and his winning the English crown against the odds only exacerbated the lie. Though his birthplace of Oxfordshire made him English under the principle of *jus soli,* he chose to grow up in Aquitaine, a part of Southern France, by his mother's side. That mother was the redoubtable Eleanor of Aquitaine (picture Katharine Hepburn in *The Lion in Winter*), who was queen of France before divorcing Louis VII and marrying Richard's father Henry II. Henry himself was not wholly English, being the son of Geoffrey of Anjou, who founded the tumultuous Plantagenet line of English kings despite being French.

Worse than his genealogy, Richard was French in heart and mind, as his loyalties or, more precisely, his disloyalties reveal. He supported Eleanor in all her quarrels with Henry, including a family revolt in 1173-74 to unseat the King, and which ended with Henry's imprisoning the recalcitrant queen for fifteen years. While he was Prince of Aquitaine (a dole from Henry), he resisted with military force efforts by Henry and his English barons to Anglicize his French dominions. In a brazen display of treason against the English throne, he swore fealty to Philip II of France in the Franco-English war of 1186-88. Finally—as the most telling of Richard's preferences for the French—he communicated almost exclusively in their language, hardly bothering to learn a word of English.

Another misconception about the Lion-Heart has to do with his sexual identity. Some say Richard's marriage with Berengaria, which was childless, was most likely not consummated because of the very little time the couple spent together. But others suggest a different reason, one "in the area of certainty rather than probability," namely, that Richard failed to reciprocate Berengaria's ample love because he was gay, or at least a bisexual who spent more time in bed with men.

Apparently, there's enough historical muck to show that Richard's imposing stature (he was well above 6 feet in height), his noble mien, his vaunted bravery and heroic feats on the battlefield, and the stories of rape and debauchery that attended his conquests, were only parts of a false front that masked his uncommon sexual preferences. According to one source, Richard confessed at a local church just weeks before his wedding that he was a homosexual, and *five years later* the king had a short one-night stand with Berengaria because this was what the confessor priest had ordered him to do as penance! His rumored lover was the French minstrel Blondel, who is credited by tradition for having discovered Richard imprisoned in a lonely castle and convincing England to ransom him. Before that, according to Boswell's translation of some passages from Roger of Hovedon, there was an affair with Philip II of France, whom Richard supported in the two-year war Philip waged against Richard's father Henry of England.

3. Mismanaging by Proxy

Myth! Prince John mismanaged the kingdom and proved disloyal to Richard during the king's long absence from England.

That the myth of the evil John lives on is evidenced by the BBC History's choice of this Plantagenet in 2006 as the 13th century's worst Briton. In reality there is probably no worse king in the history of Britain than John's own brother Richard. An absentee monarch who spent a mere six months of a ten-year reign

34

in England, all he did was bleed his country dry to pay for his military campaigns.

In contrast, John was an effective administrator, fair-minded and well informed, "often acting as judge in the Royal Courts, and his justice was much sought after." He was the foremost contributor to England's maritime power in his century, building more shipyards and harbors than any of his predecessors, making major improvements in ship design, and creating the first big transport ships, called buisses; for these accomplishments, he is credited by current historians as the founder of the modern Royal Navy. This is not to mention that the historic charter called the Magna Carta was literally signed, sealed and delivered during his tenure.

It is not entirely true that John was disloyal to Richard when he was king-in-waiting while his brother was away. During the better part of his surrogate rule, John assiduously performed all the tasks Richard delegated to him, most significantly that of raising the considerable amount needed to finance England's participation in the Crusades. Only after Richard's departure for the Holy Land, when it became known that he had designated his nephew, the young Arthur of Brittany, to be his successor, that John began to intrigue against the errant king's authority. On his return, Richard, apparently realizing he had not been fair with John (who was still rankling from the fact that their father Henry had unjustly deprived him of his share in the family's continental holdings), pardoned his brother, and they lived on not unfriendly terms for the next five years. On his deathbed Richard, reversing his previous arrangements, caused his barons and allies to swear fealty to John, although the hereditary claim of Arthur was clearly superior under the law of primogeniture.

Upon his elevation to the throne in 1199, the new king, despite the cruelties attributed to him, became an even more efficient administrator, one of the best England ever had. But this did not dissuade his nobles from rebelling against him in 1216, on which occasion he was reportedly killed. Actually, all he lost were some men and his entire royal hoard when, on the run, he crossed the River Welland and escaped barely with his life. John died a week later, the rumor being that a disgruntled monk had poisoned him. Shakespeare propagated this belief in his play *King John*, which showed a monk squeezing the poison of a toad into a cup of cider, not knowing that toads hold no venom. It wasn't until 1653, more than 400 years after John's death, that the real story came out. The physician who disemboweled the King found no evidence of poison, and ruled that he died from overeating unripe peaches and beer, which probably induced dysentery.

4. Brother John hates Brother Hood

Myth! If Richard was Robin Hood's champion, Richard's brother John was his bête noire.

Claude Rains never did a better gig than when he portrayed the slimy Prince John in *The Adventures of Robin Hood* (1938). Some say the actor wouldn't have been so inspired had he known that John as the scourge of Robin Hood was pure myth and the two were never contemporaries.

In popular culture Robin Hood is a loyal follower of Richard who is driven to outlawry by John's 'evil' reign in the 12th century after Richard leaves for the Third Crusade. As history, however, the connection between the characters gained currency only in the 16th century and has very little scholarly support. The oldest surviving ballads about Robin Hood, which are set in either the 13th or the 14th century, make no mention of either Richard or John. Conceivably, writers during the Age of Exploration, seeing some literary or cultural benefit from the contrast between Richard's 'chivalrous' exploits in foreign lands and John's reputed oppression of his brother's allies at home, used this as a backdrop for reworking the legend of Robin Hood.

5. The King had a Weak Constitution

Myth! By signing the Magna Carta, King John became the first royal to allow the democratic concept to gain a foothold in the British monarchic system.

Sir Edward Coke, claiming he found the document on an old

36

dusty library shelf, established the thinking that the Magna Carta deserves to be hailed as the 'Great Charter of English Liberty' because it gave Englishmen rights the sovereign couldn't take away. Most historians are less enthused, contending that if the Magna Carta gave anything to the people, it was something they already had. In fact, by limiting some of the already existing rights, such as trial by jury, habeas corpus and parliamentary control of taxation, to freemen, it made the public's situation worse. Considering that five-sixths of Englishmen in 1215 were serfs, it was obvious that the masses would be benefited only very gradually over the centuries.

It is not readily known that what actually initiated the idea of democratic rule in the otherwise authoritarian British setting was the earlier Charter of Liberties, which King John's grandfather, Henry I, granted to the baronage in 1100 when he ascended the throne. In the Charter, Henry proposed to have himself bound to laws that effectively ceded certain civil liberties to the church and the English nobility. What makes Henry's act truly meaningful is that it was wholly voluntary, whereas the Magna Carta, a large part of which was copied almost verbatim from the 1100 Charter, was forced on John by his barons in a brash effort to limit his powers by law and protect their privileges. The Magna Carta was the result of a compromise that the nobles wangled after entering London forcibly in June 1215 to present a set of demands in response to John's perceived failures and abuses. No wonder Shakespeare failed to mention the Magna Carta in his play *King John*. As late as the 16th century, the document for which his character is best remembered was considered "not as a triumph for liberty, but rather as a shameful attempt to weaken the central monarchy."

Historians question why the Magna Carta should be accorded so much honor when it was never really enforced as originally worded. John renounced all its provisions as soon as the barons left London, plunging England into a civil war called the First Barons' War. Pope Innocent III denounced the document and released John from his oath to obey it. After John died, the charter was reissued in emasculated form, three times during the reign of his son Henry III and the fourth and last time in 1297 under Henry III's successor Edward I. Although the Magna Carta is normally understood to refer to a single document, that of 1215, in fact it is the 1297 version that has remained extant in the statute books of

England and Wales. Today the only cognizable portions of the agreement forged in Runnymede are those dealing with the Writ of Habeas Corpus.

The manner in which King John approved the Magna Carta accounts for yet another misconception. For a long time, schoolchildren have been told that John had to affix his seal rather than his signature to the charter because he lacked the ability to read and write. Modern researchers say this textbook inaccuracy "ignored the fact that King John had a large library he treasured until the end of his life," and that "John received one of the best educations of any king of England." The misunderstanding could have been due to the practice, observed by royal and Church dignitaries during the time of the Plantagenets, of signing with crosses as illiterate people would later do; this was in compliance with the legal (and religious) norms then prevailing and not because they could not write their own names.

It is very likely, thus, that John did some signing on that fateful day of June 15, 1215, as shown in old illustrations and sometimes in non-conforming stage presentations of Shakespeare's *King John*. What he signed, of course, would not have been more than the draft of the charter that the negotiating parties hammered out in Runnymede. Although authenticated by the king's signature, this draft took legal effect and officially became the Magna Carta *only one month later,* or on July 15, 1215, when the royal chancery created the formal document recording the agreement and *affixed* the great seal of the king to an unknown number of copies for distribution to the appropriate officials.

IV

Kings' Row

On British Kings

"We are, by the sufferance of God,
King of England; and the Kings of
England in times past never had any
superior but God."

•

Henry VIII

1. Post-marital Syndrome

Myth! Henry VIII assumed the title of 'Defender of the Faith' after abandoning Catholicism and converting to the new Anglican religion that he had founded.

It wouldn't be surprising if even some of the most ardent Anglicans believed that Henry VIII founded the Anglican Church; that he did it in retaliation for the pope's refusal to grant him a divorce from Catherine of Aragon; and that he abandoned Catholicism and embraced Anglicanism before he died. This has been the popular tradition ever since Henry signed the Act of Supremacy in 1534 appointing himself as head of the Church of England.

Actually, before that redefining moment, Anglicanism was just another name for Roman Catholicism as it was practiced in England under the authority of the pope. If it had a founder, this could only have been St. Peter, the first Catholic prelate, or St. Augustine who, in the sixth century, was commissioned by Pope Gregory the Great to bring a more disciplined apostolic succession to the Celtic Christians in Britain. Thereafter, the British maintained a principal role as part of the Church laity—until Henry VIII came at odds with the pope on various issues for most of his reign, and decided it would be better for Britain to separate the Anglican arm from its Roman Catholic body. The divorce issue, as most historians note, was only one in a series of acts that collectively brought about the schism.

Many wrongly assume that, as a result, Henry VIII became the first Protestant monarch of England and the original Defender of the Faith for the Anglican Church. In fact, it was the pope who, shortly before Henry's fall from grace, bestowed the title of Defender of the Faith on the king for his utmost devotion to Roman Catholicism and its rituals. Henry stayed a Catholic to the very end, and only after his death did his successors begin using the originally Catholic title in their official capacity as defenders of the Anglican faith. Despite the reformation he began and its consequences after his rule, the Roman Catholic Church continued to play a vital part in English life and remained important to Henry, as most of his countrymen were Catholic. Henry denied the supremacy of the pope, closed the monasteries, shut down the nunneries and divorced several wives, but at the same time, he denounced Martin Luther and approved of the persecution of Protestant reformers in his book "Defence of the Seven Sacraments." In 1539 he prevailed on Parliament to pass the Act of Six Articles, which made it a crime punishable by death to deny transubstantiation, the Catholic belief that the bread and wine served at Holy Communion indicate the presence of Christ. He also insisted that Anglican priests, like their Roman Catholic counterparts, remain celibate.

The preponderance of historical documents on the matter attests to the fact that Henry never abjured Catholicism on his deathbed, as many think he did. On the throne, he consistently advocated Catholic ceremony and doctrine, and it was only after he was gone that his heirs, the devout Edward VI and the renowned Elizabeth I, vitalized the English Reformation he founded.

2. Humpty Dumpty Sat on a Throne

Myth! King Richard III was a hunchback with a withered left hand.

Most of Richard's detractors, writing under the auspices of his mortal enemies, the Tudors, pictured him as a hunchback whose left hand was withered, a depiction echoed by Shakespeare, who, writing in Tudor times, produced the play *Richard III.*

The respected Sir Thomas More saw Richard as "little of stature, ill fetured of limmes, croke backed, his left shoulder much higher than his right." But knowing that Richard died when More was only seven years old, this description is almost certainly hearsay. Lacking a categorical statement that Richard was a hunchback and cripple, it was more likely that More was referring to a slight unsymmetrical development of his shoulders, with one rising higher than the other. For no hunchback cripple could have waded into battle with as much gusto as this king, or rode a horse, swung a mace and broadsword, and generally commanded respect as he unquestionably did.

Of the many portraits of Richard III, there is only one showing the monarch with anything remotely resembling a hump. But X-

41

rays have shown that the hump had been painted on years after the original painting was completed.

3. The Spider's Stratagem

Myth! According to legend, a spider spun a web across the entrance of the cave in which the Scottish Robert the Bruce was hiding, effectively protecting him from his pursuers.

He wasn't just Robert the Bruce, for there had been seven others with that name before he came onto the scene in 1274. He was appropriately Robert I the Bruce, the 'I' signifying that he was the first of his line as king of Scotland. He grabbed the throne when the English-appointed suzerain died, and led his forces in a series of military encounters that broke the feudal hold of England.

The anomaly of Robert I the Bruce lies in his being the national hero of Scotland without having the proper pedigree for it. For his line was really French, having originated from a Norman knight probably named Robert de Bruis who landed in England with William the Conqueror. The connection with Scotland began only when the lordship of Annandale was granted to a de Bruis descendant, who died in 1141. Several generations later, the 4th lord of Annandale married a granddaughter of King David I of Scotland and sired the sixth Robert the Bruce, one of the 13 claimants to the Scottish throne in 1290-92. Robert I the Bruce, who revived the claim and became king in 1306, was the sixth Robert's grandson.

Robert I the Bruce's most famous episode in his fight for independence involves his mythical encounter with a spider. The story is strangely similar to that of Mohammed, who was fleeing from Mecca, the Koreishites close upon him, when he hid in a certain cave. Suddenly an acacia in full leaf sprang up at the mouth of the cave, a wood pigeon had its nest in the branches, and a spider wove its net between the tree and the cave. When the Koreishites saw this, they were convinced no one could have entered recently, and went on.

With Robert I the Bruce, there was no tree or bird's nest—only the spider's web—between him and his pursuers. Moreover, the crawler's objective, it appears, was not to protect the fugitive from his enemies, as it did in the case of Mohammed, but to teach him about perseverance. When Robert the Bruce saw the spider fail six times to fix its web before succeeding on the seventh try, he was so inspired that he left the island determined to win against the English. This he achieved in 1314 at the great victory of Bannockburn after numerous small successes.

Incidentally, Mohammed and Robert the Bruce are not the only heroes who, in their legends, have had to deal with a spider in order to survive their ordeal of the moment. In a modern retelling of the story, Frederick the Great was saved from being poisoned when a spider fell into his cup of chocolate and died.

4. Oxford Don Alfredo

Myth! Alfred the Great authored two monumental histories and founded England's venerable Oxford University.

Alfred may have won the war against the Danes, but his destroying the Danish fleet off Swanage has been disproved as a forgery inserted in 1600 in Asser's *Life of King Alfred*.

While celebrated for his military acumen, Alfred is better known as an educator who gathered around him learned men ('Alfred's scholars') to help promote learning in his court and among his people. Gaining fluency in Latin through self-study, he began to translate Latin books into English in 887, and he later inspired the Anglo-Saxon Chronicle, a collection of English monastic accounts from the beginning of the Christian era through 1154. But he had nothing to do with Bede's *Ecclesiastical History of the English People* and Orosius' *7 Books of Histories Against the Pagans*, two monumental books of the Middle Ages that, for one reason or other, have been credited to him without the slightest proof.

Efforts to link him to the founding of Oxford, the earliest university in England, because of his scholarly reputation pose an anachronism. Oxford started only in the 12th century, or 300 years after Alfred, when students flocked in from other schools within the precincts of the dissolved nunnery of St. Frideswide and of Oseney Abbey, and from Paris in the 1160s.

43

The anecdote about Alfred and a peasant woman's burned cakes, supposedly a real occurrence during his flight to Somerset to escape the Danes at Wessex, is not found in Asser, which is the only known biography of Alfred. Most responsible historians treat the story as pure legend.

5. These Kings' English was German

Myth! All six British kings named George were of fine British stock and lovers of things British.

None of the British kings named George had more than 25 percent British blood in him because all were basically German. The first of the lot, George Louis of Brunswick-Lüneburg, sat on the English throne as George I despite being a German prince from Hanover who could neither speak nor write English. This was not unusual, of course, since William of Orange, who ruled England jointly with his wife Mary from 1689 to 1694 and as sole sovereign from 1694 until 1702, was Dutch and knew very little English. Indeed, French was the native language of the English kings for many generations after the Norman Conquest, including Richard the Lion-Heart.

Still, George Louis hated England and its people so much that he spent the greater part of his time in Germany, leaving Britain to be ruled by his favorite politicians, with whom he communicated in French. He was the first British monarch of the German House of Hanover, and reigned for thirteen years mainly on the strength of the 25 percent British blood he owed to his mother, who was the granddaughter of James I of Scotland.

The remarkable thing is that this proportion steadily decreased through the line of British succession up to George VI, starting with George II, who had 1/8 non-German blood, followed by George III with 1/32, George IV 1/64, William IV 1/64, and the last British Hanoverian, Queen Victoria, 1/128. The long reigning queen and widow of Prince Albert of the German house of Saxe-Coburg and Gotha could not pass the Hanover scepter to her heirs under Salic law, so her son Edward VII, 1/256 British, succeeded as the sole British monarch in his father's line. George V, from the marriage of Edward VII to Alexandra of Denmark, founded the House of Windsor with his paltry 1/512 British blood, and after him was his son George VI, who had more than 1/4 non-German blood mainly because his maternal great grandmother was Hungarian.

Of George I's namesakes, the last, George VI, had the 'thinnest' British blood at 1/1024. But since his queen was 'all British', the reigning Elizabeth II is slightly more British than foreign.

---

6. A Not so Great Dane

Myth! To prove he had godly powers, the British king Canute asked to be brought to the seashore, where he commanded the advancing tide to recede.

King Canute is a myth to the many who can't quite see him as a serious figure of history because of what he reportedly did. Originally named Cnut, he was not British but Danish, an invader of Britain who became king of England in 1016 until expelled by Ethelred. His reputation as a megalomaniac rests mainly on that famous anecdote in which, after having his chair carried to the seaside, he ordered the waves of the advancing tide to recede. In another version, he tried to stop the incoming tide by lashing at the waves with a whip. The story does not say how he reacted on learning that the sea was not one of his willing subjects.

The flesh-and-blood Canute was a wise and well-intentioned king who doesn't deserve his reputation one bit, and, while his legend is correctly recounted, the reason given for his apparently haughty act is false. According to the right interpretation, Canute got tired of the flattery of his courtiers, so he asked them to go down with him to the beach and watch him whip the waves into submission. His idea was to show that none of his vaunted powers as king could work against Providence or nature, and, therefore, there was no need for his subjects to toady up to him.

Henry of Huntington, who lived a hundred years after Canute and died in 1155, supposedly originated the story, but there is no way of knowing to what extent the tale is traditional or if the author invented it entirely.

7. Presumptuous Air

Myth! The heir presumptive has the strongest hereditary claim to the British crown.

Using the expressions 'heir apparent' and 'heir presumptive' interchangeably is wrong, but to regard 'heir presumptive' as a presumed or established successor, and 'heir apparent' as one whose right to succeed is only probable, is worse. English experts tell us it is precisely the opposite that's true. The heir apparent is next in line and has better prospects of ascending the throne than the heir presumptive, who serves merely in a conditional or fallback capacity.

The heir presumptive moves up front in the line of succession if a reigning monarch has no children, and therefore no heir apparent, but he or she loses this ranking as soon as the monarch begets a legitimate child. The heir apparent as the eldest living child is the guaranteed heir provided he or she survives the ruling parent.

The present Prince of Wales is sometimes called the heir presumptive, which is erroneous. He is already the heir apparent, and the two terms are mutually exclusive. Only if he predeceases the reigning monarch, and there are no other children, will an heir presumptive fall into line.

8. By Love Dispossessed

Myth! Following the rule that sovereign rulers can abdicate at will, Britain's Edward VIII left the throne without consulting his ministers and without regard to a successor.

Popular belief notwithstanding, voluntary abdication is almost anathema in Britain, where the format of modern tradition dictates that Parliament must first give its approval subject to such terms as it may set. Edward VIII found out soon enough that a king might theoretically be compelled to stay put in his throne if Parliament so decided.

Edward VIII is often regarded as the only English monarch to abdicate freely, but not a few historians insist it was still the British rule that prevailed in his case. That is to say, the erstwhile king was practically forced to do what he did, and that Parliamentary control of the abdication process was effectively used to ease him out rather than keep him. When, after just ten months on the throne, he informed Prime Minister Stanley Baldwin of his intent to marry Wallis Simpson, he was told that he could not do so without abdicating. The Constitution allowed marriage with a commoner provided she was not a Roman Catholic, but with Wallis, Parliament interposed the rather unusual objection that she was a twice-divorced woman with two living husbands. The king offered a compromise that would allow the marriage but exclude Wallis from the queenship and any issue from their union from succeeding to the throne. This was permissible in British constitutional usage and might have been acceptable to the public as well, but Parliament turned it down. Instead, it drafted the instrument of abdication, leaving the king with no alternative but to sign.

---

9. His Own King's Counsel

Myth! King Ethelred, father of Edward the Confessor, was called 'the Unready' because he was often unprepared.

Contrary to normal understanding, the epithet 'the Unready' does not mean unprepared, although Ethelred was also considered this when he left Britain practically undefended against the attacks and ravages of the Danes in 980. 'Unready' should actually read 'unrede', which means without counsel or advice, the root word being *rede* or *raed*, the ancient term for 'counsel' (Shakespeare's Ophelia, in *Hamlet* [act 1, sc. 3], speaks of one who "recks not his own rede;" that is, does not follow his own advice).

The Witenagemot was a council of elders composed of the king's advisers, whose recommendations Ethelred continually ignored in favor of his own decision. Whether it was because of this or because he was getting bad advice elsewhere, the council was annoyed and started to call him the Unrede. This was rather ironic (and oxymoronic), because the name Ethelred itself means 'noble-counsel'.

Other historians, believing Ethelred was not such a bad king and did not deserve the negative connotation, see the word not as 'unready' but as 'too ready'. They say his advisers, whom he ignored because they were disloyal and distrustful of him, considered Ethelred too rash rather than too hesitant.

10. King Leer

Myth! King Edward III, founder of England's Most Noble Order of the Garter, is that country's model for chivalry.

Edward III is written about in school history books as utterly adored by his public because he conquered a quarter of France and "gave England back her pride." The same sources relate how Edward was dancing in a crowded ballroom when a lady's garter fell to the floor. The king picked it up and placed it around his knee, muttering *Honi soit qui mal y pense* ("Evil to him who evil thinks"). Thus was born England's highest honor, the Most Noble Order of the Garter, supposedly a symbol of the "Triumph of Chastity and Chivalry over Temptation."

What Edward said to hide his embarrassment became the motto of the order, but debunkers claim Edward was actually a lustful monarch who had several mistresses. One of them was Joan, the daughter of the earl of Kent, who eventually became the first Princess of Wales as the wife of Edward's own son called "the Black Prince." The king came by the garter, so the story goes, when he slid his hand up her leg while they were dancing, and was so aroused that he forced himself upon her later. Some insist, however, that the owner of the garter was really the countess Catherine of Salisbury, who lost all interest in sex, including with her own husband, after Edward raped her.

Besides being lecherous, Edward was hated for the heavy taxes he imposed to finance his never-ending wars with Scotland and France. Those who idolized him were his aristocratic knights, after he gave them unlimited opportunity to bring back war booty from their plundered enemies.

11. Wales in the Knight

Myth! The title of Prince of Wales is acquired by inheritance.

The popular conception that the title of Prince of Wales is inherited by or automatically accorded to whoever is the heir apparent to the throne is not true. It is not inherited but conferred by the British Parliament on any member of the Royal Family, and not necessarily on the heir apparent, who need not be titled at all.

Before the time of Edward II, there had been genuine Welsh princes that ruled Wales from the tenth to the thirteenth century. The last Prince of Wales to speak Welsh and not a spot of English was Llewelyn ap Gryffydd, who was killed in battle when he rose in revolt against the English under Edward I in 1282. The title was then invested in Edward II as the first non-Welsh Prince of Wales by the Lincoln parliament in 1301, to commemorate his father's conquest of Wales and to fulfill the wish of the Welsh people for a sovereign. But this fourth son of Edward I did not automatically become heir to his father's throne, and assumed the privilege only later with the death of his elder brothers.

From the days of Edward the Black Prince, who was Edward II's grandson, Parliament or king has almost invariably conferred the title of Prince of Wales on the heir apparent to the English crown. This has established a pattern that most people mistake for tradition. Actually, once the Prince of Wales succeeds as king, or if he dies without succeeding, the title does not devolve on the next heir apparent but is extinguished and has no further existence except by fresh creation.

V

Louie Louie, Louie Louie

On the Bourbon Kings of France

"Has God
forgotten all I have done for
Him?"

•

Louis XIV

1. Marie Quite Contrarie

Myth! Cardinal Richelieu was the real master of France during the reign of Louis XIII.

Various 19th-century novelists portrayed the French sovereign Louis XIII, by nature timid, lethargic and melancholy, as the helpless instrument of the 'tyrannical' ecclesiastic Richelieu. Many modern historians don't agree, insisting that the relations between the King and his chief minister, as complex and undefined as they appeared to be, were based on growing trust and constant communication. Richelieu very subtly asserted the power of his intelligence in the crafting of policy, but the execution was usually through the King and with his consent. It was a symbiotic partnership that worked particularly to Louis' advantage because it served to conceal his weaknesses.

The real tyrant that dominated Louis XIII during his early reign was his mother, Marie de Medicis. It was Marie who practically forced her son to marry Anne of Austria in the hope of forging closer ties with Spain and the Hapsburgs, an objective she pursued with uncommon resoluteness when she was France's Queen Regent. Oddly, her chief adviser at that time was Richelieu, whom she later introduced to Louis. When Richelieu transferred his loyalty to the King, he promptly convinced the latter to denounce Marie's long-held foreign policy. This led to France's involvement in the Thirty Years War, to Louis' exile of Marie on two occasions, and to Richelieu's rise to power under the aegis of the King.

2. The Red and the Gray

Myth! Cardinal Richelieu is history's first 'éminence grise'.

The French phrase *éminence grise,* or its direct English translation 'gray eminence', has come to mean the power behind the throne, a metaphorical description of a powerful adviser or

51

decision-maker who operates secretly or unofficially. The term is commonly associated with Cardinal Richelieu, the masterful French nobleman, statesman and religious dignitary who exercised extraordinary influence over King Louis XIII and, to a lesser degree, popes Gregory XV and Urban VIII. As chief minister to Louis, Richelieu became virtual co-dictator of France, destroying the political power of the Huguenots and plunging the country into the Thirty Years War against the Hapsburgs.

Richelieu was, in a figurative sense, the *éminence grise* of his time, but contrary to popular belief, he was not called this and the phrase did not originate with him. Rather, he was known as the *éminence rouge* because of the color of his garments as a cardinal. The real—and the first—*éminence grise* was his private secretary and confidential agent, the Capuchin friar Francois Le Clerk du Tremblay (1577-1638). Also known as Père Joseph, he inspired the term from the gray robes he wore and the shadowy authority he wielded over the unsuspecting Richelieu.

Cardinal de Retz (1614-1679), who was active in the Fronde, a French civil war (1648-1653) that ultimately strengthened the monarchy, was another politically dominant Church figure, a veritable *éminence grise*. But he rose to prominence only years after Père Joseph and Richelieu had left the scene.

3. Stealing a March

Myth! Louis XIII's famous musketeers marched with muskets on their shoulders and swords at their sides.

In the film *The Three Musketeers* (1948), with dancer Gene Kelly as the swashbuckling D'Artagnan, Vincent Price's Richelieu is the evil French prime minister but there is no sign of his cardinalship or priesthood. It appears the producers decided not to go beyond the movie's portrayal of his eminence as a villainous lay cavalier to avoid references that could ruffle sectarian feelings.

The revisionist role for Price, whether intended or not, is a historical gaffe, but the movie's depiction of the King's musketeers marching proudly in cadence without their muskets is something else. Despite the word 'musketeers', says David Feldman, citing Dumas' translator Lord Sudley, the absence of this weapon on most occasions during that era was nothing unusual and did not violate any time-honored French military custom. When Louis XIII's bodyguards were formed in 1622, they had just been armed with the new flintlock, muzzle-loading muskets. But the gun, as long as eight feet and the weight of two bowling balls, turned out to be too unwieldy to be carried by horsemen and too unsteady to be shot accurately without a fork rest. Eventually, the 'musketeers' were rendered musketless and left to rely on newfangled pistols and trusty old swords.

What was actually remiss without Hollywood being aware of it is the marching. According to historians, a soldier in the early days, from the Greeks and the Romans to the knights and the men-at-arms of the Enlightenment, never marched on any occasion, in war or in peace. Armies began to march only in the eighteenth century, when the Prussians invented the practice. Thereafter, several variations have become standards for showing off the military's penchant for order and discipline (as well as pomposity).

4. State Deportment

Myth! **In defense of his extraordinary powers as sovereign of France, Louis XIV once said, *"L'etat c'est moi."***

If popular tradition is to be believed, Louis XIV said, *L'etat c'est moi* ("I am the state"), when he was a teenage monarch in 1655, while talking to a group of parliamentarians who were bent on reducing his power. On the other hand, the common verdict of historians is that he never said it. Though no other quotation is as typical of the Sun King, it was apparently the French philosopher Voltaire who invented the high and mighty words and assigned them to Louis.

But the French need not despair, for the words were indeed spoken by one of their greatest potentates—Napoleon Bonaparte. In an address to the French Senate in 1814, Napoleon perorated, "What is the throne? —A bit of wood gilded and covered with velvet. I am the state—I alone am here the representative of the people."

Incidentally, *L'etat c'est moi* is not the only saying that mythmakers have falsely attributed to Louis XIV to prove his imperiousness. Louis, who ruled for seventy-two years, took France to the height of commercial prosperity, culture, and arts and letters, but at the same time embarked on a series of conquests for new territories that led to costly struggles with Spain, the Netherlands, and Luxembourg. On one of these occasions, seeing his army being defeated, he is reported to have uttered, "Has God forgotten all I have done for Him?" Despite evidence from modern research of their being fictitious, the words still manage to get included in some collections of celebrity quotes.

5. Apocalypse Now!

Myth! Benumbed by the extravagance of his reign, Louis XV said, "*After me, the deluge.*"

France's Louis XV may have once boasted, "After me, the deluge," but nobody heard it. This third Louis was the insensitive despot who presided over the most ostentatious yet socially retrogressive period of the *ancien regime*. Whatever the line was meant to convey, it was totally suggestive of the aristocratic extravagance that characterized the period in general and Louis' rule in particular.

But according to 18th-century writer J. B. D. Depres, the relevant words were, "After us, the deluge," and they were spoken not by the king but by his much-vilified mistress, Madame Pompadour (born Jeanne Antoinette Poisson in 1721). From 1745 until her death in 1764, this pampered coquette exerted great influence on political matters in the royal court.

Later writers, not totally convinced by Depres' claim of support from the memoirs of Pompadour's lady-in-waiting, have remained divided between the king and his mistress as the source of the quote. But Burton Stevenson trumps both versions when he points out that the saying "was original with neither, for it is an old French proverb cited in many collections, and usually applied to spendthrifts," of which Louis and Pompadour were the most audacious.

54

There is no doubt, however, that Pompadour once said, "I care not what happens after I am dead," in callous reference to her lifestyle. This sends essentially the same message as the expression, "After us, the deluge," and may be Depres' reason for attributing it to the royal concubine.

6. End of the Line

Myth! Louis XVI was the last Louis and also the last king of France.

Louis XVI was not deposed by the Revolution of 1789, as is commonly believed, but continued to hold power for a limited time with the acquiescence of the Estates-General (later National Assembly). Neither was the monarchy overthrown in the popular insurrection of August 10, 1792, when the royal family was imprisoned in the Temple in Paris. Louis' powers during this period were only temporarily suspended by the Legislative Assembly, and could have been restored had Louis and his queen not committed indiscretions that led to their execution by guillotine in 1793. Indeed, the voting that imposed the death penalty by the Convention was close enough to show some reluctance to do away with the monarch.

Louis' demise, at any rate, did not end the monarchy, and he was not the last king of France, as most people think. Louis' kingship may have terminated with the establishment of the French republic under Napoleon Bonaparte, but his line was revived with the Bourbon Restoration of 1814, when a brother, Louis XVIII, resumed the monarchy under a constitution, followed by another brother, Charles X, who later abdicated. Charles, though not an absolutist, must be considered as the truly last king of France, since his successors, Louis-Philippe and Napoleon III, were not monarchs in the strict sense of the term. Louis-Philippe took the title of King of the French, while Napoleon III was Emperor of the French before being deposed in 1871 to give way to the Third Republic.

Louis XVIII was the last of the French monarchs named Louis. However, the XVIII is a misnomer, since there were only sixteen Louises who reigned before him. The one known as Louis XVII died in prison during the Revolution, and thus never attained recognition much less the throne.

7. Masked Marvel

Myth! 'The Man in the Iron Mask' was a figment of Alexander Dumas' imagination.

In the Alexander Dumas novel *The Vicomte de Bragelonne* (written in the late 1840s), the central character in the final section titled "The Man in the Iron Mask" is revealed as the twin brother of Louis XIV. A pretender who tries to usurp the throne, he is thwarted and condemned to prison for life with an iron mask on his face to hide forever the fraternal likeness. Contrary to popular belief, however, it was Voltaire, not Dumas, who first publicized details about the mystery man. In an essay ("Questions on the Encyclopedia") written in 1756, Voltaire foisted the idea of a real-life prisoner in an iron mask who "was no doubt an elder (illegitimate) brother of Louis XIV."

While agreeing that the common subject of Voltaire and Dumas had a flesh-and-blood model, historians caution that both accounts are highly romanticized adaptations of the real event and are quite misleading. Documents have shown, for instance, that the mask wasn't iron at all, but was made out of black velvet (or waxed cloth) stiffened with whalebone and fastened behind the head with a padlock or by steel springs. The novel gives the impression that the wearer languished in one prison the whole time; in fact, he was kept in various cells before being deposited in the Bastille in 1698. Convenience and logic dictate that it was probably only during his transfer from one institution to another that he had his face masked. The real prisoner had never been tried or sentenced, and did not stay imprisoned for more than 40 years, having been jailed first in 1669 at Pignerol and died in 1703.

Finally, there is the question of the man's identity and of why he was detained, hidden behind a mask, for such a long period of time. According to the most persistent rumor, which found support in the Voltaire/Dumas versions, the man was a close relative of the King whose royal affinity posed a grave scandal or threatened His Majesty's tenure; it had therefore become necessary to render him powerless and incommunicado for at least the duration of the King's reign. Aside from the twin brother and the elder half-brother mentioned by Dumas and Voltaire, the suspected identities included Louis XIV himself (his candidacy as 'The Man in the Iron Mask' was relaunched recently by Leonardo DiCaprio in a movie of that name) and his illegitimate son the Count of Vermandois. A strange though not implausible suggestion (allegedly from data recorded by Pulitzer Prize winners Will and Ariel Durant in their multi-volume *The Story of Civilization*) was that Louis XIV imprisoned his natural father to prevent the public from knowing that the King was illegitimate and his putative father Louis XIII was homosexual.

The modern trend, however, has been to veer away from the theory that the masked man was related to Louis XIV or that he was a recalcitrant member of French royalty. Two names have been found to fit the new mold: Eustace Dauger and Antonio Ercole Matthioli. It is said Dauger, the valet of a French Huguenot who was publicly tortured and executed for plotting against the throne, knew too much about his master's agenda to be left alone, hence the psychological pressure of a burdensome mask during a long incarceration to make him talk. Matthioli, on the other hand, was of dubious origin, a foreign diplomat who reportedly embarrassed Louis no end when he double-crossed the Duke of Mantua and the Republic of Venice in a deal that France brokered. After being kidnapped following Louis' orders, he was placed in 'perpetual' seclusion and deprived of all means of communication as a special punishment. Interestingly, Matthioli's death at Sainte-Marguerite in 1696, long before the 'Man in the Velvet Mask' showed up in the Bastille, would give birth to yet another theory: that Dauger was actually the valet of Matthioli, and both master and servant, one after the other, became the mysterious masked man, their separate histories combining into a single myth.

8. Louis-Philippe's Fillip

Myth! France never had a sovereign of common stock before or after Louis-Philippe.

Contrary to the belief that France's 'Citizen King', Louis-Philippe, was a commoner, he was the duke of Chartres at the time he supported the Revolutionary Government. Seeing that the nobles didn't have any chance of being fully reconciled with the Revolutionists, he deserted the French army in its war with Austria, later automatically becoming duke of Orleans when the Jacobins executed his father. He fled to America and lived the life of a drifter for three years, taking on the image of an ordinary Frenchman by dwelling most of the time in a small room over a bar in Philadelphia.

After returning to France on the restoration of the Bourbons, he accepted the crown when Charles X was forced to abdicate by the Revolution of 1830. Actually, it was not this popular uprising that catapulted Louis-Philippe to power, as most people assume, but the ensuing victory of the nobility or upper bourgeoisie against the extremists on both sides. Louis-Philippe was given the unkingly title of King of the French as a compromise between the right-wing extreme monarchists (the Legitimists), on the one side, and the socialists and other republicans (including the Bonapartists), on the other.

The only French sovereigns of common stock in the modern era are Napoleon Bonaparte and Napoleon III, both of whom are styled Emperor of the French (rather than Emperor of France) for having come to power by coup. However, since Bonaparte is Corsican by birth, only Napoleon III is a true citizen sovereign, perhaps the first and the last of his kind.

9. A Mass to Win the Masses

Myth! Agreeing to assuage his Catholic subjects by attending mass, the Huguenot Henry IV said, *"Paris is worth a mass."*

Henry IV, the first of the Bourbon kings of France, uttered the witticism that underlies the modern political slogan "A chicken in every pot." Henry's words were: "I desire that every laborer in my realm should be able to put a fowl in the pot on Sundays." The royal pledge was good enough for the Hoover Republicans to refine it into a campaign gimmick in the presidential election of 1928.

Ironically, Henry is better known for saying, "Paris is worth a mass," a statement of dubious authenticity and significance. As the leader of the Huguenots and protector of the Protestant churches, Henry had waged a series of civil wars with the Catholic elements of France. Eventually he became reconciled with the Catholic King Henry III, his brother-in-law, and succeeded the latter when he was assassinated. However, he could not enforce his jurisdiction over the strongly Catholic cities and towns, so he decided to abjure Calvinism in 1593, an act that brought quick results despite many remaining unconvinced of his sincerity. Important towns submitted in growing numbers, until finally, on March 22, 1594, he entered Paris, purportedly making the comment, "Paris is well worth a mass," before proceeding, amid cheers, to hear the *Te Deum* at Notre Dame. Most historians question the veracity of the episode about the mass, and consequently of Henry's subtly impious remark, attributing them to the folktales generated by the Wars of Religion that ravaged France during Henry's time.

VI
Personality Complex
Or Complex Personality?

On Napoleon and the Duke of Wellington

"France has more
need of me than I have need of
France."

•

Napoleon

1. Mens Sana in Corporal Sano

Myth! Napoleon was a warmongering megalomaniac.

Historians say that, although Napoleon was extremely ambitious, it was never clear that he was mad for power or turf. At his fall, he left France surprisingly smaller than what it had been at the outbreak of the Revolution in 1789, disproving the claim that his driving passion was the military expansion of French dominion. Despite his military successes, he had been magnanimous with his defeated enemies and had received grants of territory only in exchange for cessions of his own. According to his secretary, Las Cases, the emperor was in truth a republican opposed to war and had fought only when Europe forced him to fight in defense of freedom.

Napoleon's reputed aggressiveness to compensate for his equally reputed shortness of stature is said to have inspired the term 'Napoleon complex'. But Freud suggested that what could have been the real affliction of the general was a Joseph complex—after the Biblical character Joseph—from a compulsive desire to outdo his older brother, who was coincidentally also named Joseph. There was no cause for Napoleon to compete, however, since much of his sibling's power was derived from his own. After Napoleon's fall, Joseph could only manage to immigrate to the US in 1815 and remain there practically incognito until 1832.

2. The Corsican Father

Myth! Napoleon was of fine French lineage.

However anomalous Napoleon's coronation may have been, it accorded him world recognition as Emperor of the French. But was he truly French?

Napoleon was born of parents of Italian descent in Ajaccio, Corsica in 1769, when the place was an Italian enclave that had just come under French control. This puts him in much the same situation as some equally famous personages, e.g., Marco Polo and Joan of Arc, who have been fated by geopolitical circumstances to be born outside their chosen homelands.

Corsica fought for years for independence from France, and Napoleon's father, Carlo, who was friendly with rebel leaders, was urged to flee to England when the French threatened to jail the insurgents. Carlo decided not to leave and ingratiated himself with the invaders to the point that a French general sponsored Napoleon at age nine to the Military Academy of Brienne. This was Napoleon's first brush with *La France*, at which time he spoke Italian frequently and was having trouble with the French language.

His graduation from the Academy (ranking 42nd in a class of 51) notwithstanding, he joined the Corsican freedom fighter Pasquale Paoli in 1789. Fortunately, he was not fully accepted because his father had deserted the cause. In January 1792, after his appointment to the post of lieutenant colonel of the Corsican National Guard, he had a falling out with the commander-in-chief and deserted. His offense was forgiven when France declared war against Austria and he was recalled to active duty.

---

3. A Political Stunt?

Myth! Napoleon was shorter than the average Frenchman.

Napoleon is famously called the 'Little Corporal', a pet name his troops gave him after winning in the Italian campaign against armies four times bigger than his own. And yet, he was never a corporal, and he was definitely not short.

Most of Napoleon's portrayals, artistic as well as literary, project a man of unusually short stature—not more than five feet two inches on the average. Many of his biographies, in fact, have a tendency to attribute his ambitiousness to his short height. But Hollywood actors such as Marlon Brando (in the 1954 *Desiree*) should feel vindicated by Shenkman's revelation that the man they played in the movies was of average height and not short by contemporary standards.

62

The confusion about Napoleon's height apparently stems from his having been measured at a mere 'five feet two' during his autopsy. It also didn't help that, during the Napoleonic battles, our hero was often seen with his Imperial Guard, who were above average height, and this contributed to the perception of his being short. The hostile British Tory press exacerbated the image further by caricaturing him as "a tyrant small in both physical and military stature." As it turns out, the coroner's 'five feet two' was based on an antiquated French system called *pieds de roi*, popular for measuring cadavers, particularly royal ones. The more modern British standard recognizes the difference between the French *pouce* (2.71 cm) and the British inch (2.54 cm)—enough to boost the Little Corporal's true height to about 5 feet 7 inches, average for the period.

---

4. The Emperor's Old Groove

Myth! Beethoven showed his ambivalent feelings for Napoleon by renaming a composition to spite him, naming another in his honor, and dedicating yet a third to his loss at Waterloo.

The story is told that Beethoven, a contemporary of Napoleon, put 'Bonaparte' on the front page of Symphony No. 3 in E-flat Major as its original title to honor the Corsican for championing liberty in Europe. But upon hearing the news that Napoleon had declared himself consul for life, Beethoven burst into tears and ripped up the title page in a tantrum. He then changed its name to the more impersonal 'Eroica'.

The change of name did happen, but the rest of the story, particularly about the reason for the change, is libertarian hype. In fact, Beethoven continued calling his work *eigentlich Bonaparte gennant*, or 'really named for Bonaparte', long after Napoleon's proclamation as virtual dictator. The supposedly destroyed page still exists with Bonaparte's name neatly crossed out. Although Beethoven changed the title to 'Eroica' (or Heroic Symphony), he deigned to add "—composed to celebrate the memory of a great man."

Although Beethoven had originally meant to dedicate his Piano Concerto No. 5 in E-flat Major to the Corsican, he had nothing to do with its being named 'Emperor'. It was an unidentified publisher who provided the elegant label, but nobody knows whether he did so in reference to Napoleon or because he was inspired by the overall majesty of the music itself.

Some patriotic types believe Tchaikovsky produced his 1812 Overture to commemorate the Battle of New Orleans, which Andrew Jackson won against the British in the War of 1812. Actually, the Russian composition was a comment on Napoleon's monumental setback in Russia in 1812. The music popularly believed to have been inspired by the Corsican's more famous loss at Waterloo is Beethoven's Battle Symphony, but this is also wrong. Unlike Tchaikovsky, Beethoven could not bring himself to show disrespect to Napoleon by memorializing any of his defeats. While Battle Symphony was undoubtedly in celebration of a Wellington victory over a Bonaparte, this was the one achieved by the duke over Napoleon's brother Joseph at Vitoria.

5. Not Feeling Nappy Tonight

Myth! Napoleon, kept busy by his extra-marital affairs, consistently dismissed his wife's frequent sexual overtures with a curt *"Not tonight, Josephine."*

No one knows if Napoleon really said the words at some low point in his romance with Josephine, as neither character left any memoirs of the seamy side of their relationship. The line has been traced to music-hall comedy in Victorian times and is now practically a standard item in sex farces.

Nevertheless, there are indications Napoleon may have expressed himself in this manner to Josephine on some occasions. It was an open secret that Napoleon could not keep up with Josephine's sex drive, which often had to be gratified extra-maritally. Napoleon's denial might have been his way of punishing Josephine for her indiscretions. More likely, he was not up to it.

A profligate in his young days, Napoleon began to exhibit homosexual behavior in his later years and eventually became impotent. How he succeeded in having a child with Marie-Louise remains a question, since, as his autopsy revealed, glandular problems had caused feminization of his body. This could have been the reason for Josephine's failure to conceive despite her having had two children from a previous marriage.

Television's treatment of Napoleon's marriage to Josephine as 'the greatest love story ever told' is an obvious attempt to cover up the real reason behind the phrase, "Not tonight, Josephine." The hype it has promoted—that the harmony between the marital couple thrived on sexual compatibility rather than political convenience—easily forgets that the ambitious Napoleon married Josephine mainly for her connections in Corsican high society and the circles of the ruling elite.

6. The Taste is Napoleon, But...

Myth! Napoleon said, "*God is always on the side of the big battalions,*" and, "*An army, like a serpent, travels on its belly.*"

Like most other great men, Napoleon is credited with sayings that turn out to be fake or unoriginal, and two of the noteworthy ones have pertinence to the art of war.

The first, "God is always on the side of the big battalions," is suspiciously similar to Tacitus' statement (*History*, Book IV, 17, *ca* 1st century) that 'the gods are with the stronger (side)'. In the 17th and 18th centuries, Frederick the Great and Madame de Sevigne were among those who used the expression, however obliquely.

An almost identical line, "God always favors the biggest battalions," was contained in Voltaire's letter to Monsieur (or Abbé) le Riche dated February 6, 1770. Historians initially thought this was not true, and that what Voltaire actually wrote in the letter was the famous statement, "I disapprove of what you say, but will defend to the death your right to say it." Research later showed that this otherwise brilliant metaphor for free speech, long identified with Voltaire, was the spurious one, and had been planted surreptitiously in his work by Norbert Guterman, a translator and essayist, for unknown reasons.

The second of Napoleon's dubious contributions to military science is the saying "An army travels on its stomach." When first heard from him at an army briefing, it was already obvious he had lifted the line from another source. For Frederick the Great once said, "An army, like a serpent, travels on its belly," although the thought behind the words was probably not original with that great militarist either.

The saying, "From the sublime to the ridiculous there is but a step," is often attributed to the French statesman Charles Maurice de Talleyrand-Périgord, who actually heard the quotation first in one of his conversations with Napoleon and subsequently included it, with an accreditation to the monarch, in a book. The Emperor was discussing how recent developments in the War of 1812 were beginning to decimate his troops, and he kept repeating, *Du sublime au ridicule il n'y a qu'un pas*, in agony over the sudden downturn in the campaign. Talleyrand never quite realized that the remark was conceived by Thomas Paine, and was one more proof that Napoleon's real talent was for popularizing rather than coining immortal phrases. In his *Age of Reason* (1795), the American pamphleteer wrote, "The sublime and the ridiculous are often so nearly related that it is difficult to class them separately. One step above the sublime makes the ridiculous, and one step above the ridiculous makes the sublime again."

7. Ants in his Pants or Pest in his Vest?

Myth! Napoleon's hand-in-vest gesture had psychological undertones.

Biographers suspect that Napoleon's idiosyncrasies were not always psychological in nature. Thus, while the popular belief is that ambition was what pushed the emperor to indefatigable activity, they think the real reason was a hyperactive thyroid or pituitary gland.

One persistent claim about Napoleon's odd behavior is that his characteristic pose, his hand stuck smartly in his vest, betrayed a heroic delusion. But many biographers debunk the famous 'hand-in' gesture as a myth perpetrated by Jacques-Louis David's painting, *Napoleon in His Study*, and two imitations of this 1812

66

work. Some add that, even assuming the gesture was genuine, the stimulus was physical and not psychological or emotional. The pose was a way of keeping Napoleon's hand on his upper stomach to help relieve chronic pains in that part of his body.

8. Cold Napoleon

Myth! Napoleon's most memorable military debacles were caused by the harsh Russian weather.

It is claimed that Napoleon was at fault for underestimating what even his lowliest soldier knew: that the great Eastern campaign would turn on how well the French army could cope with the unpredictable Russian weather. But debunkers say Napoleon had no reason to be apprehensive about natural conditions that time of the year, since the signals were for a mild winter in 1812. And the signals were indeed right during the period that mattered. When Napoleon retreated from Moscow in October, it was a good eleven days before the first severe frost arrived and 24 days before the first big drop in temperature. The countryside thawed in late November and did not experience below zero temperature until December 4.

Analysts believe disease more than the cold brought misery to the French, who had only 41,000 of the 100,000 troops that left Moscow on October 19 remaining relatively free of ailments by November 12. The heat was even worse, particularly in the Russian summer of 1812, when it was so hot that tens of thousands of French soldiers died from heat exhaustion and sunstroke.

But in the end, Shenkman writes, it was the size of the Grand Army rather than the weather or disease that defeated it. The number—655,000 strong at the outset—was just "too big to lead through a hostile land, making it impossible for Napoleon to feed and supply his force properly." Because no amount of logistics could have supported such a march in such vast territory in any weather, only 30,000 of the dictator's once magnificent army were able to return to Paris alive.

67

9. Short Nap not Agreeable to Pope

Myth! Napoleon was Christian if not Roman Catholic.

Napoleon was reputedly a Catholic, or at least a Christian, since he was raised a Catholic and was sentimentally attached to that religion. Not only did he sign a concordat with the pope making Catholicism the state religion of France, he also demanded that the pope himself consecrate him as emperor.

These events, however, are not what they purport to be. The concordat Napoleon signed with the pope was actually an admission of the freedom of worship and the lay character of the state. His invitation to have the pope crown him had no religious significance but was only for show, to make his coronation outshine that of the kings of France. The emperor's real reason was revealed when, at the last moment, he took the crown from the pope and set it on his own head. Napoleon had no religious awe for the papacy, which he regarded as a mere political office and a threat to the stability of his reign. He had Pius VII arrested in Rome in 1809 and held prisoner at Savona for three years. He also had the Sacred College of Cardinals moved to France in 1812.

Napoleon's upbringing may have convinced him to become a theist—one who believes in God and an afterlife—but not necessarily a Catholic. He thought religion was highly moral, agreeing with Voltaire that the people needed a religion, but he was personally indifferent to it. The little faith he had was inconsistent with Christianity, for he saw Christ only as 'a man' and the Gospels as 'beautiful parables'. In Egypt, he said that he wanted to be a Muslim.

10. Sneezing the Life out of his Prisoners?

Myth! Napoleon was notorious for his harsh treatment of prisoners-of-war.

A newspaper once published a 'stranger than fiction' feature headed by the words 'Napoleon coughed and 1,200 people died'.

68

The item reported that the Corsican, a general in the Middle East in 1799, had just decided to release his prisoners when the cough came. Napoleon exclaimed, *"Ma sacrée toux!"* ("My confounded cough!"), but this was heard as *"Massacrez tous!"* ("Kill them all!") by his officers, who thereupon executed the prisoners, 1,200 in all.

No records of this tragicomic episode exist, since not even pseudo-documents can possibly support its ludicrous details. The execution of so many prisoners, even by mistake, is far-fetched and illogical, particularly when viewed in the context of Napoleon's character. Despite his awesome powers, the Corsican was known to be tolerant, showed respect for human life, and was extraordinarily lenient to prisoners-of-war and refugees. These qualities filtered down to his men, who showed them admirably in peacetime as well as in war.

As far as is known, Napoleon personally ordered only one execution as a perfectly justifiable act of self-preservation. But even this he would later admit to be an egregious mistake. Suspecting that the duc D'Enghien was heading a secret conspiracy to assassinate him, Napoleon had the duke kidnapped and shot after a quick trial. Soon afterwards, it was claimed that Napoleon would have changed his mind had he known of a letter purportedly written by the duke, but it was proved conclusively in 1901 that this document was fake.

---

11. Ruling with an Iron Duke

Myth! After being titled duke of Wellington for his role in the Battle of Waterloo, the English commoner Arthur Wellesley went on to become one of the most successful British prime ministers of the 19th century.

There are several false impressions about the duke of Wellington despite, or because of, the fame he achieved from defeating Napoleon, the world's erstwhile conqueror.

First, Wellington was not English but Irish, having been born in Dublin in 1769. Much of his political and military beginnings were spent in Ireland, as, for instance, in 1790-97, when he held the family seat of Trim in the Irish Parliament. *Second*, he was not a commoner, his original name being Arthur Wesley, the fifth son of Wesley, the 1st duke of Mornington. He was already a 29-year-old commander in India when he changed his name to Arthur Wellesley.

Third, he was not yet formally a duke when he fought the Battle of Waterloo, and would be awarded his patent of nobility only upon his return to England after that event. The title was a belated reward for another battle preceding Waterloo, that of Toulouse, which ended the Peninsular Wars and caused Napoleon's banishment to Elba.

Fourth, the duke was a flamboyant failure and a heavy gambler in his youth, and owed his initial success in India to a position earned through nepotism (his brother Richard was the viceroy). Before this, he gained several promotions, one to major and another to lieutenant colonel, by purchasing the rank. *Fifth*, contrary to Napoleon's claim that he was a mere 'Sepoy general', Wellington returned from India to England in 1805 with a knighthood. But his reputation took a turn for the worse when he was tried by court martial for repatriating the defeated French army at Vimeiro.

Finally, after he was acquitted, he entered British politics and rose to become the country's *worst* 19th-century prime minister. His anti-reformist stance while in power and his ironhanded discipline made him extremely unpopular. At some point he was called the 'Iron Duke', but modern historians have objected to the nickname on the ground that he was actually likeable and was neither cold nor hardhearted. Few realize that the epithet 'Iron Duke' arose not from his using a firm hand but from the fact that his residence at Apsley House had been a target of window-smashers and iron shutters were installed to protect against further damage.

12. Who Else was in the 'Loo?

Myth! Though greatly outnumbered, the English managed to defeat Napoleon's forces at the Battle of Waterloo.

Everybody knows Napoleon lost the Battle of Waterloo, but who won it is not as easily answered. What is generally taught in

English-speaking countries is that the English under the duke of Wellington provided the force that broke Napoleon's back in that historic event. The Germans claim a major share of the credit for Field Marshall Gebhard Leberecht von Blücher of the Prussian army, who came to the rescue of the English in their most critical moments. Not to be outdone, the Belgians assert that victory could not have been achieved without their help, noting particularly that had not one of their generals ignored Wellington's order to retreat, the battle would have been lost.

The statistics of the battle tell the real story. The duke's forces, about 94,000 men, were outnumbered and would not have withstood the might of Napoleon's elite Imperial Guard numbering 198,000. The turning point occurred when the Prussian troops of more than 50,000 fierce and competent fighters under von Blücher's command arrived to reinforce Wellington's men. Still, the Prussians, who were the same group that had just been defeated by Napoleon in a previous encounter, were not enough, and additional Dutch, Belgian, and Austrian support had to be called to increase the figure to about 215,000. This outside combination spelled the end for the Little Corporal, and together with the duke's men, they rallied in one great charge and overwhelmed the French

---

13. Killing Room

Myth! **British agents most likely caused Napoleon's death by poisoning to prevent him from causing another European war.**

Initially, the suspicion was that British agents under Sir Hudson Lowe, administrator of the St. Helena facility, painted the poison on the wallpaper of Napoleon's bedroom, from which the emperor inhaled the invisible exudations. The wallpaper, like St. Helena's soil, was found positive for arsenic, and early analysis of samples of Napoleon's hair, which he had asked to be shaved from his head and distributed among his friends, showed signs of arsenic, antimony, and lead. Later, another theory sprang up: the poisoner wasn't the British at all, but a French member of Napoleon's household who aimed to inherit most of Napoleon's estate.

On the other hand, recent reports claim that extensive FBI testing showed hairs taken from Napoleon six hours after he died did not reveal any trace of arsenic. How the FBI got into the picture more than a century after the fact has not been explained. Nevertheless, scientists believe that any symptoms of poisoning would have been due to the fact that these same substances were prescribed in some form or other as medicines by Napoleon's doctors.

The official medical report was that Napoleon died of stomach and liver cancer, although not a few historians see medical neglect and incompetence, which hastened Napoleon's condition, as the real cause of death. He had been vomiting blood from his stomach ulcer, for which doctors gave him a poisonous emetic mixed with lemonade to induce more vomiting, believing this to be a palliative. Others insinuate that it was actually more than medical miscalculation: Napoleon felt such pain and his state was so desperate that the doctors deliberately gave the emperor a fatal dose of a mercury-based laxative to end his suffering.

14. The Knight who Hated Black Mail

Myth! When a publisher wrote threatening to expose Wellington's sexual escapades, the duke dashed the words 'Publish and be damned!' in red ink across the letter before returning it.

The duke of Wellington was a very attractive man, and so popular that many women threw themselves at his feet. One of his unwelcome admirers was a playgirl named Harriette Wilson, who wrote her romantic memoirs and sent it to a Paris-based publisher named Stockdale. Seeing a quick opportunity for profit, the unscrupulous Stockdale made a thinly disguised blackmail attempt in a letter indicating that, for a financial consideration, all references to Wellington in Wilson's memoirs could be edited out.

In another version of the story, wholly unproved, the blackmailer was a young French actress named Mademoiselle George, who claimed to have slept with both Wellington and Napoleon but preferred the duke as the better of the two. She wrote her memoirs and sent a note to every man mentioned therein that for 500 pounds, she would delete the victim's name prior to publication.

In both versions, Wellington's supposed reply was "Publish and be damned!" In the first, he challenged Stockdale to a duel, then dashed the line across the letter in red ink before returning it. The duke's biographers concede the essential truth of the Stockdale incident, but maintain that Wellington's response of "Publish and be damned" was in a separate letter and there was no challenge to a duel. Stockdale's original letter is kept at Apsley House with nothing on it to show that the text has been defiled by a vengeful message.

15. Club Wellington 1, Team Napoleon 0

Myth! On a nostalgic visit to his alma mater, Wellington observed, *"The battle of Waterloo was won on the playing fields of Eton."*

Wellesley's own descendant, the seventh duke of Wellington, didn't think the line was genuine. Most historians agree with the younger duke that the statement is "more Gallic, almost Napoleonic in tone," a style alien to Wellington, and he simply had no reason for saying it.

Wellington, who had to drop out of Eton because of mediocre academic performance, was never able to develop any spirit or loyalty for the school. Moreover, Eton had no playing fields or organized team games during those days, and the duke himself was known to have been too withdrawn to participate in such sports. He also had no opportunity to make the remark, since he returned to Eton only twice after his defeat of Napoleon. The first time was to attend his brother's funeral in 1842, which was too brief, and the second was to accompany the British queen and the French king Louis Philippe, when it would have been impolitic for him to mention Waterloo.

It was the French count Charles de Montalembert, in his 1855 book *De L'Avenir Politique de L'Angleterre*, who quoted the duke on a visit to Eton as saying, "It was here that the battle of Waterloo was won." Later, Sir Edward Creasy was heard to comment, "There grows the stuff that won Waterloo, " as he passed groups playing cricket on the school's playing fields. In 1889, or 37 years after the duke's death, Sir William Fraser, in his compilation *Words on Wellington*, borrowed the Montalembert passage and combined it with the one of Creasy, producing the agreeable but spurious result: "The battle of Waterloo was won on the playing fields of Eton."

16. Carved with Pride

Myth! When Wellington asked the commander of the French Guard, Baron Cambronne, to surrender, the Baron replied, *"The Guard die, but do not surrender."*

In another account of the famous incident, the enemy surrounded the Guard on all sides when an English voice rang out in a brief hush, demanding that Cambronne surrender. The heroic reply common to both versions, *La Garde meurt, elle ne se rend pas* ("The Guard die, but do not surrender"*)*, was later inscribed on the base of a statue of Cambronne in Nantes. This despite the Baron's insistence, after he was taken prisoner at Waterloo, that he did not say it. At an 1835 banquet in his honor, he remarked, "In the first place, we did not die, and in the second, we did surrender."

In Victor Hugo's *Les Miserables*, the Baron's response to the English demand for surrender is reduced to one word, *Merde!*, a quote that researchers say was not meant to be fiction. There is evidence that the classic remark "The Guard die, but do not surrender" was uttered near the end of the battle by a major in one of the shattered squares, and was overheard by a French reporter, who attributed it to Cambronne as a whitewash of the Baron's own scatological answer. Whatever his source was, Hugo's version seems to be the most believed, as *merde* is now one of France's most familiar cuss-words, popularly known as *le mot de Cambronne*.

17. Queen Creole

Myth! Napoleon's wife Josephine became politically and socially influential despite being only a Creole.

Josephine was indeed a Creole, but contrary to what the word popularly signifies, she was not of mixed blood. Rather, she was a pure white born of French parents in the island of Martinique.

In a broad sense, Creoles are not necessarily of mixed white and black blood. Particularly in Louisiana, where the term is most familiar, it originally meant anyone born there whose ancestors were French and had come to that state to settle. In the West Indies and Spanish America it meant a native descended from European stock, usually Spanish, as distinguished from immigrants, blacks, aborigines and natives of mixed blood. Eventually the designation was broadened to include persons born in the New World, but of some non-indigenous race, regardless of color. Thus, 'Creole' came also to refer to a black born in the Americas, as distinguished from a black brought from Africa.

In New Orleans today, there are 'Creoles of color' as opposed to white ones, and they maintain their own enclave below Canal Street. Pure blacks are also called Creoles in Brazil, and in Alaska the word was once used to designate persons of mixed Russian and Indian ancestry.

18. 'Able was I ere I Saw Elba'

Myth! After his final battle at Waterloo, Napoleon was exiled to the island of Elba in Tuscany, Italy.

The hectic last years of Napoleon's reign were so confusing as to create the illusion that the emperor was sent in exile to Elba after surviving the Battle of Waterloo. The truth, however, is that the Allies imprisoned Napoleon in Elba a year before the battle in consequence of his defeat at Leipzig and abdication at Fontainebleau in 1814. He escaped from the island in February 1815, regrouped his forces, and met his enemies at Waterloo in

June of the same year. After his monumental rout at the hands of Wellington, he was again exiled, this time to the island of St. Helena, where he remained until his death in 1821.

Incidentally, we are used to calling Napoleon's final debacle the Battle of Waterloo without realizing it wasn't fought at Waterloo at all. The French and English forces engaged at a point converging on the villages of Plancenoit, La Belle-Alliance and Mont St. Jean, in a tiny hamlet called La Haie Sainte between four to seven miles south of Waterloo in Belgium. It was at La Haie Sainte (meaning 'holy hedgerow' in French) that the French Guard made its last catastrophic charge, and it was there where it began its retreat to signal the demise of the Napoleonic Empire. The battle borrowed the name from Waterloo only because Wellington had camped there the night before and returned to it again shortly after the engagement to write his communiqué announcing the victory.

19. French Spirit

Myth! Wine manufacturers call their special edition 'Napoleon brandy' to honor the monarch, placing certain marks on the neck or side of the bottle to indicate its high quality.

In common usage, the word 'Napoleon' denotes supremacy in a particular sphere, as in the phrase 'a Napoleon of industry', 'a Napoleon of media', or 'the Napoleon of crime'. The emperor's name is often appropriated commercially to give various merchandise the mark of superiority or distinction, on the premise that Napoleon had these qualities. The same goes for the use of stars, the number of which is supposed to denote the level of quality of any commodity, which may range from wines to films and hotels. Five stars normally mean it's the oldest or the best.

However, connoisseurs who rely on star markings for wine will be disappointed to learn that they are decoration, pure and simple, in spite of the widely held belief that each star represents five years in the age of the brew. It is also not surprising that the most respected term of all—'Napoleon brandy'—has no special significance, although many manufacturers would want us to think otherwise. Like the stars on the neck of the bottle, the terms 'Napoleon' and 'V.S.O.P' (which means, presumably, 'Very Superior Old Pale') have no conventional meaning and can be used by anyone who wants to add an air of class to his spirits.

Except for the vintage year and the region or district in which produced, there is nothing on the label of a bottle of brandy to classify it in terms of age, taste, quality, alcoholic content, or any other characteristic.

20. Only the Sphinx Knows

Myth! Napoleon caused the destruction of the Sphinx' nose and the tip of the Great Pyramid.

It is said that the 4,500 year-old Great Pyramid was rediscovered more than two hundred years ago when, on July 21, 1798, Bonaparte set his sights on it. The French had just ousted the Mamelukes at the Battle of the Pyramids, and for the first time, the valley of the Nile, now liberated, opened itself to the scrutiny of Western eyes. Napoleon's initial reaction, according to a story spread mostly by Arab extremists, was to order his troops to destroy the face of the Sphinx and the tip of the Great Pyramid 'to leave his mark on them'. The soldiers supposedly fired cannon balls—explosives had not been invented yet—and broke off its nose.

The Internet says countless teachers around the world have passed on this bit of 'history' over the years despite its being utter nonsense. The most plausible explanation for the Sphinx' missing nose is the one offered by the Encyclopedia Americana: "In 1380 A.D. the Sphinx fell victim to the iconoclastic ardor of a fanatical Muslim ruler, who caused deplorable injuries to the head. Then the figure was used as a target for the guns of the Mamluks." Arab scholars propose that the nose might have been vandalized as early as 1378 A.D. by Mohammed Sa'im al-Dahr, a "fanatical sufi of the oldest and most highly respected sufi convent of Cairo." It was rumored that the residents in the neighborhood of the Sphinx were so upset by the destruction that they lynched the fellow and buried him near the great monument he ruined.

77

In fact, says another report, the war-bitten corporal was so completely awed by the majesty of the super structure that from a vantage point on the pyramid, he told his men: "Soldiers, reflect that from the summit of these pyramids forty centuries look down upon you." Once again, historians are doubtful anything of the sort happened, citing materials that describe how Napoleon, upon being invited by the generals and scholars who were with him that day to climb to the top of the structures, begged off because "he had other things to do and would attend to it later." The inspiring words his men supposedly heard from him while he stood on Cheop's apex were never delivered, although they were mentioned in an anonymous 1803 document. The line he sanctioned at St. Helena in the Memoirs he dictated to General Bertrand is believed to have been something he spoke at a different location.

What really happened, we are told, is that on first being confronted by the sight of the pyramids, Napoleon acted quite calmly though in a manner still worthy of his reputation. He appraised the structures and measured them with his eagle eye, then declared to those surrounding him that the mass of stone composing the group of three "seemed to him enough to build a wall one foot wide and nine feet high round the whole of France." When the famous mathematician Gaspard Monge, who was conveniently present, heard this, he confirmed its exactness by means of a few measurements and simple calculations. Critics brand the story as apocryphal at most, saying it was an obvious attempt by French sycophants to show off the Corsican's pharaonic wisdom.

VII

The Hand That Rocked The World

On Adolf Hitler and the Nazis

"Any alliance whose purpose is
not the intention to wage war is
senseless and useless."

•

Adolf Hitler

1. Self-made German

Myth! Hitler was German by birth.

Hitler was not German by birth, nor was he German at the time he wrote Mein Kampf in Landsberg Prison, nor even when he came into power as Fuehrer. He became German only through an involuntary process he himself implemented—the 1938 Anschluss uniting Austria with Germany.

An Austrian of peasant stock, Hitler was born in 1889 in the town of Braunau am Inn, across the border from Bavaria. Outside the German empire and in the eyes of the Allies, he remained an Austrian until the day of his death. Hitler's obsession from the very beginning that there should be no border between Austria and Germany did not *ipso facto* make him a German. Neither did his service with the Bavarian Army, which his detractors claim he joined out of economic necessity more than patriotism.

The question whether Hitler was German confronted the US courts when he brought suit for copyright infringement against Alan Cranston, an American journalist. Cranston, who would later distinguish himself as California senator, had published an English translation of excerpts from *Mein Kampf* without Hitler's authority. The courts decided that, for purposes of the suit, Hitler was a 'stateless German' at the time he had the book published. All this meant, of course, was that Hitler was German by race, a status that entitled him, despite his being a non-German citizen, to the protection of US copyright laws.

2. Portrait of the Nazi as a Painter

Myth! Hitler was a housepainter and paperhanger before becoming an artist.

Historians say the Fuehrer was never a housepainter or a paperhanger but an artist, although an inferior one. Notwithstanding his aspirations to become better, he failed the entrance examinations to the Vienna Academy of Fine Arts in

80

1907. He had to take on odd jobs during the next few years as a laborer in the building trades, which is probably what gave rise to the myth about his profession. Between 1909 and 1910, he improved his position somewhat by drawing or painting little pictures of Vienna, copying them from other works and selling the crude output at great trouble for ornamentation and advertising to support his miserly existence.

Critics believe the 300 or so paintings he left behind are at best comparable to the amateurish productions of Churchill and Eisenhower. Still, to the very end, Hitler thought himself an artist, willing his collection "for the establishment of a picture gallery in my home town of Linz on the Danube." A 'Hitler' watercolor, one of 21 pieces of artwork that were auctioned for $223,000 in England some years back, is said to have been discovered in a farm house in Belgium, where Hitler sojourned as a young soldier. Though its authenticity remains in question, the seller has been criticized for making money off the Fuehrer's art.

According to the academy that failed him, Hitler had some raw talent for architecture. Experts nonetheless surmise that Mozart's musician would have been a better painter than the Fuehrer on the premise that true artists are more versatile than ungifted ones. The Renaissance is known to have produced many artistic geniuses whose talents straddled several fields. This goes to prove that a true artist in one field, such as Mozart, is more likely to be good at any other art than either a non-artist or a pseudo-artist like Hitler.

---

3. Heil Schicklgruber!

Myth! Hitler was an illegitimate child whose real name was Adolf Schicklgruber.

For a while, it wasn't just Indiana Jones' scriptwriters but also David O. Selznick who thought Hitler's first name was Adolph. Chris Gore, in *The 50 Greatest Movies Never Made*, recounts that three days after America's entry into World War II, the legendary producer wrote a memo to his story editor, Katherine Brown, instructing her to go to the Hays Office and register the alternative titles 'Mein Kampf', 'Life of Adolph Hitler', and 'My Life, by Adolph Hitler'. It was in preparation for a movie Selznick was

81

producing based on the Fuehrer and *Mein Kampf*. "I hope there will be no nonsense about whether (Hitler's book) is copyrighted or non-copyrighted work," Selznick stressed. Had it been produced, the movie would have been noteworthy if only for having the misspelled name of Adolf Hitler in its title. Fortunately or unfortunately, it never got off the ground.

The Fuehrer's first name was not Adolph, and neither was his last name Schicklgruber (although it could have been). And regardless of so much wishful thinking that he wasn't, he was definitely a legitimate offspring. Schicklgruber was the maiden name of Hitler's paternal grandmother Anna, not of his mother Karla, and it was his father Alois who was illegitimate and was surnamed Schicklgruber in his birth records. After Anna married Georg Hiedler, a wandering miller of Lower Austria, in 1842, Alois, who was born five years earlier, was sent off to live with Georg's brother Johann. Adolf, among others, would later claim that the widowed Georg reappeared in 1876 after thirty years of absence to swear before notaries that it was really he who had sired Alois.

At about this time Alois' records were changed to reflect his acquisition of the surname Hiedler, later Hitler, although it is not entirely clear if this was from Georg or Johann. When Alois, a shoemaker turned customs officer, and his third wife Klara, who was 23 years his junior, brought forth Adolf, Alois was already validly surnamed Hitler. Had he remained a Schicklgruber, the Nazi world would have had to bear a sound altogether different from 'Heil Hitler'. Still, this would not have changed the fact that Der Fuehrer was born legitimate.

4. The Fuehrer had a Ball

Myth! Hitler had the normal number of testicles.

"Hitler has only one big ball"—so goes the first line of a doggerel that British Tommies sang during World War II to the tune of the 'Colonel Bogey March'. It seemed there was no truth to the song, and that soldiers sang it solely to deride the Nazi leader.

82

Later, evidence began to emerge that the satire had some truth to it after all. As a soldier in the German army during World War I, the future dictator was hurt in the Battle of the Somme in October 1916. Some hinted that the wound was in the thigh or the groin and could have resulted in an impairment that contributed to Hitler's lackluster sex life. The Fuehrer's World War I company commander said he had learned about his missing testicle as a result of a wartime VD exam. Other than this, no one suspected that Hitler's insistence to the last that he be completely cremated after his death was because he did not want the location of his war wound revealed.

Fortunately, the Russians exhumed the bodies at the bunker and examined them in 1945. In 1968 a published excerpt from the autopsy report stated that Hitler's "left testicle could not be found either in the scrotum or on the spermatic cord inside the inguinal canal, or in the small pelvis." In 1972 Dr. Reidar Sognnaes, a dental expert at UCLA, tested the Russian data against Hitler's proven medical history and pronounced the former—with its finding on the Fuehrer's missing testicle—genuine.

5. Like Kissing Hitler

Myth! Hitler had an active sex life and a fulfilled relationship with Eva Braun.

The claim that Hitler had numerous heterosexual liaisons—Glenn Infield's *Hitler's Secret Life* mentions at least eleven—is based largely on the statements of some of the women themselves. A few, were they alive today, might make matters even more interesting by suggesting rightly or wrongly that Hitler was gay or bisexual.

Nevertheless, Eva Braun, who married Hitler at the last minute, would probably deny the widely held belief that she had been his mistress before. Very few Germans actually knew about Eva and her relationship with Hitler, and those who did claimed the relationship was entirely platonic. That is to say, the two were extremely loyal to each other, but neither cared for sex with the other before or after the marriage.

The celebrated silent film actress Pola Negri was also rumored to be a Hitler mistress, but what apparently fueled the talks was nothing more than the Fuehrer's personal devotion to his favorite film, which starred Negri. The sultry Polish-American had a reputation for exaggerating her love affairs to promote herself. In Hitler's case, however, she took the matter one step backward by winning her suit against the French cinema magazine *Pour Vous* for alleging the existence of a clandestine affair.

Another purported Hitler mistress was his own niece, Geli Raubal, daughter of his widowed half-sister Angela. When Angela came to keep house for him in 1928, she brought Geli along, and Hitler, it is said, fell in love immediately. She was clearly flattered by his attention, but many doubted that she reciprocated his love or that he ever expressed himself sexually. He practiced a bizarre kind of paternalism over her, and when she objected, she was found shot dead in her room. Regardless of Hitler's strange behavior in the intimate company of women, there is no direct or clear evidence that he was ever attracted to a man.

6. Chief Execution Officer

Myth! Hitler founded the Nazi party.

According to the real story, he had absolutely nothing to do with the creation of the Nazi party. On a spying mission for the army in September 1919, Hitler attended a meeting of the German Workers' Party in Munich, presided over by a locksmith, Anton Drexler. The gathering of some 25 persons in a beer cellar did not impress Hitler at first, and he was prepared to forget about the visit. The next day, he was surprised to receive a postcard saying that he had been accepted in the organization. The future dictator went to the next committee meeting with the intention of explaining why he wasn't joining, but ended up changing his perception of the shabby group debating in the ill-lit back room. Forming a decision in his barracks later that evening, he became the party's seventh member.

The enterprising Hitler endeavored to build up the group's membership and eventually usurped its leadership. The party name was officially changed to the Nationalsozialistiche Deutsche

Arbeiterpartei, which was shortened to the one word 'Nazi' when the full nomenclature became too difficult for the average person to pronounce. Proving successful in advocating and popularizing Hitler's ideas, the nickname would eventually be written in blood in the pages of history by the Fuehrer and his followers.

Some wonder how things would have been had the party stuck to its original and true abbreviation—'Naso'. The anti-Nazi German writer Konrad Heiden devised the corrupted form 'Nazi', the Bavarian equivalent of 'simple-minded', to poke fun at the organization, but the word caught on despite the objections of its members.

7. Morpheus Ascending

Myth! Hitler "prepared for his life role as ruler of the world while in prison mulling over the German humiliation at Versailles."

As some history textbooks would have it, Hitler laid out his program in three stages: first, unifying the Germanic states; second, combining all of Europe as one empire; and third, placing the rest of the planet under German ascendancy or hegemony. But critics say this is as misleading as the belief that Germany prepared deliberately and meticulously for its impending confrontation with the Allies.

Mein Kampf admittedly contained some of the repellent and atrocious details of the Third Reich and of the New Order that Hitler would later inflict on conquered Europe. However, except for the unification of the Germanic states, including Austria, Poland, Hungary and Czechoslovakia, it did not indicate that the prime objective was a single European state under one leadership. Neither was a power axis or the eventual domination of the world by the Nazis hinted at. What Hitler aimed for was German influence that would propagate Aryanism and ethnic cleansing in Europe.

Military historian A.J.P. Taylor wrote in 1960 that Hitler had drifted into World War II one victory at a time and was himself surprised the early triumphs came so easily. These were in the beginning only random efforts to gain living space for Germany,

85

but their audacity soon led Hitler to invade the Soviet Union and engage in World War II in general. Hitler may have become aware at some point that a war of some ferocity and scope would be the necessary consequence of his nationalism, but he never thought for one moment that he might have to manage diverse conquered territories as a result of his actions.

8. From Hynkel to Hister

Myth! Centuries before the fact, Nostradamus predicted the rise of Hitler and the role he would play in history.

A quatrain in Century Two of Nostradamus' famous work draws a warlike scenario featuring a protagonist called Hister. "Beasts wild with hunger will cross the rivers, / The greater part of the battlefield will be against Hister, / He will drag the leader in a cage of iron, / When the child of Germany observes no law." In light of the allusions to a despot and soldiers engaged in a great war, and the suggestion in the last line that Hister is "the child of Germany (who) observes no law," the similarity between the names Hister and Hitler seems more than a coincidence.

Those who believe the portentous words can be explained in less spectacular fashion see Hister as just another name for Ister, Latin for the lower Danube. Nostradamus uses 'Hister' elsewhere in his prophecies to indicate the river, and in the quatrain in question he could be thinking of some battle sequence being fought there.

Both Hitler and Napoleon are commonly described as 'little corporals' whose military genius allowed them to build European empires. This parallelism has caused confusion in the interpretation of some of the prophesies, e.g.: "In the deepest part of Western Europe, a child will be born of poor family, who by his speech will entice many peoples. His reputation will grow even greater in the Kingdom of the East." If "deepest" means lowest, the place described is Napoleon's Corsica, otherwise it is Austria, where Hitler was born. The "Kingdom of the East" could be Japan, hence appropriate to Hitler, but it could also mean the Middle East or Egypt, where Napoleon became renowned.

86

Nostradamus' resort to obscure language, entangled metaphors and double entendres that can fit various situations seems to be why his prophecies are eerily accurate and familiar.

9. Ice in his Veins and Malice in his Heart

Myth! Northern Europe is the homeland of the Aryan race to which Hitler belonged.

The modern reference of the word 'Aryan' is not to people but to language. It used to have an ethnic signification, when it described a people that were actually not fair-skinned but black-haired and dark-skinned, and who thousands of years ago inhabited the Iranian plateau, moved into North India, and mixed with the groups there. Though their ethnicity has long been lost through assimilation, their basic language has served as the mainframe for the various Indo-European tongues throughout the two continents.

Strictly speaking, if there are any Aryans today, these are the Indians and the Iranians, whose ancestors used the word 'Aryan', meaning noble (from the Sanskrit *arya*), to characterize their language. Unfortunately for humanity, racists like Count Joseph Gobineau and Richard Wagner picked up the concept and refined it into what ultimately became a Nazi credo. Gobineau, who was not German but French, wrote in his *The Inequality of Human Races* (1855) that the Nordic peoples were the rightful heirs of Aryanism, and warned against their 'semitization' through interbreeding with yellow and dark-skinned people. When Wagner agreed, it was enough for Hitler to adapt the idea to his own purpose and to shift the Aryan homeland to the European heartland. In the end, Hitler would use the term to describe anything or anyone non-Jewish, including even the Japanese, who became honorary Aryans when they joined the Axis.

Some psychologists believe Hitler became paranoid about the Jews because of the suspicion that he himself might be of Jewish blood. The Gestapo had earlier reported that they could not find evidence of Hitler's Aryan beginnings. There were indications that his father Alois, who was born out of wedlock, was the son of a Jew, possibly a Rothschild who had employed Alois' mother as a housemaid. Alois grew up with his adoptive father's brother Johann von Nepomuk Hiedler, and ended up marrying Johann's daughter Klara to eventually beget Hitler. Since Johann von Nepomuk happens to be the name of the national saint of the Czech people, some historians see a Czech connection as well in the Hitler line. It is said this 'stain' in Hitler's supposed Aryan background is the reason for Der Fuehrer's life-long hatred for the Czechs, culminating in his destroying that nation.

Whatever be the truth in these speculations, Hitler was undoubtedly of inferior stock, not because of any alleged racial impurity but because illegitimacy, incest and commonality ran rampant in his genealogy. Alois was illegitimate, and Hitler's mother Klara, who might have been Alois' first cousin, worked as a household servant at the time of their marriage. Of the five Hitler siblings, only Adolf and a half-sister survived infancy. The latter, Angela, was a cook in a Jewish charity kitchen, and one of her two daughters who would later serve with her as Hitler's housemaids would be rumored as his lover and would die by murder or suicide because of it.

10. Fahrenheit 1938

Myth! Hitler once attended a giant book-burning rally with Nazi soldiers in Berlin in the late 1930s.

After scanning an early version of the movie *Indiana Jones and the Last Crusade*, we noted the double gaffe in the scene where Indy meets Hitler and brassily asks for the Nazi's autograph. Actually, it should have been a triple gaffe. The scene itself is a glaring historical inaccuracy as it tries to reenact the May 1933 book burning that occurred in Berlin a few months after Hitler became Chancellor. The effort falls flat, considering that the real event was a midnight affair attended by thousands of students, not soldiers, at a square on Unter den Linden opposite the University of Berlin. The flames consumed some twenty thousand books, among them the works of Mann, Einstein, Remarque, Sinclair, Freud, Gide, Zola and Proust. Hitler was absent, and in his place stood Dr. Goebbels, the Propaganda Minister, who announced the new Nazi hypocrisy when he declared with no inkling of the

88

forthcoming tragedy: "The soul of the German people can again express itself. These flames not only illuminate the final end of an old era; they also light up the new.

---

11. New Twist on an Old Symbol

Myth! Hitler invented the swastika symbol and designed the Nazi flag.

Neither Hitler nor any of the other Nazis invented the swastika, which got its name from the Sanskrit word *svastika*, meaning well-being and good fortune. The symbol dates back to ca. 2500 BC in India and in Central Asia (Buddha's footprints were said to have been swastikas). Long before the Germans stumbled on the strange shape, it had made appearances in some parts of Europe and the US. Navajo blankets were woven with swastikas, while synagogues in, of all places, Hartford were built with swastika mosaics. A 1933 study reveals that, from India, the swastika crossed Persia and Asia Minor to Greece, reaching Italy and Germany, probably in the first millennium B.C. In the 1870s the German archaeologist Heinrich Schliemann found artifacts with swastikas in the site of Homer's Troy on the shores of the Dardanelles, establishing a link with the swastikas he had seen near the Oder River in Germany.

In the twentieth century, the Germans were among several nationalities that found the symbol exciting. According to Steven Heller ("The Swastika; Symbol Beyond Redemption,"), the Germanen order, an anti-Semitic group that wore helmets with Wotan horns and plotted against "Jewish elements in German life," used a curved swastika on a cross as its insignia. By 1914, the Wandervogel, a militarist German youth movement, made it a nationalist emblem, and six years later the Nazi party laid its undisputed claim on it.

While most authors agree that it was Hitler himself who chose the swastika as the national symbol of the movement, the only proof of this is his statement, made post facto in *Mein Kampf* (1925), that he had searched for a Nazi symbol and had toyed with the idea of using swastikas. In the same book, Hitler also mentioned that the Party finally decided to adopt the swastika

89

based on a submission by Friedrich Krohn, a dentist from Starnberg. The design, Hitler added, was similar to his own, except that Krohn's swastika "curved clockwise" and was "composed into a white disk." This 'swastika in a disk' eventually became the Nazi flag, with Hitler's only contribution being a reversal in the swastika's direction so that it appeared to spin counterclockwise.

12. A Reich Staged Fire

Myth! Germany's economic blight brought about by rampant inflation precipitated the rise of Nazism in the 1930s.

It is not readily taken into account that inflation had come and gone before Hitler came into power. Hitler was still in prison when a financial wizard by the name of Hjalmar Schacht stabilized the currency and ended its ruinous depreciation. The more believable reason for the growth of Nazism, albeit controversial, is a concrete one—the Reichstag fire, which gave the Nazis an excuse to exploit people's fears of social chaos and Communist agitation.

William Shirer reports "there is enough evidence to establish beyond a reasonable doubt that it was the Nazis who planned the arson and carried it out for their own political ends." An underground passage built to carry the central heating system ran from Goering's Reichstag President's Palace to the Reichstag building. Through this tunnel on the night of February 27, Karl Ernst, who would later become the Berlin SA leader, led a small detachment of storm troopers to the Reichstag, where they scattered gasoline and self-igniting chemicals.

But A.J.P. Taylor exonerates the Nazis, laying the blame instead on a Dutch Communist named Marinus van der Lubbe, who confessed to the crime and was beheaded after conviction at a trial. It was obvious that German sentiment at the time favored Taylor's theory, since at the general election held just a week after the fire broke out, the Nazis were rewarded with a working majority in parliament.

13. Heil to the Dark Chief

Myth! All German soldiers automatically became members of the Nazi Party, and were obliged to execute the unique Heil Hitler salute.

It is wrong to assume that the German armed forces were completely Nazified during the years of the Third Reich. Only a few, mainly officers, joined the party and as a result wore the swastika armband and did the various things expected of a Nazi.

The typical rank-and-file soldier was not a Nazi and should not be called such, and at least for this reason the Nazi salute was not an official gesture of the German military until the last days of the Reich. The throngs seen in pictures executing the salute in unison at Nuremberg and other ceremonial places were generally not Reichwehr contingents but Hitler's brown shirts (SA) or black shirts (SS). The Nazi salute was imposed throughout the German armed forces only nine months before the war ended in Europe and ten years after Hitler became absolute ruler following Hindenburg's death.

It has been noted that the Nazi salute copied the way Americans paid obeisance to their flag—right arm extended, hand slightly raised, but with the palm up—from the time it had become fashionable to do so and until World War II, when Congress had it replaced with the right-hand-over-the-heart gesture to avoid the embarrassing coincidence. Similarly, the goose-step style of marching that one still sees in some Middle Eastern countries and in the former U.S.S.R., though credited by many to the Nazis as their invention, was copied from armies that had used it thousands of years before World War II.

14. No Fences Tempt Bad Neighbors

Myth! At the instigation of Hitler and the Nazis, Germany gobbled up Austria through the Anschluss of 1938.

A well-planned coup d'état by the Austrian Nazi Party in March of 1938 gave the signal for the Wehrmacht to enter Vienna

91

and enforce the Anschluss. Long a part of Hitler's dream of empire, the Anschluss was carried out despite the treaties of Versailles and St. Germain, which specifically prohibited the union of Austria and Germany.

However, the verdict of history that it was Hitler who decided the merger of Austria with Germany may not be fair at all. Despite the opposition of the League of Nations, the Allies and Austria's Chancellor Kurt Schuschnigg, Austrians even more than Germans wanted to have the boundaries between the two countries removed permanently. According to impartial reports, 99.75 % of Austrians and 99.08 % of Germans voted in favor of their unification at separate plebiscites held that year.

Historians who claim the Austrians were intimidated in 1938 forget that earlier, in March 1931, a free Austria had voted 90 percent in favor of merging with its German neighbor. When Germany failed to react—it had its hands full with Nazi and Communist rebellions at the time—the Austrian government followed up with a proposal for a German-Austrian customs union by the end of the year. The Allies opposed the move, claiming that a customs union involved infringement of Austrian sovereignty and violated obligations assumed by the Austrian government. Germany and Austria had no choice but to renounce the project on September 3, 1931.

Going back farther, on November 12, 1918, the day after the armistice, the Provisional National Assembly in Vienna, which had just overthrown the Hapsburg monarchy and proclaimed the Austrian Republic, tried to effect an Anschluss by affirming that "German Austria is a component part of the German Republic." This was the earliest indication that an Anschluss had always been popular with the Austrians, but that the Allies would defy it for as long as there was no Hitler to contend with.

15. Black God, White Devil

Myth! Hitler snubbed Jesse Owens after the black American won his first gold medal at the 1936 Berlin Olympics.

92

According to news reports, Hitler was pleased with the results of the 1936 Berlin Olympics because the Germans won more than all the other countries combined. Nevertheless, he snubbed Owens after the latter had just won his first gold medal, and he left the Olympic Stadium in a huff, apparently miffed that a black man had prevailed against his Aryan competitors.

This may have been the impression given to the papers, but it's contrary to what Owens later admitted and which others on the scene corroborated. After shaking hands with all the German victors on the first day of competition (at which time Owens had not yet earned any medal), Hitler had been told by the Olympic Committee that to maintain Olympic neutrality, he would have to congratulate everyone or no one. Hitler chose the latter, hence, on subsequent days, he did not honor Owens or any of the other participants, including the German winners.

The Fuehrer did ignore a black athlete—Cornelius Johnson—on the first day by leaving the stadium before the awarding ceremonies. But Nazi apologists explained that there were also white medalists he failed to congratulate on that occasion because he had a prior engagement.

---

16. Mutant Ideology

Myth! Nazism was an all-new ideology shaped by Prussian militarism and Nietzsche's concept of the superman.

Students of the Third Reich say Nazism was nothing new, as it was simply an alter ego of virulent Germanism—racist, militaristic, expansionist and dictatorial. According to E. H. Dance, "Most of the Nazi teaching about history was not Nazi at all. It is German—and it can be found in German history books published long before Nazism was born."

However, this should not necessarily mean that the Germans, and by extension the Nazis, were militaristic because of Prussian influence, or, for that matter, that Prussianism was a form of militarism. Shenkman argues that through most of history, Germans were not really any more aggressive than their neighbors, and even if they were, they could not have been influenced by the Prussians, who were not war-like by tradition as

93

they are imagined to be. In fact, the Prussian leaders who eventually supported the Nazis were not originally Prussian, since their roots were in southern Germany, and neither were they Prussian enough when it came to some of "the old Prussian virtues," such as racial tolerance.

The two historical figures who contributed more than any other in shaping the Prussian image were Frederick the Great and Otto von Bismarck, but both are relatively modern-day developments and were founders rather than inheritors of Prussian military tradition. Frederick's rape of Silesia was actually considered "unPrussian-like, Frederick's forebears having achieved a deserved reputation for docility." And while Bismarck's militarism was undeniable, he did not rule in the name of Prussia's old guards, the Hohenzollerns, who were in fact regarded as stumbling blocks to Bismarck's plan for a grand German state.

The belief persists that Hitler used the writings of the German philosopher Nietzsche to promote the aims of Nazism, particularly as these were related to the idea of the superman. What only a few have come to realize is that most of these writings were not by Nietzsche at all, and the few that he did write were misinterpreted to entertain the notion of Aryan superiority or Semitic subservience. It was not even Nietzsche but Goethe who invented the word 'superman' (*übermensch*), the latter using it in his *Faust* (1808, 1833) to refer to an extraordinarily gifted person. Nietzsche adopted the term for his transcendent man in *Thus Spake Zarathustra,* and George Bernard Shaw later popularized it in his play, *Man and Superman* (1903). Nietzsche himself was not only vehemently opposed to anti-Semitism, he openly favored intermarriage with the Jews to improve the German race. He ended his long friendship with the composer Richard Wagner, whose bigotry he eventually found insufferable, and hated Bernhard Förster, husband of his sister Elisabeth, for his virulently anti-Semitic ideas.

The culprit who fed Hitler with tainted copies of Nietzsche's writings was Elisabeth, who had acquired her husband's strong prejudices. The Försters opened a 'pure' Christian German colony in Paraguay, but after Förster's suicide due to a financial scandal, Elisabeth returned to Germany purportedly to edit some of her brother's writings and notes. Instead, she forged documents to misrepresent Nietzsche's thoughts after his death in 1900, meriting for her, oddly enough, a Nobel Prize nomination in literature.

17. Christian Heart

Myth! The non-Jewish King Christian X of Denmark showed his disapproval of the Nazi-imposed "yellow badge" armband by wearing one himself.

Popular history has made much of the legend describing how King Christian X, a non-Jew, thwarted the Nazis by opting to wear the so-called 'yellow badge'—a white armband with a blue Star of David and the word 'Jude' stamped on it—when the occupiers ordered Danish Jews during World War II to identify themselves in this manner. It is said all of Christian's non-Jewish subjects showed sympathy for the monarch and their Jewish countrymen by donning the armbands as well.

The legend has long been debunked, a few times by the Danes themselves, including Queen Margrethe II, who has been quoted as saying it is "a beautiful and symbolic story" but is not true. Although the Danes undertook numerous heroic efforts to oppose the Nazi regime and protect their Jewish compatriots, there is no real-life example to prove that the 'yellow badge' incident was one of them. Neither King Christian nor any Danish citizen, Jew or non-Jew, ever wore the badge, and no German official ever issued an order requiring Danish Jews to display it.

The legend obviously has multiple historical and other sources, not the least of which is the shameful practice of Christian and Muslim countries in the past of segregating their Jewish citizens from the rest of society by forcing on them a public means of identification. The various Nazi regimes of Europe set a notorious example in World War II when they required ghetto residents to sew patches that contained distinct Jewish symbols and elements on armbands or other prominent parts of their clothing.

The legend could also have derived partly from reports, mostly true, of how the King and his subjects reacted adversely to the Nazi occupation of Denmark. For instance, to show their defiance for this trespass on their sovereignty, they started wearing four coins tied together with red and white ribbons in their buttonholes. Red and white are the Danish colors, and four coins totaling nine ore represented the date of the occupation, April 9. For his part, King Christian was a known liberal and democrat who "rejected many aspects of the occupation, made speeches against the occupying force and became known as a protector of the Jews." Biographical notes often describe the King's habit of riding his horse alone through Copenhagen every morning, unarmed and without escort, to underscore his personal belief that "all Danes are equal."

The general perception of how the Danish king would have handled a 'yellow badge' situation is yet another source of the myth. One scenario was offered by a Swedish cartoon (cited in *Snopes.com*), in which the former Danish prime minister asks the monarch, "What are we going to do, Your Majesty, if Scavenius (the German-anointed prime minister) makes all the Jews wear yellow stars?" The King's reply: "We'll all have to wear yellow stars." Another was provided by Margrethe II, who said: "The myth about the King wearing the star of David ... I can imagine that this could have originated from a typical remark by a Copenhagen errand boy on his bicycle: 'If they try to enforce the yellow star here, the King will be the first to wear it!'"

18. One-Step Victory

Myth! Hitler danced a victory jig after France signed the armistice containing the terms of her capitulation to Germany in World War II.

Barely more than a week after the Allies withdrew from Dunkirk, the Germans occupied Paris, forcing the French to sue for armistice. Hitler laid down his terms: the armistice must be signed on the same spot where Germany had capitulated to France and her allies on November 11, 1918. German army engineers pulled the old railway car in which the signing had taken place onto the tracks in the center of the clearing in the woods at Compiegne. On the afternoon of June 21, 1940, Hitler arrived in his big Mercedes and entered the railroad car, passing the granite marker in which was engraved the World War I German surrender.

Later, newsreels would show Hitler dancing a victory jig apparently in celebration of the French capitulation. Millions of viewers who saw this in reruns of the newsreels took it for granted that Hitler was doing his silly little dance upon learning the news that France had surrendered. Only a few would learn later that the incident never really happened, whether at Compiegne or elsewhere. The original film had been shot by the Germans and showed Hitler jumping once in astonishment at something that was never disclosed. But Allied propagandists cleverly looped the 'jumping' segment and were able to produce the illusion of Hitler gloating merrily over the defeat of the French.

19. Child of the Damned

Myth! Propaganda minister Joseph Goebbels once posed Hitler with 'the perfect Aryan child' for a photo to be used on a German postcard.

Hitler and his cohorts were then promoting within their sphere of influence the philosophy of Aryan racial supremacy upon which Nazism was grounded. The postcard was to spread the idea that the Fuehrer was as genetically pure as the German child, and both, as models of the Aryan race, were the new hopes of the fatherland. It was irony of the grandest order, for evidence would later be unearthed that neither subject was qualified for the project. The similarity between Hitler and the child was in fact not in their Aryanism but in their Jewishness.

In their haste to do their master's bidding, the propaganda people came up with a perfect Aryan-looking child, not knowing that what flowed in its veins was pure Jewish blood. As for Hitler, the Gestapo would submit a report at the height of his power that the Fuehrer himself may have been tainted with Jewish stock from his grandfather. It was one more providential proof that Hitler's purported Aryanism was a farce.

Except for the part that raises doubts about Hitler's genealogy, the anecdote has nothing to support it and appears to be just a rumor aimed at discrediting Hitler and the Nazis' claim to racial ascendancy. Historians nevertheless believe that the Nazis were indeed obsessed with the theme of the 'Perfect Aryan Child' and were prepared to carry it out in one form or other. Their research has recently uncovered a Hitler-sponsored social program codenamed 'Lebensborn', which called for the kidnapping of thousands of children from occupied countries and their eventual 'Nazification' by the German state. The purpose, as Goebbels' postcard project no doubt intended to propagate, was to create "the perfect Aryan race to rule the world for 1,000 years."

20. Nutsy Nazi

Myth! Hitler hated Chaplin for his role in *The Great Dictator*, the first Hollywood effort to place the Nazi leader in an embarrassing light.

The genius of Chaplin, though already on the wane in 1940, was still evident in *The Great Dictator*, a satire on totalitarianism and a biting commentary by 'Chaplin the Jew' on the Nazis' anti-Semitic stance in Europe. The Fuehrer, according to witnesses, rankled at the mere mention of the film, and it was rumored that, for this 'indiscretion', Chaplin had been placed on the Nazi hit list. But others claimed having seen Hitler sneak into his private screening room to view the film on at least two occasions, and the speculation was that, as a confirmed movie buff, a true admirer of Chaplin's genius and a lover of slapstick comedy, he just couldn't help paying homage to it.

While *The Great Dictator* was Chaplin's first full talkie and the first to show him in a dual role, many thought the real distinction was that it was the first major film to make fun of Hitler—and Mussolini to boot. This was fallacious, of course, for although the film was banned in several places, including Chicago, where a large segment of the population was German, it was not the first time Hitler and his cohorts were mocked on the screen by popular comedians of the period. The first to razz the Fuehrer was Moe Howard of the Three Stooges, when this classic slapstick trio starred in a short, *You Nazty Spy*, nine months before *The Great Dictator* made its debut. Moe played the dictator of a country called Moronika, but his uniform, moustache, and hairstyle betrayed the intended similarity with Hitler. Curly Howard and Larry Fine portrayed shady characters that looked suspiciously like Hitler cronies Goebbels and Goering.

98

VIII

Majorities Of One

On Notable Despots

"The greatest and noblest pleasure
which we have in this world is to
discover new truths, and the next
is to shake off prejudices."

•

Frederick the Great

1. Alexander's Wartime Bent

Myth! When Aristotle asked why he was weeping, Alexander the Great replied, "Because there are no more worlds to conquer!"

The two best known legends about Alexander the Great may have really happened, but not in the way they have been recounted over the centuries as part of popular lore. The first involves his encounter with the Gordian Knot, which had presented a 'knotty' problem that no man before Alexander could solve by any method. It is said that when the Phrygians were without a monarch, an oracle decreed that the next man to enter the city driving an ox-cart should become their king. A poor peasant, Gordias, fulfilled the prophecy and was declared king by the priests; in gratitude, his son Midas dedicated the ox-cart to the Phrygian god and tied it to a post with an intricate knot of cornel bark. Alexander, while wintering at Gordium in 333 BC, saw the ox-cart still standing in the palace of the former Phrygian kings, and thereupon attempted to untie the knot. Unable to find its end, he sliced it in half with a stroke of his sword. Enthused by this brutal yet clever performance by their hero, Alexander's biographers claimed falsely and in retrospect that an oracle had prophesied that the one to untie the knot would become the king of Asia.

Almost all sources from antiquity confirm that Alexander was confronted with the challenge of the Knot, but do not agree on the means by which he solved it. Plutarch brands the claim that Alexander sliced the Knot with his sword as false, and relates that according to Aristobolus of Cassandreia, a Greek historian who accompanied Alexander on his campaigns, the Macedonian pulled the Knot out of its pole pin, exposing the two ends and allowing him to untie the Knot without having to cut through it. While some classical scholars regard this as more plausible than the popular account, it is the latter that has become entrenched in general usage as a metaphor for an intractable problem ('the Gordian knot") requiring a bold stroke ("the Alexandrian solution") to unravel.

The second legend, which somehow shows our hero up for his ambitions, tells about the time Aristotle chanced upon Alexander weeping. When the great teacher asked why the tears, his pupil gave the famous reply, "Because there are no more worlds to conquer!" The Macedonian champion, having subdued the Greek city-states and conquered the whole Persian Empire, was expressing his boredom at the lack of further prospects. The quote has been attributed without any specific citation to the English poet John Milton (1608-1674), who makes some references to Alexander in both *Paradise Lost* and *Paradise Regained* but never in the same context or in words matching the quote in question. Researchers, citing W.W. Tarn in his *Alexander The Great II* (1948), insist that neither the incident nor the quote occurs anywhere in ancient writings, not even in the Alexandrian romances. Their conclusion, which has remained unwelcome to most Alexander fans, is that it never happened.

Modern debunkers say the more plausible view is that the whole thing happened, though in a different light—Alexander cried out of frustration not because he had no more worlds to conquer but because he had not yet won any new territory. In this account, a Greek Sophist named Anaxarchus was needling Alexander, reminding him that there were a great many other worlds besides the Eastern to mock his ambitions. To which Alexander said, "Do you not think it worthy of lamentation that when there is such a vast multitude of worlds, we have not yet conquered one?" An Internet forum has suggested Aelian (170-230 A.D.), in *Historical Miscellany*, translated by Nigel G. Wilson, as possibly the oldest source for this remark and the incident in which it was made. But an even better reference is Plutarch's essay in his *Moralia* entitled "On Contentment of the Mind," which recites the true version in full. Notable paraphrasing appears in Samuel Butler and John Calvin's works.

Although Alexander had spread Hellenism to much of the East, the great commander still would have wanted the whole of India but couldn't because of a mutiny of his men. He had yet to conquer as well Asia Minor, Arabia and the Caspian, all of which were foremost in his plans when he died. Thus, uttered at this point, Alexander's complaint to Anaxarchus assume greater probity than the one popular tradition says he addressed to Aristotle.

2. The Last Days of Shahdom

Myth! The Shah of Iran's noble lineage dates to the days of Darius the Great, while Ethiopia's Haile Selassie, a commoner, descended from Solomon and Sheba.

Supporters of the Shah of Iran claim he never lost his inherited titles and names, including Mohammed Pahlavi, King of Kings and Sun of the Aryans, when the Ayatollah Kohmeni ousted him from the throne of modern Persia. The Shah's father, Reza Pahlavi, was himself the Shah until he gave way to his son under pressure from the Allies during World War II.

What is not readily known is that the name Pahlavi, from an ancient Persian language, sounds incongruous when applied to Reza, who was just a donkey driver before becoming an army private and later cavalry officer. He rose to become war minister of Ahmad Shah, finally taking over in a military coup that abolished the monarchy, and then proclaiming himself the new shah after restoring the monarchy four years later.

On the other hand, Haile Selassie, also called Black Napoleon, Lion of Judah and Might of the Trinity, was born Ejarsa Gora or Tafari Makonnen. Later known as Lij Tafari, then Ras Tafari, he was not exactly a commoner but a great grandson of King Sahle Selassie of Shewa (Shoa), a province of Ethiopia, and son of a chief adviser to the Ethiopian emperor Menelik II. Formerly a provincial governor, Ras was named regent and heir to the throne when the daughter of Menelik became empress in 1916.

However, Ras' direct descent from King Solomon of Israel and the Queen of Sheba of the Aksumite Kingdom is pure hokum. Ras himself created the sham connection when, after becoming emperor in 1930 as Haile Selassie, he formulated a constitution that affirmed his Biblical lineage. The provision established succession to the throne by male primogeniture and vested full sovereignty in the emperor, all as part of the Rastafarian beliefs that Selassie and his supporters developed for Ethiopia and the region.

To his followers, Selassie's descent pursuant to the constitutional fiat is as much a matter of faith as the celebrated meeting between Solomon and Sheba. In 1 *Kings* 10 and 2 *Chronicles* 9, the "queen of the South" (Saba in southwestern

102

Arabia), having heard of Solomon and eager to test his wisdom with "hard questions," went to see him in his kingdom. Rastafarians suggest Sheba was black and had an affair with Solomon, but there is no real evidence of these. Noting that she brought some goods with her on her visit, most other interpreters are convinced that all she really wanted was to establish trade channels with Israel before returning to her own country.

3. Wise as an Owl, Poor as a Dormouse

Myth! The historicity of King Solomon is proved by the three most magnificent structures he built during his reign—his Temple, his Mines and his Stables.

The renowned Temple, Mines and Stables have long been attributed by tradition to King Solomon, but there are historical and archaeological indications that they were not really his.

Although the Temple was built during his time, Solomon only contributed some men to the project, which was planned and implemented overall by others. His father King David, who also stockpiled the materials used for the edifice, provided the concept, while the actual designers and builders were Phoenicians under the direction of King Hiram of Tyre.

The Temple has since disappeared, but the ancient mineshafts believed to be King Solomon's Mines could still be seen in the sheer cliffs of a massive rock formation in Wadi Timnah in Israel. Archaeologists have shown that these mines were worked at various times before and after, but never during, Solomon's reign. They are copper mines, and should not be confused with the fictional diamond mines set in H. Rider Haggard's 1892 novel *King Solomon's Mines* on the borders of present-day Angola, Zaire and Zambia.

Finally, it has been conclusively proved that Solomon's Stables, the 'chariot cities' along the frontier where highly mobile troops similar to the Cossacks and the Bengal Lancers of more modern times were stationed, were organized only after Solomon's death. Potteries found in these sites indicate that the buildings were built a century later, during the reign of King Ahab. But the revelation has not prevented tourists from flocking to the ancient ruins in

Hazor, Megiddo, and Gedser in Israel to gaze at what is believed to be the first garrison system built for border defense.

4. The Bad, the Good and the Bohemian

Myth! King Wenceslas of Bohemia was the model for Good King Wenceslas of Christmas carol fame.

The traditional Christmas carol "Good King Wenceslas" sings the virtues of a real man. The whole trouble is there were four monarchs with the same name who ruled Bohemia from the early 13th century to the close of the fourteenth.

The identity of Good King Wenceslas is further confused because, although Wenceslas I, II, and IV were generally good, the one most often mistaken for Good King Wenceslas is the dissolute Wenceslas III. This rogue loved his hunting dogs more than his wife, and did so even after they had killed her while she slept.

The popular Wenceslas I (1205-53) brought Austria under his dynasty's rule while using the influence of German colonists and artisans to keep Bohemia strong, prosperous and culturally progressive. The strong and efficient Wenceslas II (1271-1305), who also became king of Poland, overcame a powerful faction of nobles, then ruled his Bohemian kingdom ably and spread his influence into Poland and Hungary. Wenceslas IV (1361-1419), concurrently the German king, was weak, submissive and largely incompetent, but as a peace-loving man, he is seen by many as the best suited among the four for the role of Good King Wenceslas.

Encyclopedists and historians prefer a fifth Wenceslas, albeit he was not a king but a prince-duke of Bohemia who died a martyr at age 22 and was canonized as patron saint of Czechoslovakia. Saint Wenceslas (c. 907-929) was a pious man and an avowed virgin, but the non-Christian members of the nobility, antagonized by his efforts to spread Christianity, induced his own brother Boleslav I to waylay him right at the church door.

5. Buttons and Bows

Myth! To cure his men of the habit of brushing their mouths and faces with their sleeves, Frederick the Great ordered buttons sewed on the sleeves of all uniforms.

The same quaint story of how Napoleon revised a fashion in military uniforms is told of Frederick the Great. The latter, so the story goes, was very particular about the way his troops appeared in the field. One day, he noticed that when his soldiers sweated, they mopped their brows with their coat sleeves, and after a hard session out, their sleeves would be covered with unsightly stains. Frederick finally thought of the perfect solution: sew buttons on the sleeves so that the soldiers would scratch their faces open every time they tried to use their coats for handkerchiefs.

It is said that sleeve buttons were the first items in military style to be carried over to civilian dress, but there is no real evidence to support this or the claim that Napoleon or Frederick invented them. The fashion world has a simpler and more convincing explanation: men used to wear their sleeves very tightly, and buttons were sewed on their top sides so that the wearer could unbutton them to get his hands through.

6. Gay Warriors

Myth! No two modern figures are more aggressively masculine than Frederick II the Great of Prussia and Kaiser Wilhelm II of Germany.

Standard history books tell us that both men were pillars of militarism and believers in territorial expansion through conquest. Known for his rape of Silesia, Frederick II got involved in three major conflicts, one after the other—the War of the Austrian Succession, the invasion of Bohemia and the Seven Years' War. But his violent streak could not quell a homosexual tendency that began during his teens with his first big love, a handsome lieutenant named Hans von Katte. When Hans' head was chopped

105

off in front of him at the instance of his father, Frederick William I, he was so terrified that he submitted himself completely to the absolute authority of William until, at 21, he was forced to marry Princess Elizabeth Christine of Brunswick-Bevern. Although she was pretty and only eighteen, he neglected her and spent most of his time "fondling his valet and his flute."

Kaiser Wilhelm II, on the other hand, is popularly regarded in Allied circles as the prime instigator of World War I. But what you will only hear from forthright German tourist guides is that his war-like quality masked a sexual preference that was less than masculine. Though he managed to have six sons and a daughter, Wilhelm, Queen Victoria's grandson, enjoyed the company of men much more than of his wife. There was, in particular, his beloved friend Philip, Count Eulenburg, who was later charged with molesting young boys in 1907. Victoria seemed to have been aware of Kaiser Bill's predilection, but was afraid her stopping it could erupt into a scandal. His vice was eventually forgotten "when he lapsed into becoming a war criminal instead."

---

7. Straddler on a Horse

Myth! Rising from the masses, Rodrigo de Vivar became Spain's national hero by championing the cause of the Christians against the Moors using the Spanish nickname El Cid.

Rodrigo has been the subject of a biography that inspired the spectacular movie *El Cid* (1961), but both biography and film have not dealt correctly with some aspects of this hero's life. For instance, de Vivar is described as a man of the masses who worked his way to the top, yet he actually had an elite social background. This consisted of his direct connections on his mother's side with the great landed aristocracy, and in his early life with the court of Ferdinand I as part of the household of that king's eldest son, the future Sancho II of Castile.

Contrary to the popular tradition that he was appointed commander of the royal troops despite his indifference to Sancho's design to annex his brother Alfonso's kingdom of Leon, he was an out-and-out supporter of Sancho and his help was instrumental in

Alfonso's defeat. Later, when Sancho was assassinated, the previously dethroned Alfonso took over and did his best to win Rodrigo's allegiance. However, El Cid was unwilling to come to terms, belying the claim of many of his biographers that he was run out of favor with the new king by the intrigue of jealous landed interests.

Most people think El Cid was the champion of the Christians against the Moors. But far from giving assistance to his fellow Christians, Rodrigo actually waged battle with some of them, enough to have him banished from the kingdom. It was during his exile that he offered his services to the Muslim rulers of Saragossa, whom he served loyally for almost a decade, fighting and defeating their Christian enemies. As a result, he acquired the Arabic nickname El Cid, for 'Lord'; his Spanish nickname was, ironically, El Campeador (The Champion).

---

8. The Man from Five Corners

Myth! Simon de Bolivar founded Venezuela and four other countries in the Americas, freeing them from the Spanish dictatorship in a campaign that lasted until his death.

Bolivar wasn't originally a Venezuelan but a Spaniard born in Greater Colombia. The latter was the only state Bolivar ever founded after winning the land from Spain in 1819.

Peru was then another Spanish-held territory that included Upper Peru, or what is now Bolivia. Peru and Bolivia had their own sets of founding patriots, and would never have come under Bolivar's influence had they not asked him for help in their fight for liberation from the Spanish. Although it was mainly his forces that drove out the royalists, Bolivar was not well liked by the Peruvians and Bolivians because of his distinct bias for Colombia, where he ruled as dictator. For this reason, he was discouraged from tarrying in either country to participate in its political processes.

When Venezuela, hitherto a part of Greater Colombia, seceded in 1829, Ecuador remained a department, but it, too, seceded in 1830, the year Bolivar died, leaving only Colombia and what would later be Panama. Bolivar obviously did not found

Venezuela and Ecuador, as they were instead formed in reaction to his rule. Panama is sometimes included as one of those he established, but our hero had long been dead when this country gained its independence from Colombia.

The supreme irony of Bolivar, which is also his glory, is that freedom fighters in the region who could not be reconciled to his dictatorial style and his firm belief that the states should be ruled by a president for life continued to regard him as the greatest libertarian ever.

9. The Iron Giant

Myth! Called 'The Iron Chancellor' because of his dictatorial and warmongering ways, Prussian premier Otto von Bismarck coined the slogan 'blood and iron'.

Wordsmiths believe Bismarck was called 'The Iron Chancellor' not because of his governing style but because of his fondness for the phrase 'blood and iron'. Bismarck used the words in this sequence after he got tired of saying them in reverse, as what he did in a speech to the Budget Commission of the Prussian House of Delegates on September 30, 1862: "It is desirable and it is necessary that the condition of affairs in Germany and of her constitutional relations should be improved; but this cannot be accomplished by speeches and resolutions of a majority, but only by iron and blood [*Eisen und Blut*]." A different source (*The Columbia Dictionary of Quotations*, Columbia University Press, 1993) notes that Bismarck said almost the same thing the day before, on September 29, 1862: "The great questions of the day will not be settled by means of speeches and majority decisions... but by iron and blood."

Obviously, Bismarck liked the metaphor so much that he repeated it often, although it was by no means original with him. The earliest known user of the phrase was Quintilian, the Roman orator of the first century AD, whose Latin *sanguinem et ferrum* is rendered in English in the statement, "Warfare seems to signify blood and iron."

108

10. Mummy's Boy

Myth! Tutankhamen, a revered and powerful Egyptian pharaoh who died after a long and peaceful reign, was buried in a magnificent tomb alongside part of his fabulous wealth.

The reality is that Tutankhamen (aka Tutenkhamon or King Tut, c.1350 BC) was an improbable king who never led his army into battle, having become pharaoh at age 9 and dying some 10 years later. His sole accomplishment was the eradication of the monotheistic influence of his father-in-law, Akhenaten or Ikhnaton, the previous pharaoh who worshipped the sun god Aten. This he achieved by destroying Aten's temple and transferring Egypt's capital to Thebes, the sacred abode of the god Amon.
　　Even this deed is suspect, however, since, as most historians believe, Tutankhamen was just a naive and powerless figurehead whom the priests used as a front and who was murdered when he became recalcitrant. He would never have become a historical celebrity had Howard Carter and the earl of Carnarvon not discovered his tomb almost intact in 1922. Further archaeological investigation has brought to light that Tut died from a head wound; that he was poor relative to the other pharaohs during this period; and that his tomb looked fabulous only because his murderers hastily stuffed it with things connected with him in their desire to get rid of the king as quickly as possible.

11. Frankly Franco

Myth! With US moral support, General Francisco Franco successfully defended Spain in a civil war fomented by leftists and the liberal elements of the Roman Catholic Church.

It is wrongly assumed that General Franco led the established government of Spain during the Spanish Civil War. What is true is the exact opposite—Franco and his forces were the

109

'revolutionaries' who rebelled. The misconception apparently arose because two traditional bastions of conservatism, the established Church and the army, assisted Franco, whereas the Popular Front, or Loyalist government in power, was championed by various liberal and radical elements.

It is also not true that the US came to the aid of Franco during this period. Not one American who got involved in the war had the official blessing of the US government, and practically none went to the side of Franco. About 2,800 Americans—acrobats, trade unionists, professors, artists and actors among them—traveled to Spain in 1936 to volunteer in the Loyalist army of the shaky young Republican government, just five years free of its ancient monarchy and now threatened by well-armed rebellious Fascist military leaders. Technically a battalion, the American unit was called the Abraham Lincoln Brigade, or informally 'the Lincolns'. Few of the Americans had military experience, and more than half died in the three-year conflict.

12. The Duke of Railroads

Myth! Italy's Benito Mussolini coined the rallying phrase "make the trains run on time" to commemorate his achievement of making the trains run on time.

Some of Mussolini's critics had a kind word for him: "At least he made the trains run on time." This was a way of saying that Mussolini succeeded in replacing Italy's anarchic situation after World War I with the regimentation and efficiency of his new order. He had every reason not to fail, for in 1925 he had installed himself in five of Italy's top cabinet posts—premier, minister of foreign affairs, minister of war, minister of air, and minister of marine—and he also functioned as minister of agriculture, a non-cabinet position.

Apparently, it was Mussolini himself who had vowed "to make the trains run on time," although it is doubtful that he coined the phrase, as there is no known speech by him in which this appears. Although Axis propaganda claimed that he fulfilled his promise, this has been refuted by people who lived in Italy between the March on Rome (October 1922) and the execution at Como (April

1945). In their view, Mussolini made no significant impact on Italy's railroad schedules, which were as notoriously inefficient as they had ever been. One historian, Bergen Evans, who was in Italy in the summer of 1930 ("Mussolini's heyday, when a fascist guard rode on every train"), said that he was "willing to make an affidavit to the effect that most Italian trains on which (he) traveled were not on schedule—or near it."

It seems it was the Tokyo trains that ran safely and efficiently during World War II, even more than the sabotage-prone railway system of the Nazis.

Founding Fathers, US Presidents & British PMs

I

By George He Did It!?

On George Washington

"I hope I shall possess firmness and
virtue enough to maintain what I consider
the most enviable of all titles, the
character of an honest man."

•

George Washington

1. Lost Days of Youth

Myth! **Washington's birthday on February 22 is a national holiday in the US.**

If one were to go back in time to ask young George when he was born, he would surely get an answer that's not anywhere near February 22, the date we celebrate as Washington's birthday. For George was born on February 11, 1732, under the Julian calendar then in effect. His birthday shifted automatically to February 22 when the British Empire and its American colonies scrapped the Julian calendar in 1752 in favor of the Gregorian system. The British action was a belated compliance with what had come to be known as the Gregorian, or New Style, calendar, which Pope Gregory XIII established in 1582 to rectify the accumulated error under the Julian, or Old Style, scheme. The switch was accomplished by the simple expedient of eliminating eleven days from the month of September and adding eleven days to the remaining dates as compensation.

Washington was twenty years old at the time of the calendar change, but strangely, his birthday began to be observed on February 22 only when he was already 64. This was in 1796, the year he left the presidency and retired to his private home at Mount Vernon. Odder still is that the New Style was not supposed to apply retroactively, yet Washington's birth date was changed whereas the other events in his early life remained unconverted.

Most patriotic Americans who feel for the father of their country are inclined to think February 22 is a national holiday, but this is wrong. In the first place, while the federal government and its employees are legally bound to observe Washington's Birthday, it is an ordinary day for all the states and for the private sector. And in the second place, by enacting the Monday Holidays Act in 1968, the US Congress moved the official observance of Washington's Birthday from February 22 to the third Monday in February.

It doesn't help, of course, that the third Monday of February is now sometimes called 'President's Day' to honor not only Washington but also Lincoln, whose true birthday is February 12. The concept of a President's Day had been proposed—and

114

rejected—during the legislative deliberations on the Monday Holidays Act, but the belief that it was approved has held mainly because the third Monday of February is always after Lincoln's and before Washington's birthday without ever coinciding with either. 'President's Day' is currently used almost regularly on calendars, in advertising, and by many government agencies. Since states are not obliged to adopt federal holidays, a dozen of them officially celebrate Presidents' Day while most others have adopted Washington's Birthday alone or separately from Lincoln's Birthday.

2. The Politician in Washington

Myth! Washington had no political experience prior to his election to the presidency.

A good part of the Washington mystique has been the belief that he was never dirtied by political grease on his way to a record-setting win at the first Electoral College. Nevertheless, it is not true that he was a greenhorn in that sector, with no experience in the art of the compromise, when he was inaugurated president of the United States on April 30, 1789. Washington held high public offices as often as he held military ones, and it was probably from these stints that he gained the skill for bargaining with Congress during the bleak days of the Revolutionary War.

Washington's political life is made even more impressive by the fact that it spanned all three branches of government. He was a member of the Virginia House of Burgesses between 1754 and 1774, a justice of the peace in Fairfax County, Virginia, in 1770, and a delegate to the First Continental Congress in 1774. He was again a delegate to the Second Continental Congress in 1775, which named him commander of the Continental forces after the outbreak of hostilities with the British. He presided over the second Federal Constitutional Convention in 1787, where his prestige and reputation proved incalculable in the adoption of the US Constitution.

Washington had tried to remain aloof from partisan politics, and would have succeeded had he not come under the influence of Alexander Hamilton.

115

3. George Makes a Pitch

Myth! Washington threw a silver dollar across the Potomac.

Tradition tells us that Washington once threw a silver dollar across a wide expanse of the Potomac. In one version this happened when he was a boy, and in another while he was involved in a military campaign during the Revolutionary War. Despite its hallowed place in American folklore, most critics regard the story as fictitious. Again, the reputed source is Weems, who claimed that Col. Lewis Willis, Washington's playmate and kinsman, often saw him "throw a stone across the Rappahannock, at the lower ferry at Fredericksburg." The location was shifted to the Potomac in consideration of the river's prominent role at certain critical points in the Revolutionary War.

Weems' account, though hearsay, is more patently logical than the legend it evolved. Unlike the Potomac, the Rappahanock has several narrow spots, one of which could have been 'the lower ferry at Fredericksburg'. The feat could only be achieved on the Potomac, which is more than a mile wide, if it was done from a boat navigating near the shore. Also, according to historians, it was more likely that a stone was used than a silver dollar. For one, silver dollars were not minted in Colonial America, and for another, "everything else we know of Washington argues that it would have been most unlike him to throw away a Spanish dollar, then worth five or six shillings, and important money in that day. Washington is neither careless nor profligate with money."

4. Two Rivers Ran Through It

Myth! Washington stood beside a standing American flag on a boat as it crossed the Delaware.

In 1776, George Washington led his troops across the Delaware to defeat German mercenaries allied with the British in the Battle of Trenton. Oddly, it took another German, Emmanuel Leutze, to

116

render the event on canvas in the patriotic painting *Washington Crossing the Delaware.*

It's a wonder that Americans who get a chance to see Leutze's masterpiece as it hangs in the Metropolitan Museum of Art are not turned off by the glaring anomalies that mar the famous painting. Experts say proper research could have helped bridge the time and distance separating the German artist from the 1776 event that he painted in 1851, but Leutze obviously felt his imagination would do just as well.

Leutze did the picture entirely in Dusseldorf, most likely using the Rhine as a model, and would not see the Delaware until his return to the US with the finished painting. Not knowing that the boats Washington used for his sneak attack on the British were Durham types (these were wide open boats 40 to 60 feet long and could comfortably carry at least 20 persons), he painted much smaller ones. Thus, he had to show Washington's boat filled to capacity, despite historical records indicating there were plenty of boats and only a few men at the time. George, if he were worth his salt, would have decided against using such boats, as he would never have made it to the other side. Leutze made it all feasible by conveniently painting out some of the major hazards that beset the real-life crossing, e.g., the darkness, the unfavorable weather, and the ice sheets (not ice caps or crags) on the water.

It is well known that one of the rowers with Washington was a black soldier named Oliver Cromwell, but he is absent in the painting. In his place is another black rower identified as Prince Whipple, despite lack of documentation to support the latter's presence. Leutze proved himself a pure artist, but totally devoid of military sense, when he depicted Washington assuming a flamboyant but dangerous stance in the bow of the boat. The general stands so casually that he could rock the boat or become a sitting duck to enemy fire, while the soldiers behind him are negligently holding their rifles with the barrels pointed upwards, ready to catch the falling snow. Topping it all is the anachronism of Leutze's American flag, which had not yet been adopted by Congress and was not officially in existence at the time.

The greatest misconception about Leutze's vision of Washington crossing the Delaware has nothing to do with its lack of authentic detail, nor with the fact that it was executed entirely in Germany. It is the belief that Leutze should be held high in the esteem of Americans because he painted the historical event to stir

117

up their patriotic feelings. There was actually no need for him to do so in the 1850s, when the United States was relatively at peace with Britain and the rest of the world. At least one historian, Ann Hawkes Hutton, maintains that Leutze' real intention was to agitate the rebellious spirit of his German compatriots. He hoped that the painting of an event that had rallied Americans against their British colonizers would incite the German people to rebel against the conservative governments that had recently crushed the Revolution of 1848

5. A Lot of Weemsy

Myth! Little George chopped down a cherry tree and confessed it to his father, saying, "Father, I cannot tell a lie."

One of the most enduring—and endearing—legends in American history is offered as a thesis on honesty to schoolchildren. It's about George Washington who, when a little boy, chopped down a cherry tree and admitted it to his father. We owe this vignette to the American cleric and writer Mason Locke Weems.

Parson Weems' first work on George Washington, written two months after the patriot's death, was a sell-out. But it made no mention of the two most common fixtures of the legend, which were the hatchet and the cherry tree. That story would be included only in the fifth edition eight years later, when Weems' 80-page pamphlet had expanded and began to look like a book.

A few references, including an old edition of the Encyclopedia Britannica, surmise that there may have been some factual basis for the cherry tree story. Weems' description of the event was undoubtedly overblown, but there has been no evidence to this date to disprove it. The Parson claimed he had received the gist of the tale from an aged lady who was a distant relative of the Washingtons and who spent much of her time as a girl with the family. It was only natural that Weems wouldn't get any more witnesses or other reliable sources of information at the time of his writing, since George was only six when it happened.

The verdict nonetheless is that while George was honest, Parson Weems was not. Researchers claim that Weems, seeing a

118

need to beef up his character study of the president, lifted the story from James Beattie's book *The Minstrel*, published in London in 1799.

It would not be fair to blame Weems for all of our misconceptions about Washington and the tree. For sure, he never said George chopped down the cherry tree, merely that he "hacked and barked it" so that the tree, though severely damaged, remained standing. Also, we are told that when confronted by his father, little George said: "Father, I cannot tell a lie. I did it with my little hatchet." As reported by Weems, George's confession was, "I can't tell a lie, Pa; you know I can't tell a lie. I did cut it with my hatchet."

6. Washington Confidential

Myth! The phrases 'Washington slept here' and 'father of his country' have acquired a sexually derisive meaning because of this president's reputation as a womanizer.

There is no clear evidence that George ever got sexually involved with anyone other than his wife, and the charge that he slept with Sally Fairfax and Mary Gibbons, among others, is rejected by his most responsible biographers.

As a young colonel, George used to hang around Belvoir, a place owned by his good friend Fairfax, and keep company with Fairfax' wife Sally. Just before he married Martha, George wrote to Sally promising lifelong devotion, and when she was 68, he wrote to her again hinting at a relationship that, according to him, gave him his happiest moments. These facts were good enough to launch a rumor, but lacking corroborative evidence, none has convinced historians that George's sentiments ever went beyond the platonic stage.

Another rumor claimed that Washington had kept up an affair with Mary Gibbons, a New Jersey woman, while he headquartered in New York during the Revolution. But the story originated with a pamphlet that had every indication his Tory enemies were promoting it.

The talk that Washington had an illegitimate son who became a well-known officer in the Continental Army was also wholly unsupported. It was not uncommon during the Revolution that a letter would circulate accusing George of certain sexual indiscretions, but would later be determined to be fraudulent and a product of British propaganda.

The term 'father of his country' is sometimes used to allude snidely to Washington's false reputation for sowing wild oats. Victor Emmanuel II (1820-1878), first king of Italy, was popularly given the title also because of his alleged progeny of bastard children, but unlike Washington he deserved it.

7. Dollar Economy

Myth! Washington was so poor he had to borrow money to travel to New York City for his inauguration.

Some of Washington's biographies reveal that he turned down a salary from the Continental Congress and asked instead that he be paid only for his expenses as commander-in-chief. This conflicts in spirit with the story that he had to borrow his travel fare for New York City for his inauguration in 1789. Nevertheless, both stories are apparently true.

Washington was one of the wealthiest politicians in his day, being perhaps the biggest landowner due partly to Martha's wealth and partly to his own predilection for accumulating real estate. But he did not manage his cash flow well—any excess cash, if not hoarded, went into further investment. It is quite likely that Washington borrowed money for his inauguration because of this neglect and was short of cash that day.

Contrary to what has been written, however, neither his being wealthy nor his special concern for the national budget had anything to do with why he preferred an expense account to a salary. Washington was a shrewd financial administrator, and knew that if he had accepted the salary, he would only have received a total of $48,000 for his entire tenure. On the other hand, his expense account during eight years of war came to $447,220, according to the smallest estimate. One report included

120

in this total, sums for a new carriage, expensive saddles, and imported wines for his headquarters.

8. When Push comes to Pull

Myth! Washington was appointed the first US commander-in-chief on the strength of his record as a strong military leader and brilliant strategist.

Washington is recorded in the history books as the first commander-in-chief of the US Armed Forces by virtue of his being the first commissioned officer to head the American revolutionary army. But he probably was not, in light of the fact that in 1775, just before he was installed, Artemus Ward had been commissioned general and commander-in-chief of Massachusetts' troops. These forces, which began the siege on Boston, were effectively the American revolutionary army at that time.

It has always been the belief that Washington was appointed to his post because of his excellent military record in the field. Far from it, Washington had no distinction to speak of for most of the pre-revolutionary part of his military career. He was even painted as reckless and lacking in military acumen during his early years; in one account, he had just been appointed a lieutenant colonel in the militia when he impetuously attacked a French scouting party and "accidentally started the French and Indian War."

It is almost certain that Washington's appointment as commander-in-chief was due to political and economic considerations. Washington was a Virginian and this was propitious because, with all the fighting centered in Massachusetts, special care had to be taken in order to insure full southern support for the cause. As one report puts it, "since (Washington's) appointment had to be justified on paper, it was his rather dull performance in the Seven Years War that was glamorized and cited for the purpose."

The views about Washington's military leadership during his tenure as commander-in-chief have been mixed. Traditionalists say he was a strong-willed and well-respected general to be ranked with Napoleon and Alexander the Great. He held together a ragged, poorly outfitted army by sheer force of will, chose his

121

commanders well, and inspired fierce loyalty among them. By bargaining expertly with Congress, he saw to it that he was given enough money to arm his men. The same view holds that he was a master of the strategic retreat, and tricked the British into believing his point of attack would be New York when it was actually Yorktown.

Revisionists claim, on the other hand, that Washington was an unduly harsh leader who maintained brutal discipline in the ranks. His men did not love him; there were frequent mutinies for the suppression of which he kept a well-fed and trained group of militia. He nearly lost the war several times, only to be saved by the French or the greater incompetence of the British. He was better at politicking and dealing with intrigues than commanding. More a survivor than a strategist, he had never intended to attack Yorktown until he saw the French doing it.

Close associates didn't think of Washington as the superior commander and field general that his legend portrays. Jefferson himself characterized the general as being "a failure in the field— not a great tactician," while to John Adams he was "an old muttonhead." And one edition of the Encyclopedia Britannica went so far as to accuse him of "grave military blunders."

9. This Washington Bridge was all Wood?

Myth! Washington had white hair and wore wooden dentures.

Those parts of Washington's physiognomy that have aroused the most curiosity among his biographers are his teeth and his hair.

By the time he was fifty, George had lost all of his teeth save one—the lower left premolar, which he held on to for another fifteen years. Looking prematurely aged, he went to Dr. John Greenwood, a New York City dentist, for a set of dentures. Most accounts claim he had the false teeth made of wood, but this would have been impractical. In fact, the doctor fashioned several sets, which combined human teeth with artificial ones carved from either hippopotamus or walrus ivory, and none from wood. There is doubt that George used any set for chewing, although it is believed he wore at least one while he sat for the famous Gilbert

Stuart portrait. Unfortunately, that set may not have served its cosmetic purpose well because it actually pushed his mouth out of shape and became a notable flaw in the Stuart painting.

There is hardly any portrayal of Washington—by Gilbert Stuart, Emmanuel Leutze or any other—that does not show the man sporting white hair. True, he obscured much of his hair under a fashionable white wig, but many accounts describe the hair underneath as also white. The little known fact, of course, is that his hair, though he wore it powdered white, was sandy brown.

10. When Washington was in New York

Myth! Washington was the first president to occupy the White House.

People tend to believe that Washington, being the first president, was automatically the first occupant of the White House. This may be true, but only in the sense that the White House is not a specific building but the generic name of the official residence of the US president. In the early years, this was a building located at No. 1 Cherry Street in New York City, where Washington lived during his incumbency. It was not known as the White House then, and became so only when the president's residence moved to Washington, D.C. some years later, with James Madison as the first occupant. Apparently, the term did not come into being until after the new building was torched by the British during Madison's presidency, when portions were rebuilt and the exterior painted white over the original gray to cover the burn marks. But White House historians and curators cite contemporary evidence proving the use of the term in reference to the Madison residence "well before the British marched in," suggesting that the repainting and whitewashing of the structure after the attack had nothing to do with the coinage.

Still, there was one White House in which Washington lived even longer than he had at No. 1 Cherry Street, New York. This was the residential edifice in Martha Washington's Virginia plantation, which she had inherited from her first husband, Daniel Parke Custis, and which was also called the White House. It was

123

here, in fact, that she and George were married. Of course, as all this happened long before George even thought of becoming president, his situation was not any more exceptional than those of other ordinary Americans who lived in white houses. The same goes for John Adams, who shared his residence with his wife Abigail in his own private 'White House' in Brattle Square, Boston, prior to Adam's rise to the presidency.

11. Plain Ole George

Myth! Washington is one of the few American presidents who had no middle name.

Although most people are not used to seeing a US president with only two names or without at least a middle initial, there is nothing peculiar about Washington having no middle name. Middle names were not the vogue in the days of the founding fathers as they are now. The next four US presidents after Washington, namely Adams, Jefferson, Madison and Monroe, were also lacking a middle name. Patricia Lee Holt entitled her compendium of strange historical tidbits *George Washington Had No Middle Name* (1992), but she should have called it *John Quincy Adams Had a Middle Name* instead. For the real oddity in this regard was John Quincy, who, needing to distinguish himself from his father John, became the only president from Washington to Martin Van Buren to adopt a middle name ('Van' counts as part of Martin Van Buren's last name).

Of the 24 US presidents elected before the 20th century, only eight had middle names. Two of the eight—James Knox Polk and James Abram Garfield—were not in the habit of using their middle names, and one—Stephen Grover Cleveland—officially discarded his first name. This leaves only five who can be said to have had active middle names. In the 20th century, there were more presidents with middle names or initials than with none, but two are not easy to categorize. Like Cleveland, Thomas Woodrow Wilson and John Calvin Coolidge chucked their first names at some point in their lives and settled for just their middle and last names.

124

12. Unfounded Fatherhood

Myth! Washington treated his slaves unfairly and took sexual advantage of some of them.

Washington kept such a large number of slaves that he could not avoid rumors of having fathered several illegitimate children with them. One, which is still in circulation after more than two hundred years, was started by an angry army officer, Major General Charles Lee, who was humiliated after his court-martial for unnecessary retreat in battle. Another claimed that a disease, possibly pneumonia, which Washington caught after meeting a black concubine one stormy night, caused his death. It was later revealed that the incident had really happened—not to George but to his lusty plantation manager named Lund Washington, who was known to have fathered a child by a black mistress. George himself would not have died from anything had he not been subjected to excessive bloodletting by inept doctors for what was apparently just a strep throat.

There is absolutely no evidence that Washington treated his slaves other than with respect and compassion, or that he ever made any advances toward them. The indication, if at all, is that George couldn't have fathered a child with anybody. While Washington always said he wanted children, he and Martha never had any, the difficulty almost certainly being with George and not Martha. In her previous marriage, Martha had several children within a relatively short span, the last child just two years before her marriage to Washington. In view of Martha's proved fecundity, it appears logical to conclude that George was sterile.

George and Martha Washington reportedly had 300 black slaves, all of whom were freed in accordance with George's will. Or so we are told. The fact is that George had no legal jurisdiction over most of the slaves, since they belonged to Martha. He freed only one—his old and crippled valet, William—and provided for the few others he had owned because of his marriage to be freed upon Martha's death. He also left word they should be taught to read and write, and those of suitable age be trained in carpentry or masonry.

13. Between Washington and Cleveland

Myth! Washington is the most honest US president.

Washington is one of the presidents most often identified with honesty, but that honesty is based largely on legend. Historians say Washington was not above lying if it was to soften the impact of bad news, or to avoid making offense, or for military reasons.

Worse, those responsible for molding the legend were similarly liars. For instance, his mother in her later years didn't mind lying even in public. When George was President, she accused him openly of starving her through neglect. The accusation was false, of course, but it did much to paint George as a mother-abuser and this dented his reputation further.

Parson Weems, who started the myth of George's honesty by telling the dubious story of the cherry tree, lied through his teeth when he indicated on the title page of his biography of Washington that he was "formerly rector of Mount Vernon Parish." There was no such parish, and his status as a parson elsewhere is also doubted. At best, he was an Episcopal minister who occasionally preached at Pohick Church, where Washington often attended.

Of all the presidents, Grover Cleveland had the least number of charges for misconduct or corruption during his term. It is true that William Henry Harrison suffered no accusation whatsoever, but this was because he had served only one month as President when he died. Cleveland, despite getting a good share of accusers and critics from staying long on the job, is still generally adjudged the most honest.

14. The Ninth Configuration

Myth! Washington was the first president of the United States.

To the time-honored question, "Who is the first president of the United States," the equally time-honored answer is "George

126

Washington." But George was only the first president under the federal system established by the US Constitution of 1789. Before that, the United States, already formally called by this name, was a sovereign nation under the Articles of Confederation with a duly constituted government headed by a president. Adopted by Congress in 1777 and ratified by the states in 1781, the Articles as the country's first constitution provided for a weak central government with no single executive position. Congress was, in effect, both the legislative and the executive branches, and also the Supreme Court when it came to adjudicating the rights of the states.

Those who insist Washington was the first of his kind assert that the US under the Articles was a mere confederation with a president who was not a true chief executive because his powers and functions did not extend outside the halls of Congress. On the other hand, some constitutionalists say the sole fact that the balance of power was tilted in favor of the states as against the central authority did not make the US confederation less than sovereign. Its highest official may have had little or no executive powers except within the legislative sphere, but this did not detract from his being the head of government and called the President of the United States. Such a person would not be less deserving of the position than Washington, who presided over only a handful of colonies when he was first elected and had no executive powers over the rest of the land.

Thus, unless the question, "Who is the first president of the United States," were further refined, an equally plausible answer would be, "The first of the eight presidents before Washington who were elected by Congress from among themselves." This was John Hanson, member of the Maryland House of Delegates for 24 years and elected as Maryland representative to the Continental Congress in 1781. In that same year, representatives from the 13 colonies elected Hanson 'President of the United States in Congress Assembled'. Hanson had limited powers, as did the Congress itself, and occupied a position similar to the current US Speaker of the House. He served for one year and resigned because of poor health. For the next seven years, the government, operating under the Articles of Confederation, produced seven more presidents, each serving an average of one year—in effect bringing Washington down to number 9 in the US presidential hierarchy.

127

15. Surrender by Proxy

Myth! Lord Cornwallis yielded his sword to Washington as a gesture of surrender at Yorktown.

A typical painting on the subject depicts Lord Cornwallis surrendering his sword to Washington at Yorktown. This is pure fantasy, since Cornwallis was not in Yorktown on the day set for the surrender, and it was a surrogate who did everything he was supposed to do at the ceremonies. Cornwallis had pleaded illness and had sent Major General Charles O'Hara of his staff instead.

The British surrender at Yorktown in 1781 has gone down in history as one of the greatest military achievements of an American general. Washington is consistently praised for having had the foresight to make the decision to attack Yorktown as the only way to clinch the Revolutionary War. But several historians refute this, saying that Washington practically had to be dragged against his will to attack that British bastion. What he had wanted to hit was New York, and this he would have done had not the French under Comte de Rochambeau preempted him by beginning an attack on Yorktown. George, who had relied on French assistance for most of his battles, had no alternative but to cooperate.

16. Goodbye, Columbia

Myth! Washington composed the 1796 Farewell Address, which he delivered at the end of his second term.

Contrary to popular belief, Washington never delivered his famous Farewell Address, whether in public or in private. The Address, to signalize his leaving public life, was in writing and sent to the press on September 17, 1796, six months before the end of his second term. It was published in the Philadelphia *Claypole's Daily Advertiser* for presentation to the American people.

Neither did Washington write the Farewell Address. He had asked Madison to write one for him at the end of his first term, but when he decided on another four years, he shelved the speech. Towards the end of his second term Washington revived Madison's draft and sent it to Hamilton, who, it is said, developed a different speech altogether. Because of these episodes with Madison and Hamilton, Washington became the first president to seek major assistance in the drafting of an important public address. This denies a similar claim for Franklin D. Roosevelt, whose four terms coincided significantly with the advancement of public communications in the US, and who was known to rely extensively on ghostwriters for his principal speeches.

The Address is remembered not only for discouraging further pleas for Washington to serve a third term, but also for warning against entangling alliances with foreign powers. Contrary to popular belief, however, the phrase 'entangling alliances' appears nowhere in the document and did not originate there. In fact, the expression was politically correct and already floating around during the time of the founding fathers, when the fledgling republic had just weaned itself from its European dependency. Washington did mention the idea in the Address, but not precisely in those words. He said: "It is our true policy to steer clear of permanent alliance with any portion of the foreign world...Why, by interweaving our destiny with that of any part of Europe, entangle our peace and prosperity in the toils of European ambition, rivalship, interest, humor or caprice?" George and his publicists could have used the exact words "entangling alliances" even as a heading to the speech, but they did not. Instead, his bitter enemy Jefferson, who may or may not have copied the underlying thought from Washington, formed the phrase and used it with good effect in his own first inaugural address.

17. Putting on a Cold Front

Myth! Weakened and weary from the campaign, Washington knelt in the deep snow at Valley Forge to pray.

Pictures of Washington kneeling at prayer in the deep snow at Valley Forge are based on the popular belief that it really happened. Parson Weems first mentioned the incident, saying he got it from a Quaker named Potts, "if I mistake not." The image of

129

Washington's 'Gethsemane', as the episode has come to be called, has been printed on postage stamps in the US and was cast in bronze on the wall of the Sub-Treasury Building in New York City. A shrine in Valley Forge and a private chapel in the Capitol, among others, commemorate the event, and the Potts house itself has become a place of veneration.

But historians believe Valley Forge is just one more nut from the Parson's bag of 'Weemsies' about George, like the stories of the cherry tree and the silver dollar. For one, the story does not jell in the light of Washington's pronounced aversion to kneeling. It was well known that every time Martha dragged him to church on Sundays, he would refuse to kneel even if this meant making a scene. At first, it was thought this was because, as a Deist, he was not partial to praying especially in a kneeling position. It was later realized this would not have been a sufficient reason for him to defy the religiously devout Martha in front of the entire parish. In the end, the President himself disclosed that for most of his life, he found it difficult to assume a kneeling position because of a bum knee.

18. Pater Primus

Myth! Washington was the first in the world to be called 'The Father of his Country'.

'The Father of his Country'—this is America's favorite tag for her most popular and beloved founding father, and it's almost like it was coined exclusively for him.

It wasn't, of course, since Washington is not the only one in the world or the first one to be given the title. The label was devised originally for Marcus Tullius Cicero, the great orator who martyred himself for the cause of Roman republicanism. He achieved the climax of his career when he was hailed by Catulus as 'father of his country' after he had Catiline driven out of Rome and his co-conspirators against the Republic executed. The same title would later be accorded to Julius Caesar, Augustus Caesar, Andronicus Paleologus II (c. 1260-1332), Cosimo de' Medici of Florence (1389-1464) and Andrea Doria of Genoa (1466-1560).

130

Moreover, contrary to what is believed, Washington did not become the father of the whole country when he was first elected in 1789. He initially became president of only eleven of the thirteen original colonies, the reason being that neither Rhode Island nor North Carolina had yet ratified the Constitution when Washington won the office. North Carolina gave its acquiescence only after six months, and Rhode Island officially joined the Union a year later.

19. What'd You Do During the War, Mr. President?

Myth! Washington is one of three presidents to take to the battlefield while in office.

Ask if any American president has ever taken to the battlefield during his incumbency, and the likely answer is yes. Surprisingly, not one but three names will be mentioned: Washington, Madison and Lincoln. But in fact there has been none. In Washington's case, it was not a war but police action to quell a purely local agitation. Called the Whiskey Rebellion of 1794, it was organized by farmers in western Pennsylvania to protest the imposition of the federal excise tax on whiskey. Washington issued a proclamation ordering the rebels to return home, and at the same time raised 12,000 men and rode to Fort Cumberland to stop the 'rebellion' cold.

President Madison may have been the first president to face enemy gunfire while in office and the first and only president to exercise actively his authority as Commander-in-Chief. He took command of Commodore Joshua Barney's battery at Bladensburg, Maryland, in an attempt to protect Washington, D.C. in the War of 1812 against attacking British troops. But as far as is known, no battle was fought despite a real threat of it.

Because of Lincoln's sense of commitment to the Union, the impression of most is that he must have fought in the Civil War to prove it. He didn't. It seems he had wanted to, but the burden of his office compelled him to accept the offer of J. Summerfield Staples, son of an army chaplain, to take his place. This has been mistaken by detractors as an attempt by Lincoln to hire a substitute, just like what most rich men did in those days when it was allowed by law. Lincoln, however, might have been the first to visit a battlefront as president.

II

All About Abe

On Abraham Lincoln

"A house divided against itself
cannot stand."

•

Abraham Lincoln

1. Harps and Mauls

Myth! Lincoln's favorite pastimes were playing the jew's harp and splitting rails.

According to biographer Emanuel Hertz (*Abraham Lincoln: A New Portrait,* 1931), Lincoln once said, "I will tell you confidentially that my greatest pleasure when taking a rest after splitting rails, was to play a solo on the jew's-harp." How the jew's-harp got its name is anybody's guess, but this much is certain: it is not a harp, nor has it anything to do with the Jewish faith. The player holds the lyre-shaped metal frame of this instrument against his teeth while he draws various harmonics of a fundamental tone from its steel tongue.

The quote has totally no basis and was obviously made up by Hertz, for Lincoln never played any musical instrument called the jew's-harp. Moreover, the musical organization to which Lincoln was supposed to have confided the information—the St. Marie Brass Band & St. Cecilia Society—never existed.

Abe's penchant as a young man for rail splitting may well be a myth, too. The account that he had once supported himself by splitting as many as 3,000 rails with the help of one laborer sounds too good to be true. Lincoln's reputation as a hard-fisted rail-splitter had been rather vague—until he secured the Republican nomination in 1860 and realized that for him to win the election, he needed a publicity device to endear him to the fractured masses. Thus, at a Republican meeting in Illinois, Lincoln's cousin John Hanks appeared with two rails that he claimed Abe had split in 1830. With his usual candor, Lincoln confessed he was not sure about the particular rails, but he was sure he had actually split rails every bit as good. That became a rallying point in his election.

History books and encyclopedias for the young are forever showing Abraham Lincoln splitting rails with an ax, which he undoubtedly could handle well. David Herbert Donald (*Lincoln,* 1995) recounts that during a visit to an army hospital in the waning days of the Civil War, the President shook hands with patients for several hours, after which he "picked up a heavy ax beside a log (and) chopped away vigorously for a few minutes...then, taking the ax in his right hand, extended it horizontally, holding it steady without even a quiver." Later, some

134

of the strongest soldiers attempted to duplicate the feat but failed. However, while Lincoln may have been good with an ax, he almost surely did not use one for splitting rails. Rails during his time were split with wedges, and these were hammered in with mauls. A good woodsman respected his ax too much to devote it to this kind of work.

2. Man of the Prairie

Myth! Lincoln was a true-blue Illinoisan.

Illinois is the state most closely associated with the Great Emancipator. Officially nicknamed the Prairie State, it is also touted as the Land of Lincoln. Meanwhile, we find there's a Lincoln in England, a Lincoln Sea near Greenland, and a Port Lincoln in Australia. These are only a few of the places outside the US that bear Lincoln's name but have no known affinity to the 16th American president.

At least twenty-six states of the Union have a town or city named Lincoln, some of them with more than one. Oddly, the only state with a capital city named for Abe is not Illinois, Indiana or Kentucky, but Nebraska. Odder still is that in Illinois, the only city named Lincoln was given its nomenclature without regard to Abe's political accomplishments. It was to honor him as a plain citizen, for having helped plan the city while he was still a practicing lawyer in Logan County. Lincoln had yet to attain a national or local office and was still seven years shy of becoming the 16th president when, on August 22, 1853, he christened Lincoln, Illinois, by hurling a watermelon over a stack of timber.

People from Illinois who would like to think Lincoln was born in their home state are soon disappointed that he was not. He was born on February 12, 1809, in a log cabin in the Bluegrass State, Kentucky, where he did not stay long enough to leave a mark. He spent the entire period of his adolescence in Indiana, in a rudimentary farm that he and his parents, Thomas Lincoln and Nancy Hanks, operated when he was seven. It was only in 1830 that Abe, Thomas and his second wife, Mrs. Sarah Bush Johnston, transferred to Illinois and finally settled there.

135

3. His Old Kentucky Home

Myth! Lincoln's log cabin has been preserved and is currently on display in Kentucky.

Guides point to Lincoln's cabin as the one on display near Hodgenville, Kentucky. This major tourist attraction is administered by the Interior Department and is officially registered as the 'Abraham Lincoln Birthplace Historical Site'. For some reason, it continues to be maintained in this manner despite the denial of Lincoln's son Robert that it is authentic. Records indicate that the original was destroyed by fire before 1840, and the logs saved were used as firewood. In 1865, the year of Lincoln's death, no log cabin was sighted at the old Lincoln farm.

The fake cabin appears to have been built out of logs salvaged from a two-story home near Lincoln's own. Advertised by the builder as Lincoln's birthplace, it was sold to a promoter who exhibited it in several state expositions. Later, a group of civic-minded preservationists took over and conveyed the structure to the federal government. At the instance of the Interior Department, it was returned to Hodgenville, where it was reassembled for the last time and suitably installed in an elaborate memorial building.

4. Would You Buy a Lincoln from this Man?

Myth! Lincoln was scrupulously honest.

Behind his back, people loved to call him Honest Abe, a sobriquet he earned not from lawyering or politicking, but as judge and referee at cockfights. Indeed, many of the anecdotes that demonstrate Lincoln's vaunted honesty, including those that have turned out to be myth, were set during his childhood and his early professional life. While it is generally believed Lincoln brought this trait into politics and the presidency, it is often a subject of argument whether he was actually honest in those roles. Analysts like to point out that it would have been extremely difficult for

136

even Lincoln to survive the Washington milieu, particularly during a time of great conflict, if he had been totally sincere and uncompromising.

Newsman John G. Scripps once remarked that Lincoln was "a scrupulous teller of the truth, too exact in his notions to suit the atmosphere of Washington as it now is." Yet Lincoln was known to have tolerated the use of dirty tricks in his presidential campaigns to make him win. During the 1860 Republican National Convention, his campaign managers forged convention passes to pack the galleries with Lincoln supporters, and shut out those of his opponents in the process. Moreover, after one trip to Springfield, Illinois, he filed for compensation for the 3,252 miles he claimed to have traveled, when in fact the actual length of the trip was only 1,800 miles. Critics say the worst breach of faith Lincoln committed in his public life was the Emancipation Proclamation, which he used for a political purpose rather than as a genuine measure against slavery and racial oppression

5. Lincoln's Lost Love Letters

Myth! Lincoln had an affair with Ann Rutledge before marrying Mary Todd.

The 1940 film *Abe Lincoln in Illinois* compliments some Lincoln biographers by giving credence to their story of Ann Rutledge. She was a teen-aged beauty who was rumored to be the only woman Lincoln ever loved, and who died of malaria at the age of nineteen before their affair could mean anything. It is claimed that once, unable to hide the intensity of his grief, Lincoln pointed out her grave to a friend and remarked, "My heart lies buried there."

The experts deny there was ever any such affair in the making, or that Lincoln ever did anything to suggest there was. While residing in New Salem, Lincoln became fond of the young Ann, but at no time was there a hint that theirs was anything more than a platonic relationship. Actually, Ann was engaged to someone else, and when the man abandoned her, she pined away for a couple of years. In the myth, Lincoln makes an offer of marriage to Ann, with one or the other backing out for no apparent reason at

137

the last minute. In real life, Lincoln proposed to one Mary Owens a year or so after Ann's death, then cancelled the engagement in 1837, saying he was not sure he could provide for her properly.

At the end of 1928, the Atlantic Monthly published a collection of love letters that Lincoln and Ann Rutledge supposedly wrote to each other. Paul Angle, secretary of the Lincoln Centennial Association, tested the letters in five ways and in all areas found the letters faulty. Half admitting in April 1929 that something was wrong, the magazine left the matter for the public to judge. Current opinion points to a woman in San Diego named Cora de Boyer as the one who forged the letters.

6. Honest to God

Myth! Lincoln had profound religious beliefs based on the Christian bible.

Of the hundreds of books about Lincoln, hardly any explores his religion or the lack of it. Apparently, Abe was not too demonstrative about this aspect of his private life. Hoping that he had at least verbally hinted at it, researchers constantly look for clues in his speeches and writings. Some claim they have found quotations suggesting variously that he might have been a Christian, a Deist or an infidel.

One of the earliest quotations is found in J. G. Holland's *Life of Lincoln* (1866): "I know I am right because I know that liberty is right, for Christ teaches it and Christ is God." But William Herndon, Lincoln's former law partner, was quick to dispute the idea that he said this, claiming the Great Emancipator was not an orthodox Christian and never talked in that manner.

Another quotation is in Father Charles Chiniquy's published memoirs, *Fifty Years in the Church of Rome*. Supposedly spoken by Lincoln in a conversation with the renegade priest, it read: "Now, would it not be the greatest of honors and privileges bestowed upon me, if God in his infinite love, mercy, and wisdom would put me between His faithful servant, Moses, and his eternal Son, Jesus, that I might die as they did, for my nation's sake." Unfortunately, Lincoln scholars have always considered Chiniquy unreliable, and are especially aware Lincoln "shared neither

138

Chiniquy's hatred of Roman Catholicism nor his belief in the divinity of Christ."

A line in a Lincoln collection published by Captain Osborn H. Oldroyd in 1883 purports to show that Lincoln converted to Christianity in his later years. He had not been a Christian, he supposedly told an Illinois clergyman shortly before his death, but "when I went to Gettysburg and saw the graves of thousands of our soldiers, I then and there consecrated myself to Christ." Oldroyd's source was found to be a Baptist sermon delivered by the Rev. W. W. Whitcomb in Oshkosh, Wisconsin, in 1865, with nothing to trace it from there to Lincoln.

Paul F. Boller, Jr., in *Not So!,* makes a very strong case for clearing Lincoln of the charge levied by his former law partner William Herndon that he was an infidel and an atheist. According to Boller, although Lincoln was not a member of any church, he was essentially a believer. Lincoln himself proclaimed: "I am not a member of a Christian Church...I have never denied the truth of the Scripture, and I have never spoken with intentional disrespect of religion in general, or of any denomination in particular." This confession also contradicts the claim that he denounced Catholicism once with the words, "But though not a prophet, I see a very dark cloud on our horizon. And that dark cloud is coming from Rome."

While Lincoln attended Presbyterian services in Springfield and in Washington, he declined to join any formal religion. The *Britannica* printed Lincoln's explanation for this aversion, thus: "When any church will inscribe over its altar, as its sole qualification for membership, the Savior's condensed statement of the substance of both Law and Gospel, 'Thou shalt love the Lord thy God with all thy heart, and with all thy soul, and with all thy mind, and thy neighbor, as thyself,' that church will I join with all my heart and all my soul." Again, the remark is deemed suspect because of its specific mention of the Savior. It seems that of Lincoln's many references to God in his public addresses, hardly any was to Christ.

Whatever Lincoln's religion was, there is no doubt he was a deeply spiritual man who found solace in the holy writings. Historians often wrote that when he was not at his hobbies, he was burning the midnight oil reading the Holy Book. It was his stepmother who, soon after his mother's death, had introduced him to the Bible, which was the only book his family ever owned.

139

There is no evidence, however, that he said, "I have never known a worthwhile man who became too big for his boots or his Bible." Because of Lincoln's habit in his early years of studying under an oil lamp deep into the night, some word historians thought the idiom 'burning the midnight oil' was coined in his time in allusion to his Biblical addiction. In fact, it originated in England only in 1882 and had nothing to do with Abe.

7. Northern Mind, Southern Heart

Myth! Lincoln was an abolitionist who passionately believed in racial equality.

The Emancipation Proclamation did not quite live up to its name, but it lived up to the expectations of the many Northerners who shared Lincoln's credo. According to that credo, Lincoln, far from supporting total abolition, advocated opposition only to the spread of slavery into new territories and states. He did not denounce slavery in public until 1854, and in his most critical period refused to free slaves in still loyal Border States. He seemed to have ambivalent feelings about the equality of the black man with the white, to the point that he once favored establishing mechanisms to colonize millions of free blacks in Latin America. In his debates with Douglas, Lincoln balked at the notion of allowing blacks the vote, jury duty, intermarriage or even citizenship. He said, "(T)here is a physical difference between the races which I believe will forever forbid the two races living together on terms of social and political equality." By modern American standards Lincoln was a racist, although by the standards of his day he was a liberal.

Self-anointed spin-doctors soften Lincoln's racial image by claiming that he acquired a less tolerant view of slavery after maturing in office. Lincoln is believed to have expressed his anti-slavery sentiment thus—"If I ever get a chance to hit that thing, I'll hit it hard"—but this phrase is not documented and there is no way to tell when and where the president said it. Abe is also said to have written in a letter to General James S. Wadsworth in 1864 that "(t)he restoration of the Rebel States to the Union must rest upon the principle of civil and political equality of both races; and

140

it must be sealed by general amnesty." The letter, as revealing as it may sound, does not appear in the Wadsworth Papers in the Library of Congress, and the newspaper that originally published the quote cannot be located. In the light of Lincoln's established credo, it is extremely doubtful he ever made either statement.

Lincoln did say a few things to prove that he hated slavery and believed it violated the fundamental laws of the land. But he was careful to couch them in uncertain, albeit elegant, language, betraying the fact that he was not prepared to destroy the institution. For instance, "A house divided against itself cannot stand" was a phrase Lincoln uttered before a spellbound audience on June 17, 1858, at Springfield, Illinois. It seemed at first to be a warning against slavery *per se*, but it was actually directed against the divisive effects of the slavery issue. The future president's focus was on tolerating the US as half-slave and half-free; while he was not advocating an all-free Union, he was hoping for one that, regardless of its stance on slavery, was not divided. It helped Lincoln's cause that the charismatic line originated with Jesus when he referred to Satan and his kingdom (*Matthew* 12:25; *Mark* 3:25), but in Jesus' case, there was not the smallest doubt about what he intended to convey.

8. Abecedarian Abe

Myth! 'Abe' was Lincoln's preferred form of address before he became President.

There may be something in the saying that a nickname speaks loads about the man. The simplicity of Abraham Lincoln's nickname Abe, which he must have loved hearing from his constituents, is often offered as proof of this president's humble nature. Another affirming but unverified bit of trivia: the word 'honest' was appended to Lincoln's nickname to honor his reputation for probity in and out of politics.

Lincoln loved to talk about common folk, calling them by their nicknames, but contrary to the popular yarns about the President, they did not call him Abe in return. Though Lincoln was a man of the people, he did not allow anyone to call him Abe; according to biographer Stephen Oates, "he loathed the nickname." His wife

141

Mary called him Mr. Lincoln or Father, while others called him Mr. Lincoln or simply Lincoln. When writing to friends, Lincoln routinely signed off as 'A. Lincoln'.

9. What Counts is Winning What Counts

Myth! Lincoln fared well in both politics and business.

Many see Lincoln's phenomenal rise from rags to the pomp and power of the Presidency as a typical Horatio Alger story. From the log cabin of his early days to the hallowed halls of Washington, D.C., Lincoln managed every difficult step with no more than pluck, determination, hard work and acumen. Luck, of course, was on the side of most of Alger's heroes, and many assume luck also figured prominently in Lincoln's transformation.

As it turns out, the luck our real-life hero encountered on his way to the White House and thereafter was mostly bad, so bad that it eventually ended his life and career. It is not widely known that Lincoln had suffered three business failures before he went into politics. In 1832, Lincoln lost his job in a failing business partnership. In 1833, a private business collapsed. Although elected to the state legislature in 1834, he implemented an internal improvement project that nearly bankrupted the State of Illinois.

Almost no one realizes as well that Lincoln's political debacles were even worse. He started by losing a race for the state legislature in 1832. After gaining entry into the house, he lost races for the speakership in 1836 and 1838. In 1843, Lincoln was defeated for the nomination to the U.S. Congress. He was elected to Congress in 1846 but lost his seat in 1848. In 1849, he lost the election for a land-office seat. He lost two Senate races, one in 1854 and another in 1858, and in between lost the VP nomination. He had lost a total of nine elections and nominations before he made it to the US presidency. What most people do know, however, is that shortly after getting reelected to that high office, Lincoln suffered the ultimate bad luck—he was assassinated.

10. Addressing an Envelope

Myth! Lincoln composed the Gettysburg Address on the back of an envelope during the train ride from Washington, DC, to Gettysburg.

Lincoln's son Robert made this claim in a letter he wrote in 1855, but that's all it was—a claim. Evidence discovered after the President's death shows he made various drafts of the Address—five, to be exact—before leaving for Gettysburg. On the first draft, in fact, Lincoln indicated that he had started work on it almost two weeks before the event. These copies all exist in Lincoln's handwriting, and one even hangs in the Lincoln Room in the White House. He may have continued to revise the speech on the train, but as Lincoln's own private secretary noted, the train ride was too bumpy to permit writing with or without an envelope.

Historians say Lincoln would never have dared to be so casual, as Robert made him to be, following a previous embarrassment he suffered at another Civil War battlefield cemetery. It is said that several months earlier, he was criticized for his informal and inappropriate remarks at Antietam while he was visiting there shortly after the battle. The opposition press "reported Lincoln's behavior as if he had desecrated a sacred spot." Knowing that the Gettysburg Address would provide him with the opportunity to redeem himself and express his true reverence for these memorials, he must have prepared it well in advance.

11. Debatable Results

Myth! Lincoln won his debates with Stephen Douglas during their campaign for the presidency.

One of the greatest political events to promote Lincoln's fortunes and mark his era was a series of debates held in 1858 between him and his leading opponent at the time, Stephen Douglas. The perception of many is that the Lincoln-Douglas debates were about their fight for the presidency; that more than a dozen debates on a one-on-one basis were held before capacity crowds; and that Lincoln won the debates by favoring the abolition of slavery.

The debates had nothing to do with the US presidential election at all. At stake was the senatorial seat for Illinois, and the presidential race between the two will not be until two years later. Only seven joint debates were conducted, all of them before relatively small audiences. Each speaker made many more separate appearances before considerably larger gatherings. Not that the size of the audience mattered; in Lincoln's time, US senators were not elected by popular vote but by state legislatures. Thus, it cannot be said that the debates had an impact on the outcome of the elections, or that Lincoln or Douglas won. The popular vote went for Lincoln, but he lost the Illinois Senate race to Douglas because of gerrymandering and the other vagaries of representative voting.

Since the issue was territorial slavery, the overall presumption is that Douglas was for it and Lincoln against it. Actually, it was not that simple. Lincoln insisted that Congress must exclude slavery from the territories, but he also strongly believed that the right of the slave states to maintain the status quo should not be curtailed. On the other side, all that Douglas wanted was to give the inhabitants of the territories the right to decide the slavery question themselves. The two were actually not far apart in their basic views, both taking a moderate position that was neither abolitionist nor proslavery.

12. By, For and Of the Majority

Myth! Lincoln was an unpopular president.

Some say Lincoln was an unpopular president—an irony for the man who has accomplished the greatest feat by an American leader, that of preserving the Union. Lincoln had more internal enemies than any Chief Executive, a matter readily explained by the fact that he was involved in a great civil war, where almost every rebel stood intensely opposed to his cause. This pro-Union president eventually met his death at the hands of a fanatical follower of the South.

144

Lincoln was one of the most vilified by the press even in the North. But Lincoln's time was an era of journalistic vituperation scarcely equaled before or since. It is worthwhile noting that the extraordinarily vicious comments most often reflected only the opinions of editors, like Horace Greeley, and not the public. When Lincoln was assassinated, even those newspapers that had been most bitter in their comments while he was alive poured forth a torrent of adulation.

Some think Lincoln gained the presidency in his two election bids by a close shave. In the 1860 exercise his share of the popular vote was 39 percent, or less than a simple majority. But he was running against three other candidates, each of whom he beat handily. Lincoln thrashed Douglas, his leading opponent, by more than 500,000, a margin equivalent to about 5.5 million today and greater than Franklin Delano Roosevelt's lead over Thomas E. Dewey in 1944. And when McClellan was his only opponent in 1864, Lincoln proved he was popular in his previous tenure by capturing over 55 percent of the general vote, a resounding victory by any standards.

---

13. Nobody's Fool

Myth! Lincoln said, "You may fool all the people some of the time; you can even fool some of the people all of the time; but you can't fool all the people all of the time."

Politicians and public servants all over the world love to include this populist line in their speeches, often without paying obeisance to its professed author Abe Lincoln. Perhaps it is just as well, because Lincoln probably didn't say it.

Lincoln is credited by his fans for making this observation not once but several times—in 1856 at Bloomington, Illinois; in 1858 at Clinton, Illinois; and in 1863 at Washington, D.C. But there is no real evidence, other than the typical homespun wit behind the words, that connects the phrase to Abe. Many who weren't there have sworn blindly that Lincoln said it at Clinton, Illinois, when he was campaigning for the Illinois senate against Stephen Douglas. Before then, the Bloomington *Pantagraph* had reported on the 1856 speech when it was delivered, but it did not mention the line in particular. Again in 1905 the Chicago *Tribune* and the Brooklyn *Eagle* cited several people who claimed they were present when the quote was made, but the witnesses, all well into their seventies by this time, confirmed only that Lincoln had said something generally of the quote's nature. The saying is not found in any of the president's printed addresses or published works.

The line first appeared in a 1904 book, *Abe Lincoln's Yarns and Stories,* by the Pennsylvania Republican Alexander K. McClure. In one anecdote, the President was conversing with a visitor and their talk turned to the virtue of dealing honestly with the American people. Lincoln said, "It is true that you may fool all the people some of the time; you can even fool some of the people all of the time; but you can't fool all the people all of the time." McClure did not say if the incident was fiction or fact, but chances now are that it was the former.

14. More Lincolnesque than Lincoln

Myth! Lincoln was the first to declare free the slaves of secessionists during the Civil War, and the first to free slaves on a mass basis anywhere in the North and South.

It wasn't Lincoln but General John Charles Frémont ('the Pathfinder') who first declared free the slaves of secessionists during the Civil War. To reverse his military losses at Wilson's Creek, Missouri, Frémont declared martial law and announced that the slaves of secessionists were free. Far from giving his support, Lincoln requested that the order be withdrawn, and when Frémont refused, Lincoln removed him from command.

Lincoln, as was said, never really freed slaves on a mass basis, as the Emancipation Proclamation had no teeth and the Thirteenth Amendment would be passed only after his death. But even if he did, he was not the first to do it. The honor, if a bit undeserved, belongs to Lord Dunmore, the British governor of Virginia. Like those of Frémont and Lincoln, Dunmore's motive was political. He had dissolved the Virginia Assembly in 1772, 1773 and 1774 on account of its revolutionary sentiments, and in April 1775 seized the colony's store of powder, sparking an armed uprising. Taking refuge aboard an English warship with the rebels on his

146

heels, he declared martial law and proclaimed freedom to all slaves in his jurisdiction in the hope that they would join the British. The effort didn't amount to anything, however, and he was defeated at Great Bridge near Norfolk in January 1776, after which he returned to England in July of the same year.

15. A Double's Jeopardy

Myth! Lincoln could not fight in the Civil War because, as the President, he was legally prohibited from doing so.

Not a few believe that Lincoln wanted to lead the Union on the battlefield, but being the President, he was prevented by law from doing so. Others, like Kenneth C. Davis (*Don't Know Much About the Civil War*), say that while there was no such prohibition, Lincoln had to pay another to fight in his stead because he was too busy attending to the affairs of state. Die-hard Lincolnites support this latter view except the part about the President hiring a substitute, arguing that it was beyond anyone as important as Abe to express publicly a desire to fight in the war when he didn't have to, and then turning around and paying a professional to do it for him. If at all, the surrogate would have had to offer his services voluntarily and for free.

The idea of avoiding the Civil War draft by hiring a substitute was one of the odd exemptions provided by the Enrollment Act of March 3, 1863, which called for men ages 18 to 45 to register with local militia units and be available for national service. Men like J.P. Morgan, Andrew Carnegie, Grover Cleveland, and the well-to-do fathers of Teddy and Franklin D. Roosevelt availed of this privilege, prompting the cry of "rich man's war, but poor man's fight."

Carved on a gravestone in Stroudsburg, Pennsylvania is an epitaph tending to prove that Lincoln did have a substitute to fight for him in the Civil War. The name is that of J. Summerfield Staples, who was apparently not of the professional-for-hire variety, although he may have once before substituted for a draftee and fought in his place for three months until he was medically discharged. In one version, Staples is said to have heard about the

147

President's quandary and felt he would be honored if he were to be his substitute. It is not clear whether, after rendering the service, he received the enlistment reward, or bounty, that the federal and local governments legally paid to volunteers who were not engaged by private patrons. In the version favored by the Monroe County Historical Association of Stroudsburg, the New York Times and presumably historian Davis, Staples was recruited by a Lincoln operative and hired personally by the President to serve as his "representative recruit" for a one-shot cash payment of $500. He worked for a whole year at a desk job in Alexandria, W. Va., and as a prison guard without ever seeing action on the battlefield, and then returned to his hometown as some kind of a hero.

16. Multiplier Effect

Myth! A Lincoln biographer faked the line, "God must have loved the common people, he made many of them," claiming falsely that the President had heard it in a dream.

Though this line is acclaimed as one of Lincoln's best populist quotes, many doubt he said anything of the sort. James Morgan is the one suspected of faking the phrase in his 1928 book *Our Presidents*, by making sure the words exhibit the same homely wit that runs through many of Lincoln's off-hand remarks. In his account, Lincoln quipped, "Friend, the Lord prefers common-looking people. That is the reason he makes so many of them." According to Morgan, the expression came to Lincoln during a dream in which someone in a crowd remarked that the President "is a very common-looking man."

The writer Ralph Keyes saves the day from the critics with newly uncovered evidence that the dream quote is not spurious. According to Keyes, the diary of John Hay, one of Lincoln's private secretaries, was published in 1908, and in it appeared the anecdote about Lincoln's dream. Hay had written it on December 23, 1863, and it quoted verbatim how the President reacted in the dream when one in a party of plain people noticed Lincoln and said, "He is a very common-looking man." The line as it is known today is a modern rendition of the remark.

148

17. Letter to an Unknown Woman

Myth! One of Lincoln's most compassionate writings was a letter he addressed to a widow whose five sons died fighting for the North in the Civil War.

The 1998 World War II movie *Saving Private Ryan,* about a group of US soldiers tasked to go behind enemy lines to retrieve a paratrooper whose brothers have been killed in action, tries to draw a parallel with a supposed occurrence in which five siblings died fighting for the Union during the Civil War. In one of the film's critical scenes, the group's commanding officer explains the reason for the mission by calling attention to the celebrated 'Lincoln letter' to Mrs. Lydia Bixby of 15 Dover St., Boston. In the letter, the President condoles with Mrs. Bixby as "the mother of five sons who have died gloriously on the field of battle," and offers her the consolation "that may be found in the thanks of the Republic they died to save."

Surprisingly, the original letter was never found, yet the text has survived to establish it as one of the greatest testimonials to familial sacrifice and patriotic parenthood. To this day, it has fostered the belief that Lincoln acknowledged the valiant deaths of the five Bixby brothers for the Union cause, despite convincing proof that he never did. Debunkers say both the letter, allegedly dated November 21, 1864, and its subject matter are fake, the slickest double hoax to come out of the turbulent Civil War period. The records of the War Department revealed that only two Bixby boys were killed, one deserted, one was honorably discharged, and one was captured and eventually joined the Confederate ranks. These facts had been grossly misrepresented in words that read eerily like Lincoln's, but scholars can't find any proof he wrote or signed the letter or was even aware of it.

According to Nicholas Murray Butler, whose third-hand report historians found competent, John Hay, Secretary of State to Teddy Roosevelt and former private secretary to Lincoln, confessed to having written the Bixby letter. There is no indication, however, that Lincoln signed the letter or authorized Hay to send it without his signature.

149

18. Obits and Hearses

Myth! Lincoln's dreams about his imminent death were premonitions that proved he was psychic.

Because he had been receiving numerous death threats, Lincoln began to have troubling dreams, and one of these he told his friends a few days before he died. He had been awakened in the White House by grieving cries, and on entering the East Room he saw a corpse resting on a catafalque. When he asked who had died, a soldier answered it was the President, "killed by an assassin." Ward H. Lamon, Lincoln's Illinois law partner, is believed to have confirmed this story, although when it was first published, Lincoln expressly denied it was he who had been killed.

In another dream that he had on the eve of his first election, Lincoln was looking into an old, large mirror when he noticed two distinct images of himself, one superimposed on the other. He told his friends he thought this meant that he would serve a second term as President but would die in office. The authenticity of this account is doubted despite some claims that what occurred wasn't a dream but something Lincoln actually experienced.

The two incidents are often cited to prove that Lincoln was psychic, especially about his fate. Throughout his life Lincoln believed in dreams and other enigmatic signs and portents, but this did not mean he was psychic. Dreams normally do not qualify as psychic experiences because they are mere expressions of inner fears, thoughts, and desires. Almost everyone dreams, and if only they can remember all of their dreams, they will find a very large percentage to be coincidental with reality.

19. Bearded in his Den

Myth! The most notable of Lincoln's physical features were his beard, his bass voice, and the wart on his left cheek.

A resonant bass voice and a bearded but unwhiskered face enhanced President Lincoln's imposing 6'4" presence—or so the

150

movies and TV would have us believe. These happen to be the two most common fallacies about how Lincoln looked the first time he assumed office in the White House. Raymond Massey's masterful voice in the 1941 *Abe Lincoln in Illinois* serves Abe's myth well, for it masks the fact that the real Lincoln spoke in a piercing, high-pitched tenor. Fortunately, the shrillness was not to Lincoln's disadvantage in those days when microphones were yet to be invented.

With regards to Lincoln's beard, his face was entirely clean of it on the day he was sworn in as President. Shortly afterwards, Lincoln began growing a beard, which he had for just five years until his death in 1865. According to an oft-related anecdote, it was an 11-year-old girl, Grace Bedell, who suggested in a letter that with a beard, Abe would "look a great deal better for your face is so thin." Despite our popular image of a bewhiskered Lincoln, he was clean-shaven for his entire public career until he was fifty-one years old.

A less known fallacy concerns the wart on Lincoln's face, which not a few people erroneously locate on his left cheek. Some of the President's photos do show it this way, and the explanation apparently has something to do with how those photos were taken. For lack of full-length pictures of Lincoln, photographers often put his head onto other people's bodies. When the head needed to be adjusted to fit the body they were using, they would reverse it so that the wart on his right cheek ended up on his left.

20. The Second Guest was Second Guessed

Myth! Edward Everett, the main speaker at Gettysburg, was more impressive than Lincoln, whose speech is remembered only because it was short and he was the President.

Most everything negative that has been said about the Gettysburg Address is misleading. *First*, there is no doubt Lincoln was the principal speaker that day despite the fact that his remark took approximately a mere two and a half minutes while Edward Everett of Massachusetts spoke for two hours. The President

151

prepared thoroughly for the occasion, as the number of drafts his speech went through indicated.

Second, some newspapers may have insisted that Everett, a former President of Harvard and a master orator, made a rather forceful presentation, whereas Lincoln, despite being a highly skilled and experienced speaker, was unimpressive with his delivery. But the press that mattered was not at all critical. The Associated Press, for instance, mentioned in the New York Tribune that Lincoln was interrupted no fewer than five times by hand claps, adding that following the address there was "long-continued applause."

Third, contrary to what the anti-Lincoln press reported, Lincoln did not "mumble" his remarks or failed to be heard for any other reason. He spoke with power and confidence, as the moment demanded, and although the words did not immediately register as a classic, even Everett was awed. He told Lincoln, "My speech will soon be forgotten; yours never will be. How gladly would I exchange my hundred pages for your twenty lines!"

---

21. Against all Flogs

Myth! Lincoln's Emancipation Proclamation freed all the slaves in both the North and the South.

What Lincoln is most remembered by—the Emancipation Proclamation—turned out to be fluff, but even Martin Luther King believed in it implicitly when he was alive. Since the fiat proclaimed the freedom of all slaves in regions under Confederate control, this excluded those in the slave-holding states that had chosen to stay with the Union, e.g. Kentucky and Maryland; those in border states, such as Delaware and Missouri; and those in secessionist states retaken by the Union, such as Tennessee, West Virginia, parts of Virginia, and Louisiana. The Proclamation applied only to those areas where Lincoln and the Union had no authority to enforce its terms, hence its immediate practical result was that its provisions freed no one.

As Union forces prevailed in Southern territories, some slaves were later freed as these areas came under US control. But out of four million slaves in the US at the time of the Proclamation, a

152

mere two hundred thousand or so were ever released from bondage as a direct consequence of the order. Lincoln couldn't care less, since his real purpose was to force the Southern states to return to the Union by threatening to deplete their manpower reserve in slaves. In 1862 Lincoln told them that any state that did not rejoin the Union by the end of the year would have its slaves declared free men. No state accepted the offer, so on January 1, 1863, the Proclamation, still a great humanitarian edict to many, was issued with the declared intention that it shall be "a fit and necessary war measure for suppressing rebellion."

Another objective for the Proclamation had the international community in mind. By making it appear that the Civil War was a crusade against slavery, the Lincoln gesture discouraged England and France from supporting the Confederate cause, as the South had hoped and expected they would do to save their major source of cotton.

Lincoln's true intention was revealed when he told Greeley, in reply to the latter's accusation that he had forgotten the problems of slaves in the South: "If I could save the Union without freeing any slave I would do it...What I do about slavery and the colored race, I do because I believe it helps to save this Union." At the end of the war, Lincoln paid more attention to the slaves in the North who were not touched by the emancipation than to those in the South. It took the Thirteenth Amendment to the Constitution, which the Great Emancipator missed by a year, to officially abolish slavery in 1866.

22. John: 1838

Myth! Lincoln begat the phrase, "With malice toward none; with charity for all."

On the occasion of Lincoln's inauguration for a second term as president in 1864, he delivered a speech seeking to bridge the wide rift between North and South caused by the Civil War. Anticipating victory for the North in a few weeks time, he announced the idea of reconciling with a defeated South as though nothing had happened. One phrase stands out more vividly than the rest: "With malice toward none; with charity for all; with firmness in the right, as God gives us to see the right, let us strive on to finish the work we are in...."

This line has long been thought to be unique with Lincoln, but it isn't. Although the 16th president may have expressed it better, the idea was lifted, consciously or unconsciously, from the writings of the 6th president, John Quincy Adams. As part of his 1838 response to an invitation to attend a celebration of slavery's abolition in the British West Indies, John Quincy wrote, "In charity to all mankind, bearing no malice or ill-will to any human being, and even compassionating those who hold in bondage their fellow-men, not knowing what they do..."

23. The Army Saves Face—and a Life

Myth! On learning that a Union soldier was sentenced to death for falling asleep while on guard duty, Lincoln issued a pardon stopping the execution in time.

This incident involving Private William Scott is supposed to illustrate the humanism of Lincoln, but it is an obvious case of misreporting to augment an already established presidential reputation. An investigative reporter discovered soon after it happened that Lincoln had nothing to do with Scott's deliverance. Seven captains of Scott's regiment and a Brigadier General had all petitioned for Scott's freedom, and General George B. McClellan heeded by signing the pardon. Obviously, the compassionate decision was made without Lincoln knowing about it. However, no one doubts that, had he known, the Great Emancipator would have approved of McClellan's action, which is probably why his role in the incident is not regarded as myth at all.

24. Mine, Yours and Ours

Myth! Lincoln coined the phrase "government of the people, by the people and for the people."

The second populist utterance wrongly attributed to Lincoln is the phrase "government of the people, by the people and for the people." The idea happens to be as old as democracy itself, for as early as 1382, in the General Prologue to his translation of the Bible, John Wycliffe wrote, "This Bible is for the government of the People, by the People, and for the People." And in 1830, Daniel Webster wrote: "The people's government, made for the people, made by the people, and answerable to the people."

How did Lincoln come across the elegant phrasing? In the 1850s, an abolitionist and Unitarian minister, Theodore Parker, used various versions of the credo in many anti-slavery speeches. Lincoln's law partner William Herndon, who gathered anti-slavery material for the President, included some of these in a collection of articles prepared for Lincoln's reading. According to Herndon, before composing the Gettysburg Address, Lincoln read an 1858 Parker sermon in which he marked the words "democracy is direct self-government, over all the people, by all the people, for all the people."

III

The Life And Times Of Hardy Andy

On Andrew Jackson

"Any man worth his salt will stick up for what
he believes right, but it takes a slightly better
man to acknowledge instantly and without
reservation that he is in error."

•

Andrew Jackson

1. Born in the USA

Myth! No person born outside the US has ever been elected president or vice president.

Constitutionalists swear that no person born outside the US has ever become an elective president or vice president in view of the rule that only those born in this country are qualified for either position. A naturalized citizen is not eligible, and, unless the courts should decide otherwise, neither is a person born abroad to American parents.

But historians have an intuitive sense for facts, and they suspect the rule may have been broken in the case of two US presidents—Andrew Jackson and Chester Arthur. Despite North Carolina, South Carolina, West Virginia and Pennsylvania putting forth claims on Jackson as their native son, there is no clear evidence that he was born in any of these states or colonies, as is sometimes believed. In fact, it was rumored during Jackson's time that he was born in England or Ireland, if not on the high seas.

Arthur, who was the elected vice president when he succeeded the assassinated president James Garfield in 1881, had American parents, but because they moved around so much, Arthur's birthplace has never been established. Some say he was born in Fairfield, Vermont, others in a log cabin in nearby Waterville, New York. During Arthur's campaign as vice president and throughout his presidency, his political opponents claimed he was ineligible because he had been born in Canada.

As far as is known, electoral authorities have never bothered to raise the issue of birthplace for purposes of qualifying or disqualifying any presidential or vice presidential candidate in US constitutional history. If they did, it would have been problematic for seven other presidents who, purely as a technical matter, were not born in the United States. Washington, Adams, Jefferson, Madison, Monroe, John Quincy Adams, and William Henry Harrison were all born in the thirteen original colonies before these became the United States. When Martin Van Buren was brought into the world six years after the signing of the Declaration of Independence, he became the first president to be born a true US citizen.

157

2. Taming the Great Beast

Myth! Jackson was a 'commoner president'.

Lincoln was undoubtedly the greatest of the presidents whose known roots were the masses, but it was Jackson who was given the tag 'commoner president'—for the wrong reason. Old Hickory made the mistake of inviting the hoi polloi to his inauguration, and right after his inaugural address, hundreds of the muddy-booted well-wishers stormed into the White House, overturned chairs and left a chaotic mess. The incident immediately gave Jackson the reputation of being the common man's president and a true democrat.

According to his critics, the real Jackson was far from any of these. Although he had humble beginnings—he was an orphan who had grown up on the frontier, later becoming an Indian fighter and a war hero—he changed his ways immediately prior to entering politics. He no longer sought plebeian company, and was instead brought into the upper circle by his friends in Tennessee, where he owned a good part of present-day Memphis and was treated with deference by the local citizenry. He was occasionally crude—a throwback to his early days—but generally, "he dressed sharply and had excellent manners." He was humorless, arrogant, dictatorial, over-sensitive and short-tempered—an aristocratic mien that blended well with his morality as a racist and pro-slaver. Pictured by his opponents as an ignoramus who couldn't even spell properly, his financial administration was so astute that, in his second term, the US for the only time in its history had a surplus instead of a debt.

3. Politics is Division

Myth! Jackson originated the 'spoils system' in US politics.

We are told that Jackson threw out most if not all of the Republicans under Adams in favor of his men upon his

158

ascendancy to the presidency, and by this action brought about the 'spoils system' as now observed in US politics. The phrase 'to the victor belong the spoils', referring to the practice by which the victorious party in an election rewards its supporters by appointments to public office, is generally attributed to Jackson.

Actually, Jackson was not an ardent follower of the spoils system, and he never made the remark. The 'spoils system' has been practiced by every administration from the beginning of the republic, with Jefferson as the first to use it. True, the demand for patronage following Jackson's election was unprecedented, but the 'commoner president' hardly responded to the calls as most everybody thought he did. He created very few positions, most of which went to previous jobholders anyway, and replaced only 252 out of a total of 612 officers. The presidential practice was much worse under Lincoln, who in his first year in office replaced 1,457 men and left less than 200 appointees from previous administrations.

Some historians are convinced that it wasn't Jackson but his successor, Martin Van Buren, who elevated the system to an art. Van Buren was the first politician president, and the one who invented the political machine, smoke-filled rooms, ward heelers, and rallies. When Jackson nominated Van Buren as minister to Britain before he became president, Henry Clay denounced him for having brought patronage practices he had developed in Albany into national politics. Senator William L. Marcy strongly defended Van Buren, his fellow New Yorker, and in so doing may have been the one who coined the phrase "to the victor belong the spoils."

| 4. A Degree of Literacy |

Myth! Jackson made a fool of himself at Harvard when the school gave him an honorary degree in 1833.

In a story that reinforces his image as a commoner president, Jackson is so impressed by a speech addressed to him in Latin by a Harvard luminary that he clumsily attempts a little Latin himself when it is his turn to speak. Standing before the crowd of scholars after receiving an honorary Doctor of Laws degree from the school, he strings together the only two Latin phrases he knows, and says: "*E pluribus unum*, my friends, *sine qua non.*" Although the story enjoyed credibility for a time (it was still being repeated at Harvard in the 1950s), its scenario has since given way to a more plausible one—that Jackson received his degree in eloquent silence. As one observer noted, he "never said a word, only once in a while bowed a little," following an aide's advice to "say nothing, but look as knowing as any of them." Biographers regard the Latin parody as an invention of Whig detractors, like John Quincy Adams and Charles Augustus Davis, to ridicule the President. For as a lawyer, Jackson must have been familiar with run-of-the-mill Latin phrases, and his having been invited to Harvard was recognition enough that he was an educated man who was not given to silly airs. This is why other supporters take a different tack, and claim that the President was not totally incapable of uttering the pretentious words—for a subtle purpose. *E pluribus unum, sine qua non,* they say, looks makeshift, but it can be taken to mean, "Our Federal Union, it must be preserved." By using the Latin double phrase to mock the pomposity of the Harvard intellectuals, Jackson may have been trying to send the great American message across.

5. Presidential 'Seel of Aproval'

Myth! Jackson's misspelling of 'all correct' as 'oll kurrect' gave rise to the expression 'O.K.'

There are dozens of possible originations for 'O.K.', some of these traceable to established phraseologies in black and Indian culture, like the Jamaican *Oh ki*, the Choctaw Indian *okeh*, and the Surinam *okee*. A source that stands out in popular tradition is Andrew Jackson himself, who was known as a poor speller, and who supposedly wrote the abbreviation "O.K." for "oll kurrect," his spelling of "all correct." 'O.K.' could also have been a product of the craze for comic misspellings and abbreviations that became a newspaper fad in and around Boston in the late 1830s.

US historians say that, as in the case of the 'spoils system', it was the eighth president, Martin Van Buren, who invented this most universal of all American expressions. It seems the Jackson

160

attribution was nothing but an attempt to belittle Van Buren, an ardent Jackson follower. 'O.K.' stood for Old Kinderhook, Van Buren's nickname, which was derived from his birthplace of Kinderhook, N.Y. His supporters, in an effort to improve his public image, formed the Democratic OK Club, and the word soon became a Van Buren rallying cry in 1810. 'OK', which meant that Van Buren was all right by the Democrats, quickly spread across the nation.

Why Jackson would be blamed for the crude misspelling of a simple phrase could only be due to the belief, entertained mostly by his political enemies, that he was semi-literate. Apocryphal sources have been cited claiming that Jackson actually devised a clever line, often misattributed to Mark Twain, to mask this shortcoming. "I never did make much of a man who could think of only one way to spell a word," he is supposed to have said. But most of Jackson's biographers say he could not have spoken the line, or he did it to mean something else, because, while he may have been a poor speller, he was fairly well educated and became a lawyer to prove it.

| **6. Cabin on the Sea** |

Myth! Jackson was the first of eight presidents to be born in a log cabin.

Abraham Lincoln, Millard Fillmore, James Buchanan and James Garfield were born in log cabins, but four other presidents widely believed to have been born in the same surroundings were not. Foremost is Andrew Jackson, who has been touted in almost every schoolbook as "the first president born in a log cabin." There is no proof Jackson had this distinction, and probably none will be found, since historians are not even sure in what state or country he was born.

William Henry Harrison was born in a sturdy, elegant two-and-a-half story red brick mansion located in a large plantation, complete with dormered windows and a good wide view of the James River. When an opposition paper mentioned that "all Harrison wanted in life was a two-thousand-dollar pension, plenty of hard cider, and a log cabin," his propagandists took the cue and

161

pretended that he had indeed been born in a log cabin. To portray him as a man of humble origins in the presidential election of 1840, they used the log cabin and the Battle of Tippecanoe, which he claimed to have won against the Indians, as the symbols of his candidacy.

Andrew Johnson was really poor, but contrary to his biographers' assertion that he was born in a log cabin, his birthplace was in a "small frame house, with a shingled gambrel roof, having an outside stone and brick chimney." Johnson's successor, Ulysses Grant, was likewise born in a frame house, although for some reason, the log cabin persisted as part of his 'poor boy' myth. The error was memorialized in 1922, when the federal government issued a half-dollar with Grant's face on one side and a small log cabin on the other, explaining in the accompanying literature that the general and president had been born in a log cabin.

7. Rachel Getting Married—Again

Myth! Jackson committed bigamy with his first lady.

Most of the popular accounts about Jackson claim that many people were scandalized over his marriage to Rachel Robards because it was bigamous. It seems Jackson was aware on their wedding day that she was still married to her first husband, Captain Lewis Robards, whose divorce from her would not become valid until two years later.

If anyone was guilty of bigamy, however, it was Rachel, considering that it was she, and not Jackson, who married different spouses. Jackson, moreover, acted in good faith—he relied completely on Robards's announcement that he was suing out a writ of divorce against his wife. When he realized in late 1793 that Robards had not bothered to file for divorce until the spring of that year, he tried to correct the mistake by having a new marriage bond issued in January 1794.

Some people are under the impression that the anomaly was significant because all or part of it happened during Jackson's incumbency as president. Actually, Jackson married Rachel for the second time in January 1794, or a good 35 years before

162

becoming president in March 1829. Rachel didn't even get a chance to become first lady because she died before Jackson could make it to the White House. The putative adultery had become a hot issue in the 1828 campaign and was one of the causes that hastened her death.

8. Cotton Wall Jackson

Myth! Jackson used the town's cotton bales to shore up his defenses against the British at the Battle of New Orleans.

One myth about the battle of New Orleans that has held fast is that Jackson made good use of the town's production of cotton to shield his troops from the British. There is only a small amount of truth in this. Cotton bales had been suggested to Jackson as a likely buffer against British muskets, and they were in fact put in place a few days before the battle. However, a premature British heavy artillery attack set some bales on fire and endangered the ammunition supply. This prompted a decision to have them removed, and they were no longer used in the subsequent historic fight.

IV
Tommy Knocking Tales

On Thomas Jefferson

"A democracy is nothing more than mob rule,
where fifty-one percent of the people may take
away the rights of the other forty-nine."

•

Thomas Jefferson

1. Uncle Tom in the White House

Myth! One of Jefferson's ideals was racial equality.

One aspect of Jefferson that did not ring true was his racial philosophy. Reputedly a rigid anti-slaver, he was all his life one of the biggest slave owners in America. There were 135 slaves left to him by his father-in-law, none of whom he freed. Of his subsequent acquisitions, he enfranchised only the five children of Sally Hemings, and only presumably because they were his own or were related to him. Robert E. Lee became a lesser man in the history of American civil rights by defending the pro-slave South during the Civil War, but he hated slavery and proved it by not owning a single slave ever.

Historians make much of the fact that Jefferson tried to insert a lengthy statement attacking the institution of slavery in his original draft of the Declaration of Independence. What is not said is that the attack was not against the evil of slavery *per se*, but against the British king whom Jefferson accused of foisting the slave trade on the unwilling colonists. In his only book, *Notes on Virginia*, Jefferson thoroughly discussed one of the principal obstacles to abolition—the belief that, because of inherent racial differences, blacks and whites could not live together in peace and harmony. In supporting the idea, he argued that blacks were inferior in physical beauty; that they might be lacking in foresight; that they were equal in memory but inferior in reason to the white race; that they were guided more by transient sensation than by reason or reflection; and that they were relatively lacking in imagination.

2. Slave to his Affection

Myth! Jefferson sired five offspring with his sister-in-law, a black slave named Sally Hemings.

The rumor in vogue during Jefferson's presidency was that he had a long-term affair with Sally Hemings, a black slave who happened to be the half-sister of his wife Martha. It was said that

165

he had five illegitimate children with her, all of whom he later freed as a condition set by Sally. The relationship apparently started when Jefferson was minister to France and Sally was asked to accompany his young daughter Polly to Paris. Those who believed the rumor cited a number of suspicious circumstances: Jefferson was home about the time each of Hemings' five children was conceived; at least one of them had an uncanny resemblance to him; and the children were the only slaves he freed when they turned twenty-one. Also, in later developments, two of the children acknowledged Jefferson's paternity; DNA tests conducted in 1998 attested that Jefferson fathered one of Sally's sons; and research by the Thomas Jefferson Foundation gave a similar conclusion

Jefferson's defenders claimed, on the other hand, that his only mistress at the time was Maria Cosway, the wife of a painter, and it was actually two of the President's nephews who were Sally's lovers. They couldn't quite imagine him permitting himself to do something so tawdry as to have sex with a woman who wasn't in a position to say no. Moreover, he would not have tolerated the relationship because of his views about the inferiority of the black race. In support, the Thomas Jefferson Heritage Society, reviewing essentially the same materials that had come before the Foundation, concluded that Sally Hemings was only a minor figure in Thomas Jefferson's life and that it was not probable that he fathered any of her children. It suggested that Jefferson's younger brother Randolph was more likely the father of at least some of them, and accounts for the DNA match.

It is not clear how Jefferson's case is affected by the finding that Sally was well beyond being an ordinary slave, as she was three-quarters white, intelligent and French-educated. That she was Martha's half-sister and, therefore, Jefferson's sister-in-law remains vague, but it is widely accepted that this practically freed woman was legally a slave only because her half-breed mother had to pass the bondage on to her children.

The consensus that has emerged from all these is that, despite the many circumstances pointing to a 'relationship' between Jefferson and Hemings, there is no direct or strong evidence that it was sexual or that it produced Heming's offspring. This is to say that, since the case against Jefferson is unable to carry the burden of proof, it must yield to the side of the defense.

166

3. Only on Paper

Myth! **Jefferson favored unlimited freedom of the press.**

This founding father's ambivalent attitude towards freedom of speech and the press is frequently cited as a prime example of Jeffersonian hypocrisy. He is credited with restoring these rights to the people when he became president, thus ending the celebrated 'reign of terror' of the Adams administration. Earlier in 1787, he had made the famous remark that "were it left to me to decide whether we should have a government without newspapers, or newspapers without a government, I should not hesitate a moment to prefer the latter." On another occasion, he had also said: "Our liberty depends on the freedom of the press, and that cannot be limited without being lost."

But as a politician Jefferson frequently lashed out at the press and used the government to try to put hostile publishers out of business. After becoming president, he got so fed up with Federalist criticism of his administration that he encouraged the states to prosecute Tory newspapers for seditious libel. On his second term in 1807, he was caught saying, "The man who never looked into a newspaper is better informed than he who reads them; inasmuch as he who knows nothing is nearer to the truth than he whose mind is filled with falsehoods and errors." He unleashed his wit to spite the press: "Advertisements contain the only truths to be relied on in a newspaper," and "I do not take a single newspaper, nor read one a month, and I feel myself infinitely the happier for it."

4. The Autocrat as a Liberal

Myth! **Jefferson believed in "a government that governs least."**

The saying, "That government is best which governs least," occurs in the first sentence of Henry David Thoreau's 1849 essay

"Civil Disobedience." Though Thoreau did not claim the remark as his—he put quotation marks around it—he did not identify its true source either. Those who assume it was Jefferson include the influential opinion-maker William F. Buckley, Jr., who, according to Boller and George, urged Republicans in his nationally syndicated column for November 11, 1987, to remember "the insight of the earliest Democratic President. It was Thomas Jefferson who said that the government is best which governs least..." Despite such persuasive endorsements, however, there is no proof that Jefferson ever made the statement.

Observers may have come up with a clue when they noted that the line appeared on the masthead of *The United States Magazine and Democratic Review*. Thoreau contributed to the periodical, which was almost surely his source for the quote. This makes the likeliest candidate John L. O'Sullivan, who founded the magazine in 1837 and was known to have expressed more than once the editorial view that, "The best government is that which governs least."

Jefferson did say nearly the same thing as O'Sullivan, but the trouble is, he was not completely loyal to the philosophy expressed. His "government that governs least" was good only in the hustings, so that when he was safely ensconced in the presidency, he became a strong advocate of territorial expansion, embargo and greater federal powers.

---

5. Incredibly Edible

Myth! Jefferson ate a tomato in public to prove it was not poisonous.

The Jeffersonian myth is so diverse it even includes the genealogy of the lowly tomato. According to a popularly believed story, the fruit (or vegetable, if you like) was introduced into America from Europe but remained untouched for centuries because of its botanical kinship with the deadly nightshade and belladonna (of the family *Solanaceae*). People were afraid it was poisonous—until Jefferson proved otherwise by eating a raw tomato in public.

168

The truth, of course, is something else. The tomato is native to the New World, from which it was introduced to Europe and not the other way around. And it wasn't Jefferson who made it edible fare. According to Richard B. Manchester (*Amazing Facts*), on September 26, 1830, one Col. Robert Gibbon Johnson ate a bunch of tomatoes in public to prove the fruit was not deadly. The doughty Johnson called the residents of Salem, New Jersey to a gathering outside the courthouse and there on the steps, in the horrified eyes of everyone, ate an entire basket of juicy red tomatoes. His doctor expected him to die, and when he didn't the audience cheered.

Sadly for trivia collectors, Andrew F. Smith (*The Tomato in America*, cited in *Uncle John's Giant 10th Anniversary Bathroom Reader*, p. 414) debunks Manchester's charming piece as one more legend about the New World's flora, saying that many of the colonists were well aware from the start that the tomato was not toxic. Jefferson was, in fact, one of those who believed the fruit was nutritious, showing interest in it as a farmer and noting down its first appearance in the Washington markets. This may account for why Jefferson often gets associated with the tomato when it should be the Brussels sprouts, which he introduced to the US in 1810.

6. The Elephant that Morphed into an Ass

Myth! Jefferson turned Democrat after founding the Republican Party.

While Americans in power at the turn of the eighteenth century considered themselves generally as either Federalists or anti-Federalists, they regarded organized parties with disdain and suspicion. What sowed the beginnings of real partisanship was the feud between Jefferson and Hamilton, which broke out when Jefferson and James Madison organized factions to support their growing opposition to Washington's Federalist administration.

The Jeffersonians eventually adopted the name Democratic Republicans—Republicans for short—in 1796, generally favoring a democratic, agrarian society in which individual freedoms were elevated over strong, centralized government. On the other side of the fence, Hamilton and his supporters coalesced in 1792 as the Federalist Party, working for a strong central government, promoting commercial and industrial interests, and currying favor with the elite and powerful of the nation. The Federalists held most of the power in Washington for several years to come, dominating Congress during the two Washington administrations and the Adams presidency.

Contrary to popular belief, Jefferson's venerable organization, despite its name, did not become the modern Republican Party. Instead, its members changed the name to the Democratic Party under Andrew Jackson and became the present-day Democrats. The Federalists—later the Whigs—didn't have the will to evolve into anything modern and simply disintegrated. Today's Republican Party is an entirely new one, although formed essentially along the same lines as the Federalists.

---

7. Granite Mountain Men

Myth! The Mount Rushmore sculpture of Jefferson and three other US Presidents, each representing a national ideal, is the largest in the world.

Carved on the face of the 5,600-ft. high Mount Rushmore are the inscrutable likenesses of Washington, Jefferson, Lincoln, and Theodore Roosevelt. *The Man Who Sneezed in Lincoln's Nose*, the preferred title of Hitchcock's film *North by Northwest*, is a sly reference to the immensity of the sculpture.

But the august group carved on Mt. Rushmore, in the Black Hills of western South Dakota, is not the largest sculpture in the world. That honor belongs to Rushmore's big brother Stone Mountain, on which is portrayed Robert E. Lee, Stonewall Jackson and Jefferson Davis near Atlanta, Georgia. The sculptor Gutzon Borglum had a hand in both, but it was only Mt. Rushmore that he pursued to completion before he died in 1941.

Borglum's widow claimed in an essay published by a government commission soon after his death that her husband's theme for Mt. Rushmore was territorial expansion across the American continent. Lincoln, she averred, was included because he was the "President under whom Alaska was acquired."

170

Actually, the Great Emancipator died in 1865, two years before the US bought Alaska from the Russians. Later, Borglum's son, who did the finishing touches on the figures, stated that the four Presidents were chosen because each represented a national ideal—Washington for the struggle for independence and the birth of the Republic, Jefferson for representative government, Lincoln for the permanent union of the States and equality for all citizens, and Theodore Roosevelt for the twentieth-century role of the United States in world affairs.

The truth, according to researchers, is that Borglum never gave a specific reason for his choice of the four personages. The original plan for Mount Rushmore, as suggested by South Dakota historian Doane Robinson, was to sculpt the heads of Kit Carson, Jim Bridger and John Colter, three "romantic western heroes." But as soon as Borglum was commissioned for the job, he proposed they be replaced by the four former US presidents, with nary a hint that his shifting to them was because he was impressed with their achievements. In particular, his choosing Lincoln to represent racial equality seemed laughable, considering that Borglum was an unmitigated racist who joined the Ku Klux Klan while doing Stone Mountain for the clandestine group. More likely, he thought the features of the four were easier to carve on stone, or that a monument for national figures would get wider support than one for local heroes.

8. Security Counsel

Myth! Jefferson authored the words, *"Eternal vigilance is the price of liberty."*

Whenever we come across this line in speeches and other writings, we immediately assume the source is Jefferson. The wisdom is no doubt Jeffersonian, but whether it was Tom who originated it nobody knows. We can't even be sure if the statement was spoken or written in its pristine form, although scholars agree that for Jefferson to have been the author, it must have been in writing. For as brilliant a writer as Tom was, he was a poor public speaker who mumbled his *bon mots* so much that none has been reliably preserved.

171

Since the epigram is nowhere to be found in any of Jefferson's written pieces, it is probably safe to write him off and consider other sources. Ralph Keyes notes that the first recorded use of the line, or one similar to it, was in a 1790 speech by Irish statesman John Philpot Curran: "The condition upon which God hath given liberty to man is eternal vigilance." The exact phrase attributed to Jefferson, "Eternal vigilance is the price of liberty," was spoken verbatim in the following century—in 1852, to be exact—by abolitionist Wendell Phillips, whose spontaneous delivery of stirring and passionate speeches against slavery made him one of the most brilliant orators of his day. Phillips' reputation makes it likely that he was the one who originated the saying, just as he claimed to be.

9. Jeffersonian Economics

Myth! Jefferson was a humble man with simple tastes.

Although Jefferson was not particular about social distinctions (among whites), he did not apply the average man's standards to himself. He was a lavish spender who lived beyond his means despite owning a vast plantation and one of the largest groups of slaves in America. On the day he died, he left unpaid obligations totaling more than $107,000, a fortune in those days, which he incurred primarily to underwrite his open-handed hosting, his fine horses and fancy rigs. He sold his fine library to the US Congress and made a last-ditch effort to avert bankruptcy with a lottery and public subscriptions for his financial relief, but he still died flat broke and his beloved Monticello was foreclosed.

It was reported that Jefferson, in a gray homespun suit, rode to the Capitol on horseback unattended the first time he was inaugurated. While something of the sort did happen in 1801, it did not prove Jefferson's simplicity and temperance. Edward Thornton, then in charge of the British legation in Washington, gave a correct account of the incident in a dispatch that is still preserved in the British archives. Jefferson at the time was lodging in a boarding house on New Jersey Avenue several hundred yards from the Capitol. He walked to the latter building in his ordinary dress accompanied by the Secretaries of the Navy and

172

the Treasury and a number of his political friends in the House of Representatives. It was all unintended, however, for it had been planned for John Eppes, Jefferson's son-in-law, to procure a new $6,000 carriage and an expensive velvet suit for the inaugural ceremony, but bad weather had delayed their arrival.

10. Draftsman's Contract

Myth! Jefferson relied on his own ideas when he wrote the entire Declaration of Independence.

Jeffersonians who love to brag about their idol's unique role in the framing of the Declaration of Independence, claiming he wrote every single word of that famously eloquent document, miss two exceptions in the preamble that make the tour de force less than complete. The more significant of these is the phrase "pursuit of happiness," which the founding fathers used in lieu of Jefferson's original wording, "protection of property," obviously to divert attention from their own large real estate holdings. The other is the word "unalienable," replacing "inalienable" in Jefferson's draft— apparently a case of a simple typographical error, but in fact deliberately inserted in the broadsides hurriedly printed on the night of July 4, 1776. The printer, John Dunlap, probably thinking that "inalienable" was ungrammatical, proceeded to edit the manuscript in accordance with his personal preference while setting type.

Though it may be conceded that Jefferson wrote *practically* the entire text of the Declaration of Independence, to say that he originated the ideas behind the words is another matter. Franklin and John Adams, who were both on the drafting committee, recognized the superior talent of Jefferson and let him do the yeoman work of writing. Though Jefferson insisted that he did the assignment "turn(ing) to neither book nor pamphlet" for reference, friends and foes alike, including his gadfly John Adams, would charge him years after the Revolution had been won with having plagiarized other authors, notably Aristotle, Aquinas, and the English philosopher John Locke. Jefferson finally hedged by

173

admitting that he was never tasked "to invent new ideas altogether."

V

Some Founded, Others Foundered

On Other US Presidents

"My choice early in life was either to be a piano-
player in a whorehouse or a politician. And to tell
the truth, there's hardly any difference."

•

Harry Truman

1. The Trouble with Harry

Myth! President Harry Truman was a diminutive haberdasher whose middle initial is S.

This may come as a surprise to many, but there is no middle initial in Harry S Truman's name. The S is not an initial at all but a one-letter middle name, which explains the absence of a period after it. His two grandfathers—Anderson Shippe Truman on his father's side and Solomon Young on his mother's—had names that began with S, so Harry's parents chose the S to honor both. However, in some cases, a period appears, as when the intention is to use the name as its own initial. Harry's daughter Margaret preferred the conventional 'S.' form—her biography of the President is entitled *Harry S. Truman*—because she wanted to avoid having to answer inquiries that would be asked if she left the period out. Truman himself got tired of the novelty at times, and signed his papers with a big period after the S to show his annoyance.

The public image Truman projected even during his time was that he was no more than 5'4" tall and 140 pounds heavy, particularly when shown in newspaper photos looking up to such tall men as President Roosevelt, General MacArthur and Charles de Gaulle. The press itself apparently didn't know the real score, because they persisted in calling him "little man." Actually, the 33rd president measured 5'9" in height and weighed 167 lbs.

What may have contributed to the illusion that he was a short dapper man was the manner in which he dressed—he loved bow ties and wide-lapel suits—and the type of jobs he held before he moved into politics. He had been a deskman in a series of small enterprises—the railroad, the post office and a local bank—and for this he earned the disparaging epithet "ribbon clerk" from union leader Al Whitney. One nickname that stuck to him—"Haberdasher Harry"—was an even greater exaggeration than the others. He had been in the haberdashery business in Kansas City for only two years as a silent partner, compared to the more than 25 years he spent in politics prior to his presidency.

176

2. Pass Before you Kick

Myth! The mottos, "The buck stops here," and, "If you can't stand the heat, better get out of the kitchen," are original Trumanisms.

Truman had a motto prominently displayed on the Oval Office desk during his time, which read, "The buck stops here." According to most historians, it was even "more Truman than the Truman doctrine," implying that only the President could have coined it. 'Buck' is not a dollar or a bucket, but a poker marker that is passed on by someone who does not wish to deal; a related phrase is 'passing the buck', a figure of speech that means evading a task or responsibility and shifting it to someone else. Truman, an inveterate poker player, liked the saying because it was exactly how he felt and it was couched in a language he understood. Although the slogan remained on his desk only for a short time, it provided a strong affirmation of his belief in the nature of his office as the final repository of responsibility in the entire executive department.

Unfortunately for quote addicts, biographer David McCullough discovered that Harry had nothing to do with the original expression, as it was Fred Canfil, a former Kansas judge and Truman's long-time friend, who had given him the sign. Canfil had seen one like it in the head office of a federal reformatory in El Reno, Oklahoma, and had asked the warden if a copy could be made for his friend the President.

The second expression, "If you can't stand the heat, get out of the kitchen," means anyone who can't stand criticism should not stay in public office. According to *Time* Magazine in its issue of April 28, 1952, Truman admitted that he had only heard it from others, and was immediately struck by its relevance to his decision whether or not to seek reelection to the presidency. Truman would later reclaim authorship in his 1960 autobiography, referring to the expression as something he had made up but was picked up by others. The line is now generally considered Truman's, although it's not exactly what he was used to saying in his intimate moments and sometimes even in public. It seems Harry's preferred version, which used the 's' word, was more colorful and, therefore, 'Trumanish', but it didn't look good in print and needed

177

to be laundered.

3. Not Worth a Guinness

Myth! The 1948 presidential contest between Truman and Thomas E. Dewey scored two media 'firsts'.

Two events transpiring during the electoral race for president in 1948 have gone down in history as media 'firsts', but in reality they are not. The first involves the famous mistake perpetrated by the Chicago Daily Tribune, when it published the bold-faced headline, "DEWEY DEFEATS TRUMAN," on November 2, before the true results were known. Truman, whom few in either party gave any chances of defeating Dewey, confounded the prophets—and the Tribune—when he won to become the 33rd president of the US. Actually, it was not the first or only time a major publication made such a fiasco.   On the morning of November 8, 1876, New York City residents woke up to a headline in the New York Tribune announcing that Democrat Samuel Tilden had been elected. At the time, the contest was still undecided and remained so until the electoral college finally gave the victory to Rutherford Hayes.

The second event is the television coverage given for the Truman-Dewey fight, which continues to be hyped as the first for a presidential election. But in fact, the television industry in the late 1940s was still in its infancy, and the only coverage of any kind during this period was the minimal attention given to the Republican National Convention. Television's intrusion into the election scene would not be felt until 1952, when the studios began to broadcast TV ads and live campaign speeches for the candidates and showed actual footages from the campaign trail to update the general public.

4. The General gets Brassed off

Myth! Truman fired General MacArthur for

178

insubordination during the Korean War.

News dispatches in 1951 told it bluntly: President Truman fired General Douglas MacArthur for his insubordination as commander of the UN forces in Korea. MacArthur was sacked for repeatedly criticizing the administration's policy of non-confrontation with China. The General had wanted a more aggressive posture against the country that was turning the tide against the Allies in the Korean War, but Truman preferred to be moderate for fear that anything more could trigger a nuclear war. MacArthur's attitude, it is said, so angered Truman that he would not allow the General the dignity of a resignation. "The son of a bitch isn't going to resign on me, I want him fired," he reportedly said.

MacArthur was fired all right, but contrary to the widely held belief, it wasn't Truman as Commander-in-Chief of the Armed Forces that did the firing. Army General Omar Bradley gave MacArthur his walking papers on his own authority and without invoking the name of the President. What is generally assumed may well be true—that Truman ordered Bradley to sign the order of discharge. But this did not shift the responsibility to the President anymore than it would shift it to Congress had Bradley done the firing by authority of the latter. Actually, Truman didn't have to lift a finger, inasmuch as Bradley by himself had the power as Chairman of the Joint Chiefs of Staff to remove MacArthur, or any general for that matter, from his command. MacArthur obviously knew this when he decided not to seek Presidential confirmation of the order of dismissal.

---

5. Big Trouble in Little Rock

Myth! Eisenhower sent federal troops to Little Rock, Arkansas, in 1957 to protect black students against local harassment.

Eisenhower usually gets the credit for being the first president since Reconstruction to apply the full force of federal arms to protect the rights of blacks. The facts are only partly true, however, and many question the sincerity of the president's action insofar as it addressed the racial issue.

In September 1957, the Arkansas governor posted 270 fully armed men from the Arkansas National Guard outside Little Rock Central High School to prevent nine black children from entering the hitherto all-white school. After some hesitation, Eisenhower ordered 1,100 paratroopers from the 101st Airborne to Little Rock and placed the state national guard under his direct orders, ostensibly to protect the rights of the children.

As it turned out, Eisenhower's real motive was to defend the sovereignty of the federal district court order requiring the governor to allow the children into the school, but which the governor was reluctant to follow. Northern Democrats were joined by black activists in charging that Eisenhower was not acting out of concern for the students' rights or safety, but for the integrity of federal law against state defiance or violation. Republican campaign blurbs would later fudge the distinction between the two issues, and say that Eisenhower tried to uphold the federal law because it was for the protection of blacks. Critics, however, knew better. Eisenhower had shown indifference to the racial question many times in the past, and even at the height of his popularity, he could not be relied upon to define his position vis-à-vis the newly emerging civil rights movement.

6. Good Night, Vietnam

Myth! Kennedy was on the verge of withdrawing from Vietnam when he was assassinated.

One of the legacies of America's Camelot is the thought that Kennedy was planning to withdraw from Vietnam just before his assassination. For conspiracy theorists, this was a reason for suspecting the hand of the military in the murder of its commander-in-chief. But Boller, in *Not So!*, tracks down every Kennedy pronouncement on US participation in the Vietnam War, and the picture that emerges is a President resolved to stay the course until victory in some form could be achieved. Despite lukewarm public opinion, Kennedy remained firm in his position, so much so that all his advisers, with the exception of Assistant Secretary of State George Ball, were eventually swayed in his

180

favor.

Kennedy's hawkish attitude showed through when, in Fort Worth a few hours before the assassination, he made his last statement about Vietnam. "Without the United States," he said, "South Vietnam would collapse." Boller adds that in the speech he planned to give in Dallas that day, "he reminded Americans of the military build-up he had undertaken in order to check the 'ambitions of international Communism'."

What might have given rise to the speculation that Kennedy was intending to end US military presence in Vietnam was the plan to withdraw 1,000 US troops from that country by the end of 1963. After making an on-the-spot assessment of the Saigon situation, Secretary of Defense Robert McNamara and Chairman of the Joint Chiefs of Staff Maxwell Taylor had reported that some US personnel could already be withdrawn and replaced by trained South Vietnamese. True to his feelings, Kennedy approved the recommendation but refused to associate his name with it, attributing the idea wholly to McNamara and Taylor. The assassination interrupted the plan, and it was left to LBJ to scrap it totally in favor of even greater military participation in the Vietnam conflict.

---

7. The Little Boat that Couldn't Have

Myth! The young Kennedy rescued three men from a PT boat after it was rammed and cut in two by a Japanese destroyer.

Kennedy was at the helm of a PT boat near the Solomon Islands one moonless night in 1943, on a mission to intercept Japanese vessels harassing American supply ships in the area. Visibility was virtually zero, and Kennedy's boat, PT 109, along with two others, had no radar. Suddenly, he saw a Japanese destroyer bearing on him, traveling at some forty knots. Kennedy turned right abruptly, but before he could fire his torpedoes, the vessel smashed into PT 109, cutting it in two.

This story as recounted by Kennedy himself has been held sacrosanct by many historians, and has merited for the future president both the Navy Medal and the Marine Corps Medal for heroic conduct. But others have raised questions, two of which go into the heart of the matter and suggest that Kennedy was anything but truthful. *First*, why did Kennedy claim he saved three men, when the indications are that he saved only one? *Second*, why did Kennedy say that the little boat was split in two while it was attacking a destroyer, yet interviews with members of Kennedy's crew tended to show that it was rammed during a lull in a combat zone, when he and everybody else on board were virtually napping? Experts note that PT boats were fast and highly maneuverable, and there was simply no way one with a fully alerted crew could have been struck deliberately in an offensive by a ponderous destroyer in the middle of a naval battle.

---

8. The Eagle Spreads its Wings

Myth! Teddy Roosevelt composed the proverb, "Speak softly and carry a big stick."

The Monroe Doctrine, one of the most monumental principles enunciated in the geopolitical arena, declared in essence that the US would not tolerate intervention by European nations in the affairs of the Americas, and the US in turn would not interfere with European governments and their already established colonies.

President James Monroe, after whom it was named, is generally given credit as the author, though he had nothing to do with the doctrine prior to its launching except to incorporate it in his address to Congress on December 2, 1823. He did use the full force of the American presidency to put it into effect, and for this Monroe probably deserved to have it named for him, but he did not conceptualize the doctrine. It was a recommendation by Secretary of State John Quincy Adams that he later expanded into a full-pledged foreign policy, an achievement that many now believe to be his finest ever. This is yet another misconception, however, since Adams actually grabbed the idea from its real author, British secretary for foreign affairs George Canning, who had suggested that the US and Britain unite to oppose European expansion in the West.

For helping drive the Spanish out of Cuba in pursuit of the Monroe Doctrine, Teddy Roosevelt is often cited as the first

182

American president in the 20th century to put the 1823 principle into play. Actually, the Cuban intervention, which precipitated the Spanish-American War, occurred in the 19th century, when Teddy was only Assistant Secretary of the Navy. He was still only the Vice President when, at the Minnesota State Fair in 1901, he said, "Speak softly and carry a big stick—you will go far." He had intended to capsulize the message that the Monroe Doctrine would go far if the American nation spoke softly and honed up its navy. As it turns out, the saying wasn't any more original than the doctrine was, since Teddy himself disclosed in a letter to a friend that he had only repeated a West African proverb. Carl Sandburg thought it was a Spanish adage, but whatever it was, it became Teddy's favorite.

Roosevelt extended the Monroe Doctrine later as President by issuing the 1904 Roosevelt Corollary, which asserted the right of the United States to intervene in case small states in the Caribbean and Central America were unable to pay their international debts. Although the catalyst for the new policy was Germany's aggressiveness in the Venezuela affair of 1902-03, Teddy applied the Corollary not to Venezuela but to the Dominican Republic when this Caribbean nation became hopelessly bankrupt in 1905 and faced intervention by European powers. The U.S. customs receivership that the President arranged provided fiscal control but it also brought about virtual political domination and, eventually, outright occupation by the US during that period.

9. Still Voices, Distant Lives

Myth! When asked why he annexed the Philippines in 1898, President McKinley said, "God told me so."

President McKinley reportedly told an assemblage of Methodists that he had "walked the floor of the White House night after night until midnight," agonizing over his decision whether or not to annex the Philippines, which the US had just won from Spain. "I am not ashamed to tell you gentlemen," he explained, "that I went down on my knees and prayed Almighty God for light and guidance more than one night."

According to an observer, the statement revealed McKinley for

183

what he was—a sanctimonious pretender. He noted, "An honest man, it's said, would have admitted that public opinion pushed him to keep the Philippines, that God had nothing to do with the matter." But in fairness to McKinley, the story only came out three years after his death and was told by a sympathizer, General James Rusling, who claimed he and his fellow Methodists (who did not corroborate the account) had heard it at the aforementioned meeting. A long supposedly verbatim account that Rusling later published in the *Christian Advocate* made the story even more suspicious because no shorthand reporter had helped record the words originally. Since then, many have suggested that the General was not even at the meeting and just made the whole thing up.

According to historian Thomas Bailey, this was not the first time Rusling had depicted a president as asking for divine guidance in making a decision. Rusling had earlier published a book in 1899 in which he had "Lincoln report, in suspiciously similar language, a prayerful experience on the eve of the Battle of Gettysburg."

---

10. President for a Day

Myth! The shortest tenure of a US president is one day.

Both the oldest and the youngest US president held office in the 20th century, and, as some people erroneously believe, so did the longest and the shortest tenured. Ronald Reagan was undoubtedly the oldest at 69 years, while Teddy Roosevelt at 42 was the youngest to *become* president when his predecessor died in office. The fact that Teddy was older than JFK when he was elected to his regular term makes JFK, also a 20th century president, the youngest to be *elected* to the position. The longest tenured is FDR, but the shortest is William Henry Harrison, a figure of the 19th century. Harrison, who died after only 32 days of governing the nation, hardly had time to make himself felt, thus the suggestion, quite false, that William McKinley's 6 months and 20 days in office is the shortest among the presidents. Actually, McKinley had already served a first full term as president before his second

184

term abruptly ended by assassination in September 1901.

Harrison's record has not entirely gone unquestioned, however. To his fans, David Rice Atchison, whose graveyard in Missouri reads, "President of the U.S. one day," and who has a statue erected in his honor in Plattsburg, will always be the president with the shortest term of office. Atchison was the Senate President pro tempore when President James Polk's term ended on the noon of Sunday, March 4, 1849. (Technically, a new administration starts at midnight of March 3 after the presidential election, but it has been customary for the outgoing president to continue to perform his duties until the new president takes his oath of office on March 4). However, Zachary Taylor, who was the newly elected President, did not take the oath of office until Monday, March 5. Because Polk's vice-president had resigned beforehand as president of the Senate, the claim arose that the only person qualified to be president during the interval between March 4 and 5, 1849 was the Senate President pro tempore. As it was a mere technicality, and lasted only for an inconsequential 24 hours, political pundits felt that there was no harm if the belief held fast.

It would have been a national event of unprecedented dimensions, nevertheless, but it never really happened. Atchison could not succeed Polk in the interim because his term had also ended on March 3 and he was not reelected until March 5. Moreover, there was no senate president pro tempore between Congresses because that office was filled only for a particular session. The next in line, the speaker, was on the same boat as any other elective official whose old term ended on March 3 but whose new term began on March 5. The law at the time provided that if all of the offices in the line of succession were vacant, the states were to send electors to choose a new president. This procedure, however, was not observed.

11. When Jack went Hog Wild

Myth! Kennedy's popularity plummeted when he caused the Bay of Pigs invasion, which he had engineered, to fail.

Kennedy took full responsibility for the Bay of Pigs fiasco,

185

which had been aggravated by his refusal to give air cover to the rebels who floundered on the beach and were eventually annihilated by Castro's forces. Ironically, Kennedy's highest poll rating came right after the debacle, with 82 percent of the American people rallying to support the President. Obviously, the public loved Kennedy for the concept despite the botched handling, not realizing that it was the brainchild of the Eisenhower Administration, hatched entirely by the CIA under Allen Dulles and okayed by both President Eisenhower and his Vice President, Richard Nixon. The only time Kennedy gave his acquiescence to the plan was when Dulles presented it to him just before his inauguration, but this was, technically speaking, while Kennedy was not yet president.

The invasion was not as secret as the plotters had wanted it to be. Some journalists had uncovered most of the plan, and several editors, including those at the New York *Times*, had to be persuaded by the White House to withhold the information. This weakness, according to historians, was a major reason for the failure of the plot, and was even more important than Kennedy's refusal to provide US assistance when the invasion began to turn sour.

12. The Great Silence

Myth! President Calvin "Silent Cal" Coolidge was laconic and soft-spoken.

It seems Calvin Coolidge, instead of being nicknamed Silent Cal, ought to have been called 'the talkative President'. Researchers say that far from being the quiet figure who sat mummy-like at cabinet meetings, he was an erudite, witty and friendly conversationalist answering questions in quick tempo and indulging in reparteés and anecdotes. Copies of reports of all the Coolidge bi-weekly press conferences, contained in a wooden box found in the Forbes Library at Northampton, Coolidge's last home, unraveled the myth. The transcripts showed that this president was voluble when speaking 'on background', and tended to be formal and quiet only when he didn't feel at ease with the

186

company.

One other surprising revelation: Coolidge gave more interviews to the press than any other president before him. It seemed the press painted a Silent Cal image not because Coolidge said little but because he hated to be quoted. He told reporters that he felt better if he wasn't placed on record, and allegedly advised Herbert Hoover, when the latter became president: "If you don't say anything, you won't be called on to repeat it."

Silent Cal became a frequent target of satire because of the misconception that he was a quietly dull person. Apparently, even his death could not spare him from the legendary tartness of Dorothy Parker, who, when she heard Coolidge had died, said, "How can they tell?" Alice Roosevelt Longworth, daughter of Teddy Roosevelt, reportedly quipped that Coolidge "looked as if he had been weaned on a pickle." Both would later deny authorship of these witticisms.

Another made-up story is about Mrs. Coolidge wanting to know the topic of the Sunday sermon from the President, who had just come from church. "Sin," he replied. Mrs. Coolidge asked what the minister said about sin, and Cal replied, "He was against it." Finally, there is the anecdote about the woman sitting beside Coolidge at dinner who told him that she had made a bet that she could get the President to say more than two words. "You lose," Cal said, and clammed up the whole evening. A few months after Coolidge died, his widow wrote that, although the conversation could have happened, she had no way of knowing because she wasn't present at the time.

VI
Buttling For The State
On British Prime Ministers

"Men occasionally stumble over the truth, but
most of them pick themselves up and hurry
off as if nothing had happened."

•

Winston Churchill

1. Winnie the Pooh-Poohed

Myth! Churchill was the best prime minister Britain ever had.

Churchill is undoubtedly the most popular and successful British prime minister—outside Britain, that is. The British themselves believe that men like Walpole, Gladstone and Disraeli were far greater than Churchill, whose career was shot full of holes.

Churchill was made responsible in 1915 for the failed Dardanelles campaign when he was Lord of the Admiralty. Demoted to the duchy of Lancaster, he managed the Gallipoli campaign, which cost the lives of 55,000 Allied soldiers. In 1922 he was defeated humiliatingly in the elections because of the public belief that he was risking a major war by urging a firm stand against the forcible reoccupation of the Dardanelles neutral zone by the Turks. Appointed chancellor of the exchequer in 1924, he restored the gold standard, from which flowed deflation, unemployment and the general strike of 1926. He was in and out of office during the 1920s, surviving only through persistence and doggedness, and in the 1930s made himself even more unsympathetic by opposing dominion status for India and publicly championing Edward VIII in the abdication crisis of 1936. Churchill became prime minister only when Lord Halifax, the foreign secretary, refused to accept the position from Chamberlain.

Churchill acquitted himself with his able stewardship of the country during World War II, but whether or not this fully erased his negative image from the British mind has remained in doubt. After the war's end in 1945, Churchill lost his prime ministry as his party went down in defeat at the polls.

It is ironic that Churchill's academic performance has been underrated even while his political achievements have been exaggerated. Some biographers claim that young Winston was a blockhead throughout his elementary school years, and that he barely passed his academic examinations. Others seem more credible when they say Churchill was, for the most part, a competent student whose class standing was always top drawer. Comments one observer: "His own flippant, self-flagellating

189

remarks probably contributed more to those poor-student accounts than anything else. We must remember, Sir Winston was known for his wit, including that directed at himself."

2. Unrequited Toil

Myth! Churchill coined the phrase 'blood, sweat and tears'.

The free world cheered when this doughty British prime minister finally spoke on the radio at the onset of World War II. Churchill's stirring words—"blood, sweat and tears"—spurred the Allies on and became an apothegm for the great historical events that followed.

The epigrammatic triumvirate 'blood, sweat and tears' is familiar to most of us, but they were not the actual words Churchill spoke. Addressing the House of Commons on May 13, 1940, when he became Prime Minister, he said, "I have nothing to offer but blood, toil, tears and sweat." The speech has since joined the ranks of the finest of the twentieth century, despite the report that the MPs present when it was delivered gave it a cold reception.

Popular usage discards the word 'toil' because it disturbs the cadence and the harmony of the phrase. 'Toil', an action noun, does not belong in the category of blood, sweat and tears, which are body fluids, and besides, it means almost the same as the word 'sweat'.

Churchill claimed the word ensemble was entirely his own invention. More likely, he drew it from a source in his subconscious, adding the word 'toil' for effect. The earliest known user of 'blood, sweat and tears' was the English poet John Dunne, in *An Anatomie of the World in 1611*. Lord Byron reiterated the words in 'The Age of Bronze' in 1823, and again Lord Alfred Douglas in 1919. Churchill himself used it long before his 1940 speech at the British Parliament. In his 1931 book *The Unknown War*, he wrote, "Their sweat, their tears, their blood bedewed the endless plain." He was directing his praise not at the

190

British army or any specific war, but at the soldiers of the Czar before the advent of the Russian Revolution.

3. A Few Good Men

Myth! Churchill said, "Never in the history of human endeavor was so much owed by so many to so few," in praise of the RAF.

The image of Churchill as a masterful writer is well earned, but many claim his reputation for eloquent speech is overrated. A political contemporary likened Churchill's speaking prowess to "heavy but not very mobile guns," meaning that while he excelled in the set speech, on the preparation and editing of which he would spend long hours, his performance in the impromptu was something else. Many of the anecdotes meant to showcase his quick wit and his talent for the repartee have been exposed as myth, and several of his celebrated *bon mots* are known to have been recycled from obscure sources. His manner of delivery also left much to be desired. According to the Britannica, Churchill suffered from a speech defect from which he never fully recovered, and combined with a certain psychological inhibition, this prevented him from becoming a true master of the debate.

Some of Churchill's statements made during the war differ from their popular versions and still others from the official records. For instance, as if from Churchill's own lips, we often hear the phrase, "Never in the history of human endeavor was so much owed by so many to so few." But what Churchill said to the House of Commons on August 20, 1940, to honor the RAF pilots who were turning the tide in England's favor in the Battle of Britain, was, "Never in the field of human conflict was so much owed by so many to so few." He had actually spoken the same words a few days earlier, in a conversation with General (later Lord) Ismay after a visit to the Operations Room of No. 11 Group, Fighter Command. This has provoked suspicion that the statement was not a spur-of-the-moment thought, but had been simmering in Churchill's mind ready for his prepared speech when he saw his opportunity to make it sound extemporaneous.

It is also believed Churchill's phrasing was a bit too lavish for the RAF, whose contribution to the overall British war effort is perceived to be only legendary. Richard Shenkman lists some of the disappointing statistics: a mere 15 percent of the RAF's pilots ever shot down a single plane; just 17 pilots shot down more than ten; it wasn't the RAF's English pilots who made the most kills, but an RAF Polish squadron; and of the thousands of RAF pilots, the two most successful were a Czech and a Pole. Military historians claim it would have been more apt had Churchill addressed his gratitude to the men who guided the radar, which was the real hero of that battle.

4. No Peace in Appeasement

Myth! Churchill rejected appeasement as a means of achieving peace with the Nazis.

When Churchill insisted that the Munich Agreement represented "a total and unmitigated defeat," it buoyed him to the heights as Britain's hero of the times and brought Chamberlain to the depths as its villain. Churchill, it was said, stood up to Hitler, but Chamberlain surrendered through appeasement.

It may come as a surprise to many that Churchill was as much an appeaser as Chamberlain was, and probably more so, although he was extremely careful to do it only in private. For instance, when he was publicly assuring the English that he wanted "victory at all costs," he was privately telling the cabinet he would consider giving Germany back some of its African colonies and giving Italy Gibraltar, Malta, and the Suez Canal if that would buy peace for Britain.

In fairness to Chamberlain, hindsight tells us that the Munich Agreement was not all that bad for the Allies, since it gave the Western democracies time to catch up with the Germans in rearmament. Hitler himself disliked the Agreement for having been "imposed" on him, and it legally denied him an excuse to use his Nazi troops to proceed beyond his takeover of the Sudetenland and conquer all of Czechoslovakia. It must be remembered that when Hitler finally did use the German army to annex the rest of

192

the country in March 1939, parts of it had already been ceded to Poland and Hungary through the treaty.

5. Better Deceased than Diseased?

Myth! Disraeli got the better of Gladstone when the latter predicted the manner of his dying.

Some people suspect British Prime Minister Benjamin Disraeli (1868; 1874-1880), 1st earl of Beaconsfield, was a Jew, but in fact he was a baptized Christian of Jewish descent. Known for his caustic wit, the author-imperialist lost his ministry to William Gladstone in 1868, though not the frequent exchanges of barbed repartees between the two in Parliament. It is said that on one occasion, Gladstone told the august assemblage that Disraeli would meet his end either on the gallows or from some loathsome disease. "That depends," responded his archrival, "upon whether I embrace your principles or your mistress!"

Historians say this famous put-down, though sounding very much like Disraeli, was actually made a century earlier, in 1768, by another British politician, author and wit, John Wilkes, at the expense of his adversary and one-time friend, the eponymic Lord Sandwich. While Sandwich was careful not to specify if it was venereal disease or the pox that would kill Wilkes, his acid comment was typical of the insults the two politicians traded in their debate on how the American colonies should be handled.

6. Lord of his Peers

Myth! Sir Robert Walpole was the first British prime minister.

Robert Walpole, the first to reside at 10 Downing Street, held various ministries—war, treasury, foreign affairs. His dominance at the House of Commons, his forceful character, and his influence with the King and court made him the most powerful figure of his day in Britain. He rejected the title of prime minister, which he regarded as a term of abuse, but his control of the treasury and leadership in Commons contributed to the stability and order of 18th-century politics and made him effectively the first British prime minister in the annals of tradition.

Before and during Walpole's time, there was no office of prime minister, only a chief minister from the House of Lords or Commons, who was the king's first minister and principal member of his cabinet. The role usually devolved on the First Lord of the Treasury, if from the House of Lords, or the Chancellor of the Exchequer, if from Commons. The position gradually took hold and became firmer after Walpole when Parliament gravitated towards a loyalist and an oppositionist party, the head of each eventually becoming the prime minister or alternative prime minister for a term depending on a vote of confidence by Parliament.

Stanley Baldwin formally became Britain's first prime minister when the office was raised in 1937, the last year of his stint in office. To this day, however, the plaque outside Number 10 points to it as the residence of the First Lord of the Treasury.

| 7. No Picnic for a Peacenik |

Myth! Neville Chamberlain was the first British PM to use the phrase 'peace with honor'.

On September 30, 1938, British Prime Minister Neville Chamberlain brought back from his meeting with Hitler a signed copy of the infamous Munich Agreement. From a window of his residence at 10 Downing Street, he reportedly announced to the multitude gathered below: "My good friends, this is the second time in our history that there has come back from Germany to Downing Street peace with honor. I believe it is peace in our time."

Noel Coward subsequently borrowed the phrase "peace in our time" for the title of his 1947 play, not realizing that what Chamberlain really said was "peace for our time." The true source of "peace in our time" is the familiar Book of Common Prayer, which is probably what led to the confusion. Baby boomers are

made to believe the other noteworthy phrase in the statement—
"peace with honor"—originated in those hectic days preceding
World War II, and that Chamberlain was the first to think of
appeasement and the first to use the infamous phrase. But
Chamberlain himself noted that this was not the first time the idea
had come to the country. In 1878, Benjamin Disraeli, the then
prime minister, had just returned from the Congress of Berlin. He
announced, "Lord Salisbury and myself have brought you back
peace—but a peace, I hope, with honor..." Before Disraeli was a
slew of other users, including Lord John Russell in 1853, Samuel
Pepys in his diary, Daniel Defoe in *Memoirs of a Cavalier*, and
Shakespeare in *Coriolanus*.

8. Curtain Call

Myth! Churchill was the first to use the term 'iron
curtain' to describe Russian isolationism.

In a speech delivered at Westminster College in Fulton,
Missouri, on March 5, 1946, Churchill warned, "From Stettin in
the Baltic to Trieste in the Adriatic an iron curtain has descended
across the Continent." The phrase 'iron curtain', widely regarded
as a Churchill original, had been uttered more than a hundred
years before he came to power, and had originally referred to the
fireproof metallic curtains introduced to theaters in the late
eighteenth century.

In later years the words were used as metaphors by a host of
writers and public figures—in 1823 by the Abbé de Pradt; in 1904
by H. G. Wells in *The Food of the Gods*; in 1914 by Queen
Elizabeth of the Belgians; and in 1915 by George Crile in *A
Mechanistic View of War and Peace*. It was applied specifically to
Russia and the Bolshevik Revolution by Russian author Vasily
Rozanov in the late 1910s; by German Foreign Minister Count
Lutz Schwerin on the eve of Germany's defeat; and in various
magazine articles from the 1920s to the 1940s. In February 1945,
Josef Goebbels uttered the phrase to caution the German people
against surrendering to the Russians.

At about the time of Churchill's Fulton appearance a year later,
the phrase was already in common use in the newspaper world,

195

having appeared in an article in the *Sunday Empire News* (London) on October 21, 1945, and within a month or two in leading articles. It was mentioned at least once in the House of Commons before Churchill gave it worldwide circulation.

9. Sign of Five

Myth! Churchill invented the famous two-finger 'V' sign of World War II denoting victory for the Allies.

If those two chubby fingers weren't cradling a cigar, they were being flashed in every photo op to buoy up the hopes of Allied soldiers around the world.

Churchill greatly popularized the hand sign using the upraised middle and index finger to form the letter 'V', to denote victory for the Allies in World War II. However, 'Colonel Britton' (D. E. Ritchie), the director of the BBC European news service, is believed to have had a larger role than Churchill in diffusing the V-sign propaganda throughout Europe. The Morse Code 'V' (dot-dot-dot dash), followed by the opening bar of Beethoven's Fifth Symphony, which has the same rhythm, was featured in every BBC broadcast to the continent, including those areas under the Nazi yoke.

Ironically, it was neither of these stalwarts of Britain's fight against Hitler that launched the V-sign during the war. That honor goes to a nondescript member of the exiled Belgian government in London named M. Victor de Lavaleye. In a radio broadcast from the British capital to his native land on 14 January 1941, Lavaleye proposed that the letter 'V' be substituted for the letters 'R.A.F.' which were then being chalked up on walls, posts and other public places in Nazi-occupied Belgium. The 'V', standing for the Belgian Vriehard, meaning freedom, and essentially for 'Victory' in all other European languages, was adopted enthusiastically by the Allies to bolster morale in the European theater.

It has long been told that the 'two-fingers salute' or 'V sign' derives from the gestures of English archers, who used the English longbow fighting at the Battle of Agincourt during the Hundred Years' War. The myth claims that the French cut off the two shooting fingers on the right hand of captured archers, and that the

196

gesture was a sign of defiance by those who were not so mutilated. This is, however, almost certainly untrue in light of the fact that the first definitive known reference to the 'V-sign' is in the works of Rabelais, the French satirist of the 1500s. Additionally, archers were typically commoners who were usually executed when captured.

10. The Lie about the Lie

Myth! Churchill invented the line, "In wartime, truth is so precious that she should always be attended by a bodyguard of lies."

Churchill spoke the line, "In wartime, truth is so precious that she should always be attended by a bodyguard of lies," on various occasions in World War II, but he did not originate it. He himself admitted that Stalin had provided him with the quote, saying it was a Russian proverb.

Churchill reportedly also said, "A lie travels round the world while Truth is putting on her boots." But the real source was Charles Haddon Spurgeon, an English Baptist minister, who wrote the statement in "Truth and Falsehood."

Apparently, the only phrase about truth (or falsehood) that is genuinely Churchillian is 'terminological inexactitude', which Churchill as Under-Secretary at the Colonial Office coined in a memo to answer charges that the British government was condoning the enslavement of Chinese workers in the Transvaal. Currently listed in the modern edition of Roget's Thesaurus as a humorous and long-winded doublespeak for 'lie', 'terminological inexactitude' was branded as an inefficient euphemism by Joseph Chamberlain, who said: "Eleven syllables, many of them Latin or Greek derivation, when one good English word, a Saxon word of a single syllable, would do!" As it turns out, no euphemism was intended, since what Churchill meant was not a lie but an error—he saw that the word 'slavery' would be improper terminology in reference to Chinese labor, a 'terminological inexactitude'.

11. Altered Echo

Myth! Churchill uttered the phrase 'we shall never surrender' on British radio in June 1940.

At the end of May 1940, some 338,000 Allied troops were evacuated from the Dunkirk area of northern France. It was a massive retreat following a resounding defeat at the hands of the Nazis. To hide their embarrassment, the Allies chose to look at the event as a victory. But on June 4, Churchill spoke to the House of Commons to set things straight. Recognizing the debacle and ending with a note of hope, he declared: "...we shall defend our Island, whatever the cost may be, we shall fight on the beaches, we shall fight on the landing grounds, we shall fight in the fields and in the streets, we shall fight in the hills; we shall never surrender..."

People remembered listening to Churchill on radio a few days after his appearance at the House of Commons, but never realized it was British actor Norman Shelley who was articulating the words this time. Shelley was so good even Churchill could not tell the actor's voice from his own. "Very nice," Churchill said, "he's even got my teeth right." The same ploy was used, again with Shelley as the stand-in, for Churchill's famous 'blood, sweat and tears' and 'their finest hour' speeches. The reason allegedly was that the PM did not want to waste time working the airwaves with what he had already done in Parliament. More likely, Churchill realized his minor speech impediment and rigidly formal style did not put him in good stead as an effective radio speaker.

12. Three-Headed Dog of War

Myth! From the 40s to the 60s, the 'Big Three' meant Winston Churchill, Franklin D. Roosevelt and Josef Stalin.

Even today, the impression is that Churchill, Roosevelt and Stalin were the same persons that attended all the Big Three

198

meetings in World War II, and that their influence as a triumvirate went beyond the forties and well into the sixties.

Actually, the powerhouse trio at Teheran in 1943 and Yalta in 1945 changed in composition as early as July 1945 at Potsdam, when Clement Atlee replaced Churchill after the first day of the conference and Truman took over from Roosevelt, who had died. Churchill had initiated the meetings to shape Allied strategy in the Great War, the first at Teheran to consider plans for the liberation of Europe, and the second at Yalta to carve up the new Europe into zones of political influence. But hardly had Churchill warmed his seat at Potsdam when his government was defeated in parliamentary elections, compelling him to return to England and resign. The final decisions of the conference no longer involved Churchill, whose duties passed on to Atlee as the new British PM.

Fortunately for Churchill's ego and reputation and unfortunately for Atlee's, the conference failed insofar as it proposed to reduce the tensions between Russia and the Western Allies. Quite the contrary, the meeting even highlighted their differences, which had been ignored when they were fighting a common enemy. The only accomplishments worth remembering at Potsdam were the placing of a new smaller Germany under the supervision of a control council and the issuance of an ultimatum to Japan for her immediate surrender.

---

13. Sounds Good like Winston Should

Myth! **MP Bessie Braddock and Lady Nancy Astor were both victims of Churchill's famous put-downs.**

Churchill is placed in a rather ungracious light when shown as a slayer of matronly conceit in many of his anecdotes. Fortunately, most of the stories have proved difficult of authentication if not outright false.

For instance, in one of his most famous put-downs, an outraged Member of Parliament named Bessie Braddock accused Churchill of being drunk at a dinner party. He responded, "And you, madam, are ugly. But I shall be sober tomorrow." No evidence exists that the conversation ever took place, and it is not easy to imagine this greatest of statesman as the source of such tactless wit.

199

In another legendary exchange, Lady Nancy Astor purportedly told Churchill, "If I were your wife I'd put poison in your coffee." Churchill responded, "If I were your husband I'd drink it." George Thayer, who helped Randolph Churchill research a biography of his father, discounted this rejoinder as totally uncharacteristic of the prime minister. Despite a long history and a cast of characters that vary with each retelling, the anecdote, with or without Churchill, probably never took place.

Queens,
Grand Dames
& Heroines

I

In Praise Of Famous Women

On Heroines of the Western World

"I am not afraid...I was born to
do this."

•

Joan of Arc

1. Maid of Honor

Myth! Joan of Arc, the illiterate daughter of a French peasant family from Arc, became an accomplished military leader at 17 and eventually the official patron saint of France.

What may come as a surprise to most is that, *first*, Joan of Arc, the greatest national heroine of France, was not French during her lifetime. She was born in 1412 in Domrémy when this was still part of Bar in Lorraine. Bar was then an independent duchy, while Lorraine itself did not join France until 1766.

Second, Joan's family name was Darc, but for no apparent reason this became d'Arc, falsely suggesting that she had something to do with a place or thing called Arc. *Third*, she is often described as a peasant girl born of an ordinary plowman, but in fact she was the daughter of an extremely successful farmer who was the leading citizen of Domrémy and a rabid anti-French. *Fourth*, the Britannica (1974 edition) says it was her wont to write passionate letters against the English during her military campaigns, a revelation that she was not illiterate as is generally believed.

Fifth, contrary to the common understanding, she fought not because she admired the Dauphin but because she hated the English. Ironically, it was not the English but the Parisians under the Burgundians that captured her, and she was later turned over to the English. *Sixth*, the claim that she was an accomplished military leader at the age of 17 is open to question, in the light of writings that refer to her as just being "one of many maids that followed the Army as a banner carrier on the same daily rate of pay as an archer."

Finally, the 15th-century maiden was canonized in 1920 to become one of the two patron saints of France—but only unofficially. As far as the government is concerned, there has been no such position ever since France's proclamation of the separation of Church and state in 1905.

203

2. Minute Maid

Myth! Molly Pitcher was a celebrated woman gunner in the American Revolution.

In most history books the tale of Molly Pitcher is illustrated by a picture of J.C. Armytage's engraving depicting the 1778 battle of Monmouth, New Jersey. Molly stands out in the engraving as the woman stuffing ammo into the barrel of a cannon about to be fired at the British by an American gunnery crew. The antecedent to this setting tells us Molly followed her husband to Monmouth, and while there attended to the Revolutionary soldiers by giving them water. The soldiers asked for her service by calling, "Molly, pitcher," hence the nickname. Armytage's piece celebrates the moment when she took her husband's place at the cannon after he fell wounded, and for which she was awarded a commission and several citations by no less than George Washington.

But not a few insist the scene at Monmouth is no less fictitious than the woman herself, as there is hardly any evidence that the story happened or that Molly existed. Others say there is, in fact, too much evidence, mostly pseudo-historic and spread thinly over a good number of Molly Pitcher candidates vying for the title. One of the leading contenders is Mary Ludwig Hayes McCauley, a profane, tobacco-chewing housewife who accompanied her husband John Hayes on his stint as a soldier for the Continental Army at Monmouth. Another was Margaret Corbin, a woman in the same artillery regiment as Mary and who, like her, happened to be with her husband (also named John) while he was fighting the British at the Battle of Fort Washington. Margaret, commonly referred to in patriotic literature as 'Captain Molly', sealed her reputation when, seeing John Corbin get killed, she replaced him at the firing line and fought valiantly throughout the war until captured by the British. She went one better than Mary McCauley by being the only Revolutionary soldier to be buried at the Military Academy at West Point.

Among Mary, Margaret and the many other women of that period who could easily fill the shoes of the legendary heroine, who is the real Molly Pitcher? Emily J. Teipe, in a piece entitled *Will the Real Molly Pitcher Please Stand Up?*, gives a "simple" answer—all of them and none of them. Says Emily: "The name

Molly Pitcher is a collective generic term as much as 'G.I. Joe' was a moniker for a soldier or soldiers in World War II…(It) is a common label for the countless, nameless women…who are anonymously honored for their heroic service. Because no one individual can be accurately identified as Molly, many women qualify to be called by what has come to be the honorary title of Molly Pitcher. Hundreds, perhaps thousands, of women served not only as ammunition wives, manning and firing the guns, but also in the army and colonial militia."

3. A Total Lack of Sense

Myth! **Though born deaf, dumb and blind, Helen Keller surmounted all her difficulties with the help of only one teacher.**

Contrary to what the Britannica tells us—that her disabilities were congenital—Helen Keller was actually born normal. At the age of one, she caught an infantile disease that left her sight and hearing irreparably damaged. The film *The Miracle Worker* eulogizes her teacher, Anne Sullivan Macy, who restored Helen almost whole to society, but disregards two other teachers and helpers, Polly Thompson and Winifred Corbally.

Helen was also 'mute' at an early age, but it was not because her physical faculty for speaking was impaired. In fact, Helen learned to read, write and speak, eventually graduating *cum laude* from Radcliffe College. She wrote many books and articles, and was one of the most articulate women in the world on the day she died. Helen was unable to speak only in the sense that a profoundly deaf child, though physically capable of speech, cannot learn to speak in the normal way, which is by imitating what it hears said. Thus, Helen had all her physical elements for speech intact from the very beginning, but because she was deaf and blind, she had to learn to speak without the aid of sound or the sight of the word being formed.

In one anecdote, Helen's failure to respond to an introduction elicited the wisecrack, "Oh, all Americans are deaf, dumb, and blind anyway!" It was a wrong perception of Helen's condition, and in very bad taste. George Bernard Shaw, the alleged perpetrator, quickly denied it ever happened.

4. Born to Kill

Myth! **The famous animal scientist Joy Adamson was killed by the lioness she once cared for.**

The international press occasionally reports the deaths of animal researchers as having been caused by the subjects of their own studies, and later amends the news to reveal that the victims were actually killed by animals of the two-legged variety. This was the fate of researcher Dian Fosse, who was murdered by unknown assailants in 1985 but whose demise was initially blamed on the gorillas in her care. Then there was the case of Joy Adamson, whose book *Born Free* tells the story of the lioness Elsa she and her husband George had raised as a cub in Kenya and then returned to the wild. When Joy was found dead on a lonely road, the press immediately concluded that she had been killed by a lion, most probably by Elsa herself. Later investigations established that it was really an African herdsman that murdered her. Joy's husband, George, was also killed nine years after Joy's murder, near the Kora National Reserve in Kenya. Had he been slashed instead of shot, the initial suspicion might have been that he was done in by one of Elsa's kin.

5. Night Walker with a Lamp

Myth! **Florence Nightingale earned the legendary epithet 'The Lady with the Lamp' for devoting most of her life to nursing the sick and the wounded.**

Although Florence Nightingale, the first woman to receive Britain's Order of Merit for her work as a nurse, was born in Florence, Italy (which accounts for her first name), she was entirely British. What's misleading about her is that she didn't do

206

much of the nursing that she is noted for. In fact, only about three years of her life were spent in the activity, primarily during the Crimean War with Russia, where she headed a unit of British women nurses from 1854 to 1856 to care for the sick and the war-wounded. It took no more than her first year's stint as a nurse to shape single-handedly her patients' conception of her as 'The Lady with the Lamp' and put her up as a national hero of England.

By May 1855, nursing the sick had become Florence Nightingale's secondary interest, as she began to set her sights on the welfare of the British Army and later on public health as a whole. It is in these higher tasks that her real fame rests. She was quite an administrator and innovator, establishing the rudiments of modern nursing and pioneering in preventive medicine. She started nursing schools and organized medical organizations, foremost of which was the Nightingale School for Nurses at St. Thomas's Hospital, the first of its kind in the world. She lived to be 90 years of age, but interestingly, the last forty years of it she spent in one room, never leaving, although there was no stated reason for her doing so. It is suspected that Florence Nightingale, who had no known organic illness, pretended to be an invalid to be able to devote herself night and day to her chosen pursuits.

| **6. In Pursuit of a Foggy Notion** |

Myth! Stephen Foster named a song he composed after Nellie Bly, an American adventuress who broke Phileas Fogg's record for girdling the globe.

Nellie Bly was a figure of the late nineteenth century, which is probably why she is a bit removed from modern perception. Although her real name was Elizabeth Cochrane Seaman, it was under the pen name Nellie Bly that she feigned insanity and exposed the inhuman conditions at the notorious Blackwell Island women's asylum in 1887. However, she was better known for having traversed the globe in 72 days, a feat that, by popular interpretation, was a record breaker because it beat the 80 days previously set by one Phineas (not Phileas) Fogg.

Her book *Around the World in 72 Days*, which described her real-life journeys by steamboat, rickshaw, railroad, and even

207

sampan, dispelled some but not all of the common fallacies about Bly. She was a newspaper reporter, not an adventuress, and on her world-girdling tour, she had traveled all alone, meaning there was not one witness to integrate her story. Her completing the mission in 72 days might have set a record but it did not break one, since the 80-day round-the-world adventure of Phineas Fogg was pure fiction from the pen of the famous French writer Jules Verne. Incidentally, unlike Bly, Fogg was not alone in accomplishing his feat, but was accompanied by his valet Passpartout.

After Bly's feat, flowers, trains and racehorses were named for her and songs were sung in her honor. Contrary to popular belief, one such song was not the famous tune 'Nellie Bly' composed by Stephen Foster, which was written before she was born and from which the reporter had in fact taken her name.

---

7. Freedom Rides the Rails

Myth! Harriet Tubman managed the Underground Railroad, which transported nearly a hundred thousand slaves from the South to the North and freedom.

The idea that a slave's run for freedom frequently involved the use of railways would, if it were once believed, be the most naive misconception about the Underground Railroad. The term referred to nothing more than a loose network of safe houses, with no specific escape route, no designated means of conveyance for the fugitive, and no guarantee that the operation would be successful. Modern scholars say the belief that the Underground Railroad saved up to a hundred thousand slaves was based on wildly inflated abolitionists' claims. Kenneth C. Davis notes: "The number successfully escaping—only about a thousand to twenty-five hundred a year between 1830 and 1850—was virtually insignificant in terms of making an impact on the slave economy."

The human delivery system sported the slogan 'North to Freedom', without clarifying that most of the North was often bypassed and the northernmost terminal was not in the US but in Canada. Moreover, the Underground Railroad did not begin with a slave state and end with a free state, as is commonly believed, but

208

extended from a free border state to a free Northern state. While the assistance of a 'railroad conductor' was always welcome, the conductor was in a position to guide the slave only after the latter had already made the most dangerous part of the journey himself—that which took the slave out of the South and into a border state where the railroad operated.

Davis confirms as myth the claim that the Underground Railroad was the creation of benign whites that oversaw its efficient, friendly operation. "In fact," notes Davis, "the network of safe houses, conductors and station masters consisted of mostly black abolitionists, their families and homes." Prominent in this regard was the African American Harriet Tubman, who drew a prize on her head for bringing over 300 slaves to freedom. However, Tubman is overly credited for what apparently was just a handmaid's role. Records show she had no part in supervising the 'railroad'.

8. People Movers

Myth! Pioneers Susan B. Anthony (women suffrage) and Margaret Sanger (birth control) were the first of their gender to become dedicated to their respective line of work.

History has apparently been too lax in ministering to the distaff side of achievers. Two honorees who have gotten more than they deserve are Susan B. Anthony and Margaret Sanger. Although Anthony blazed the trail for women's vote in the eastern United States, she was not the first for the whole country. Researchers believe this was Abigail Duniway, a witty, self-educated farmer's wife who had arrived on the Oregon Trail and began to etch her name there. Her speeches were instrumental in gaining the women's vote in Idaho in 1896 and Washington in 1910, and she also spearheaded the drive that ultimately won suffrage for Oregon women in 1912.

According to Tom Burnam, people who think the advocacy of birth control emerged in the twentieth century and was invented by Margaret Sanger are wrong. More than a hundred and fifty years ago, another woman, Frances Wright (1795-1852), was already lecturing on birth control, equal rights for women, emancipation of the slaves and equitable distribution of property, among others. Unfortunately, Wright had a too aggressive and unfeminine image on the lecture circuit and this did much to detract from the popularity and efficacy of her ideas.

9. The President's (a) Lady

Myth! Americans have yet to put a woman in the Oval Office, whether in an official or de facto capacity.

The US has been one of the last to remain unyielding to what is now a political reality—that the government of a major power can be run effectively by a woman. The irony of it, according to critics, is that this nation continues to claim to be the leading exponent of women's rights in the world. It hasn't lost any time trying: Hillary Clinton has just waged a difficult and intense campaign to break the gender barrier to the presidency—and failed. Although the next American vice president after Joseph Biden may be a woman, there is even less expectancy that she will eventually rise to the presidency by succession or election.

The little known fact, however, is that the highest office in the US was once run unofficially by a woman—an incapacitated president's wife—long before the idea of women's rights became popular. For the last seventeen months of his term, Woodrow Wilson was severely paralyzed and partially blinded from a stroke in 1919. Few people knew about the President's condition and the fact that the first lady, Edith, had already assumed many of the President's functions. His Vice President, Thomas Marshall, had publicly confessed that the thought of being president terrified him, and had declined to take over, allowing Edith to practically run the show until the end of the presidential term.

Lacking the Twenty-fifth Amendment to the Constitution, there was no clear direction on who should assume power in the case of a severely incapacitated—but still living—chief executive. Edith controlled all access to the President, reviewed his correspondence, and almost certainly forged his signature on documents requiring presidential approval. She held independent meetings with cabinet members, and had the final draft approval on the Administration's annual message to the newly convened

210

Congress in 1919. She often emerged from closed-door conferences with her husband to convey his views to the press, most likely making up the words herself. Edith could have been the first to break the political barrier against women, but she couldn't even vote at the time and ironically was one of those who vehemently opposed the campaign for female suffrage.

10. Flawed Gam

Myth! By sporting a wooden leg during most of her career, the stage actress Sarah Bernhardt inspired the theatrical expression 'break a leg'.

Bernhardt had her leg amputated in 1915, when she was already 72, and she adamantly refused to have an artificial one fitted. Instead, she had a chair made specifically to allow her movement around the narrow passages of theaters, as well as on the stage, where she continued to act roles that could be played seated.

The actress' condition is thought to be the basis of the theatrical expression "break a leg," meaning good luck, but the allusion is just another myth. Sarah lost her leg outside the theater and long after the expression came into being. Actually, the expression did not originate with actors but with race fans; to mislead an evil spirit that delighted in spoiling things such as a horse race, bettors began telling their horses to go ahead and "break a leg" while secretly wishing them good luck. Actors now use the same formula and say "break a leg" when wishing someone good luck.

11. Woman Under the Influence

Myth! Carrie Nation was an untiring advocate of temperance who had a fearsome reputation for demolishing entire barrooms with a man-sized axe.

211

Carry (not Carrie) Nation, whose real name was Amelia Moore, directed her crusade against alcohol and, on the side, against fraternal orders, tobacco, foreign foods, corsets, skirts of improper length and mildly pornographic art. She began her career by attacking a saloon in Kiowa, Kansas in June of 1900, but contrary to the myth this created, what she smashed were liquor bottles and a few mirrors and windows using bricks and rocks she had gathered in her own backyard. She didn't begin using a hatchet (not an axe) until sometime later, and this she wielded more for the benefit of the press or to help sell souvenir hatchets to pay her fines and damages. The 'demolition' she carried out was usually limited to glasses, bottles and cheap items that she believed she could pay for if pressed. Actually, Carry didn't have to be armed to be able to put up a threatening appearance, as she was a formidable woman—nearly 6 feet tall and weighing 175 pounds—who loved to dress in stark black and white clothing.

Little is known about what urged Carry to carry out her temperance mission, but the breakup of her first marriage after only a few months, caused by the alcoholism of her husband, could have had something to do with it. Her second marriage with a lawyer, journalist and minister named David Nation lasted 24 years, at the end of which he divorced her on the ground of desertion.

12. Angel of Mercy

Myth! Clara Barton, an American Civil War nurse, founded the International Red Cross.

A character in the 1941 Bette Davis movie *The Man Who Came to Dinner* casually mentions that Florence Nightingale founded the International Red Cross. A quote book attempts to correct the error by pointing out that Clara Barton, 'The Angel of the Battlefield' during the U.S. Civil War, was the real founder.

The correction is just as wrong, for what Barton founded was only the American Red Cross. Moreover, she wasn't a nurse, as most people think, though she has been mistaken for one because of her activities during the Civil War when she went out into the battlefields and took supplies to the Union troops. Her activities were limited to seeing that men got food and clothing, and she also cooked food for the soldiers before they were transported to the hospitals in the cities.

Neither was Clara Barton part of the Red Cross while she was doing her charitable work during the American conflict. The Red Cross movement was founded in Geneva in 1864 by a Swiss banker, Jean-Henri Dunant, and Barton got to know about the organization only when she went there on vacation in 1869. Soon she became a volunteer with the International Red Cross during the Franco-Prussian War. When she returned to the US, she campaigned to have the country become part of the movement; eventually, she called for the establishment of the American Red Cross. However, she saw to it that the latter focus on civilian disaster service, unlike the original in Europe, which was set up for military involvement. The US organization was over twenty years old before it did any military relief during the Spanish American War in Cuba in 1898.

13. I am Siam

Myth! Anna Leonowen was a well-bred **Englishwoman who served as governess for the barbarous Mongkut of Siam in 1862.**

Anna's own account in her two books—*The English Governess at the Siamese Court* (1870) and *The Romance of the Harem* (1872)—is apparently not as accurate as we have been made to believe, and this taints all works that have been derived from it, including Margaret Langdon's 1944 novel *Anna and the King of Siam*. For one, it snubs the image of the late Mongkut (1804-68) as a known reformer who modernized Siam, now Thailand, and, worse, attributes to him the barbaric deeds and atrocities of earlier Siamese rulers in history and legend. Anna may have made up her description of how two young lovers were burned at the stake on the orders of the king, a tragedy depicted in the 1946 film *Anna and the King of Siam* but replaced with a happier version in the 1951 musical *The King and I*.

For another, Anna falsifies her background, claiming she was from Caernarfon, Wales, when in fact she was an Anglo-Indian born in Ahmadnagar, India. News that she was not Welsh came as a shock to the town that had long claimed her as one of its most famous natives. Other sources say she was "a rather racy character for a Victorian governess," and could have hailed from anywhere except Britain. Her father was a poor army sergeant named Edwards, not the fine Captain Crawford she proudly wrote about, and her deceased husband, identified in her writings as Major Thomas Leonowens of the Indian Army, was actually a civilian clerk named Thomas Leon Owens. Attempts to better the family's circumstances took the couple to Southeast Asia, where Thomas landed a job as hotel manager in Penang, Malaysia.

Serious historians consider Mongkut much more civilized than Anna painted him to be. Sharing some of Solomon's noteworthy attributes, this king excelled in foreign affairs, entering into friendly relations with many countries and boosting foreign trade. He showed Solomon's tolerance for religion by welcoming Western missionaries and religious teachers into his kingdom. Perhaps it is just as well that the Solomonic feat he should be most known for has not rated much notice at all. Unbelievable as it may seem, the small and frail-looking king bested Solomon's record of 1000 wives and mistresses by having 9000 spouses in his lifetime, almost all of them legal. And he probably had as many children, for nothing less would have taxed the spirit and energy of the feisty governess.

Of course, when the same historians say it was Mongkut who assured Thailand's place as the only Southeast Asian nation that did not experience colonization, they are giving the iconic king more praise than he deserves. Old Siam used to be a kingdom with fluid borders, extending its sovereignty into what are now Burma, Laos, Cambodia and Malaysia. But for a period of fifteen years in the sixteenth century, it was colonized by a country that was neither Western nor a power—Burma. Worse, while most of the Southeast Asian countries that became Western colonies eventually recovered their territory intact, Thailand was one of the few that permanently lost territory by cession to the Western powers and, through them, to their colonies. Ironically, it was Mongkut who first relinquished sovereign rights in Cambodia by yielding part of the territory to the French in 1867. The Thai monarch and his successors obviously realized that the Western countries had the power to enforce their will on them and had little choice but to follow a concessionary policy sometimes worse than the European colonization of Indochina and Indonesia.

II

Queen's Gambit Declined

On Cleopatra

"Be it known that we, the
greatest, are misthought."

•

Cleopatra

1. Suicide Redux

Myth! Cleopatra committed suicide for love of Antony.

The central point in almost every book or film about Cleopatra is a scene in which she kills herself with style. Shakespeare popularized the foolishly romantic notion that it was all for love of Antony. Though rather surprising for one so vain and ambitious, this apparently suicidal act is not the only famous turn to promote that bromide 'love conquers all'. The list includes Queen Christina of Sweden and Britain's Duke of Windsor, two royals who committed political suicide with a flourish by abdicating their thrones for the sake of *l'amour*.

The common version of the tragedy is that Cleopatra summoned Antony from his camp, then primped herself for her suicide. On seeing Cleopatra dead, Antony ran himself through with a sword. It almost seemed like a suicide pact between the two lovers to avoid the humiliation of capture by Octavius, the enemy who had previously bested them at Actium.

As history sees it, however, Antony's death was the object of an elaborate murder scheme worthy of Agatha Christie. Cleopatra was desperate to salvage her Egyptian throne under an imminent Roman administration, so she quickly decided to do a deal with Octavius. Realizing there was no other way to dispose of Antony, she thought of tricking him into taking his own life. She sent him word that she had followed this honorable course by drinking poison, with the slightest of hint that Antony should follow suit. Upon receiving her message, the desperate Antony, without confirming the news, killed himself with his sword.

Later, Cleopatra learned Octavius was planning to take her to Rome and parade her through the streets as a symbol of his triumph. This was a grim reminder of what Caesar had previously done to her sister Arsinoe. Becoming depressed, she resolved to make the mock suicide real—an offering not to love and faith but to pride. Ironically, the rumor that she was to be fettered and paraded through Rome was a false one. It was created by the Romans precisely to convince her that suicide was the only noble alternative.

217

2. Banged-up Nile Blonde

Myth! Cleopatra was Egyptian, had tawny skin and wore her black hair in bangs.

Cleopatra has been stereotyped by the popular arts as a dark-eyed beauty with tawny skin and black hair. Afrocentrism would color her black entirely, based on the belief that Egypt was a black African society. Her fans don't seem to mind if she was black or white, as long as her hair is shown right. Says one: "Cornrows should look just as good on Cleo as they do on Bo Derek or Whoopi Goldberg, but would you put bangs on any of them?"

In fact, Cleopatra was a Macedonian Greek, possibly with some Iranian strain but with no drop of Egyptian blood in her. The first Ptolemy from whom she descended was the son of Lagos, a general in the army of Alexander the Great who seized power in Egypt and made himself king. She was probably a blonde or a redhead who wore her hair in a bun, not in bangs as shown in the movies. Hairstyles then as now dictated that bangs go only with black hair, while buns showed light colors to better advantage. A black wig, on the other hand, would not be worn in bangs but in tight curls over a shaved head, as was the royal fashion of the times. Claudette Colbert and Elizabeth Taylor, who played Cleopatra in the movies, wore bangs for reasons of their own and not because this was demanded by the script. According to gossip, Claudette had a personal fondness for bangs, while Elizabeth went with the vogue in the early 1960s when her movie was being made. A widely viewed art piece showing the Nile Queen wearing a headband that looks like bangs may have suggested the notion that Cleopatra wore that hairstyle.

3. Death at First Bite?

Myth! Cleopatra died from the bite of an asp.

Most everyone believes that Cleopatra poisoned herself with the help of a snake, which delivered the fatal payload. Plutarch, born some 76 years after the fact, insists it was an asp, but only he seems to be sure. It is wholly unusual for suicide by snakebite to occur in high places, and Cleopatra's is probably the only royal case on record. A modern equivalent is unthinkable—unless some similarity is seen between snakebite and lethal injection, which may have been the way poison was conveyed into the system of a suicidal American sex queen in the early 1960s.

The more deductive of Cleopatra's devotees agree that the Nile Queen was 'asp fixated', but doubt that the poison that killed her was administered through snakebite. For one, she would have found it easier drinking it. For another, while two small marks were discovered on her left arm, no asp was ever found in the sealed mausoleum. The only possible witnesses, the two handmaidens who attended her, were found dead in the same room, apparently from the same cause. A snake could have been smuggled into Cleopatra's chamber in a basketful of figs delivered that morning, but how it ever got out is a mystery. The asp (*vipera aspis*) was of a species that has never been found in Egypt, and Cleopatra would not have wanted its poison, which is painful, slow-acting and rarely fatal.

Although Plutarch may have originated the asp theory, he never really presented it as fact. Quite likely, he used the word 'asp' not specifically to refer to members of the viper family, but generically to include the highly venomous Egyptian cobra, or *Naja haje*. Plutarch could have had the native cobra in mind as the agent of death because of its symbolical significance to the Egyptian monarchy, especially to the royal house of Cleopatra. The latter regarded this snake as an object of veneration and believed that surrendering to its bite was an act of honor.

---

4. A Nose for Intrigue

Myth! Cleopatra had a beautiful face and a voluptuous figure.

In five mainstream films that brought her epic to the masses, Cleopatra is portrayed as a voluptuous femme fatale. Vivian Leigh, Claudette Colbert and Elizabeth Taylor were particularly striking in their role as the Serpent of the Nile. The latest to put on

219

Cleo's costume and makeup is Hollywood novice Leonor Varela, whose French-Chilean sultriness scorched the small screen in a 1999 HBO miniseries. Morphing the exotic features of all these actresses into a single face and figure promises to generate an interesting modern image of the Egyptian queen.

Unlike the movies, however, history gives no hint of the kind of figure Cleo cut. Resorting to the standards of the time, the image that emerges is that of a short, fine-boned and plumpish woman. In this guise, Cleopatra was far from the likes of the movie stars that played her (except possibly Elizabeth Taylor in her later years).

What the screen has largely ignored is her Semitic nose, a nose that Blaise Pascal said would have changed the whole face of the world had it been shorter. Pascal obviously meant her big nose made her strong of character, as the physiognomy of his century indicated, although cynics think the scientist was just being polite. Most historians agree that Cleopatra was not pretty generally, and that she captivated her two lovers less with her physical assets than with her wit and charm, not to mention wealth. Judging from the Roman coins Antony made in her honor, she was plain, with 'an ungainly hooked nose and a fleshy face'. The best thing that has been said about her physical features is a platitude from the Britannica—"a countenance alive rather than beautiful, with a sensitive mouth, firm chin, liquid eyes, broad forehead, and prominent nose."

5. Fabulously Stoned

Myth! Cleopatra dissolved some pearls in a cup of vinegar to win her bet with Antony.

No amount of history or myth would complete our unflattering portrait of Cleopatra without the business of the pearls, revealing that what she lacked in physical charms she made up with her fabled extravagance.

Cleopatra showed queenly flair in some of the most stylish performances ever cooked up by a head of state. Of the many antics she played with her Roman overlords, it would appear the most frivolous was her famous wager with Antony involving pearls in a cup of vinegar. According to Pliny, when Antony expressed astonishment at a costly meal that Cleopatra had prepared for him, she dislodged one of the two fabulously large pearls in her earrings and threw it into a cup of vinegar. This, while saying, "My draft to Antony shall far exceed it." She drank the potion as soon as the pearl had dissolved, allegedly to win a wager that she could spend ten million *sesterces* ($500,000) on one entertainment in the blink of an eye. Plancus, the umpire, immediately declared the queen winner of the wager, and refused to let her dissolve the second pearl.

Suetonius says the emperor Caligula accomplished the same feat of extravagance in an exhibition. A similar story is told of Sir Thomas Gresham, who, at the Royal Exchange, pledged the health of Queen Elizabeth I in a cup of wine in which precious stones worth £15,000 had been crushed to atoms. However, serious historians downgrade these tales to the level of legend, with the one involving Cleopatra being the most implausible. A popular science experiment has shown that pearls, which are 91.7 per cent calcium carbonate, 6 per cent organic matter and 2.3 per cent water, will dissolve in vinegar containing six or more per cent of acetic acid, producing carbon dioxide and leaving calcium acetate as dissolved salt. But even in very strong vinegar, pearls will dissolve only slowly because of their great hardness—perhaps not in less than three or four hours before they become drinkable.

6. Egyptian Needlework

Myth! Cleopatra's legacies to the modern world include the three Cleopatra Needles standing in New York City, London and Paris.

Three 70-foot-tall granite obelisks, one standing in New York City, another in London, and the third in Paris, are oftentimes held up as the only existing monuments from Cleopatra's reign. Called Cleopatra's Needles, they were built apparently under the auspices of the Egyptian queen.

In fact, the structures are much older than Cleopatra's period, having been erected by Pharaoh Thutmose III in the 16th century BC, or 1,500 years before the Nile queen was born. Standing

221

originally in front of the temple of the sun at Heliopolis, near the present city of Cairo, they were transferred to Cleopatra's favorite city of Alexandria in 14 BC by the Roman emperor Augustus. It was then that 'Pharaoh's great needles' became 'Cleopatra's needles', a name that stayed even after the structures were moved from Alexandria to their present incongruous locations in the West in 1878. The perception of many is that the Needles are fake replicas of the original, like Cleopatra's Barge in Las Vegas, but antiquarians are ready to swear they are the genuine articles that once graced Heliopolis and Alexandria thousands of years ago.

7. Angles and Incest

Myth! Among all of Egypt's queens, there was only one Cleopatra.

To most people, there is only one Cleopatra. She is the multi-faceted Queen of Egypt who was mistress to both Caesar and Antony, and who very nearly changed the whole course of history by becoming Queen of the Roman Empire as well.

Few realize that Cleopatra was only an official title for certain queens of Egypt, and that six other Cleopatras had in fact ruled the country at different times. None was Egyptian, and some were equally, if not more, successful in edifying the name. The Cleopatra we all know was not the original but the last, an unhappy position she attained when her ill-fated adventure with Antony wrote finish to her line. While she should properly be referred to as Cleopatra VII, her real name was Philopator, born in 69 BC to the Egyptian ruler Ptolemy XI. All the Cleopatras were Macedonians belonging to the line of the Ptolemys. They were Egypt's rulers for two hundred fifty years despite being native not to that land but to a mountainous area north of the Aegean Sea (what is now Greece, Yugoslavia and Bulgaria).

The second in the line, Cleopatra II, married her own brother Ptolemy Euergetes II, with whom she had two sons who became co-rulers of Egypt after the death of their father. This incestuous queen is often mistaken for Cleopatra VII, who also married her brother, 12-year-old Ptolemy XIII, and with him assumed joint regency of the empire. But she bore no child from the sibling affair, a fact that many historians presume is because the marriage was never consummated.

When Ptolemy XIII died, Caesar wanted the widowed Cleopatra to marry another brother, Ptolemy XIV. This was obviously to downplay the romance he was carrying on with her, which was attracting attention from Rome. Some say she went through this marriage while others believe she didn't. But all seem to agree that she remained a mistress to Caesar, and that after the latter's assassination, she had Ptolemy XIV murdered so that Caesarion, her son by Caesar, could share her Egyptian throne in joint rule.

The relationship between Cleopatra VII and Ptolemy XIII had so deteriorated that when Caesar arrived in Egypt, the two were preparing for war against each other. The myth was that to gain Caesar's sympathy, Cleopatra VII came to see him concealed in a carpet, which was unrolled in his presence (picture Elizabeth Taylor confronting an astounded Rex Harrison). The Roman reconciled the warring factions, but only temporarily. When Ptolemy acted up again, Caesar crushed his forces at Alexandria, where the young ruler drowned while fleeing.

8. Mistress of Foreign Affairs

Myth! Cleopatra earned the title 'Serpent of the Nile' from her fascination for snakes.

Some writers believe Cleopatra was called the 'Serpent of the Nile' because she was especially fond of pets belonging to the reptilian breed. An unverified source provides yet another reason: her uneducated subjects somehow got it into their heads that she was descended from a god that looked like a giant anaconda. According to popular lore, which is still the most cogent, Cleo earned her nickname from the way she enticed men into her bed and dumped them afterwards.

Historical evidence tends to prove the tag does not deserve a sexual connotation and is probably political. Cleopatra had only two known 'romantic' adventures—Caesar and Anthony. Like her previous incestuous marriage, political expediency rather than carnal desire motivated both.

223

Caesar's fascination with Cleopatra was only incidental to the real reason he stayed in Egypt. It was to convince her to repay what he had spent when he restored her father to the throne— 6,000 talents, an amount almost equal to Egypt's entire annual revenue. Caesar installed her as queen of Egypt because anyone else he appointed would have instantly become his potential rival.

The vaunted love affair between Cleopatra and Antony is said to have been for real, but this is not true either. Antony agreed to kill Cleopatra's sister for her and he fathered her twins as well. Still, when Antony's real wife died, he declined to marry her and instead married Octavius' sister Octavia. He did end up divorcing Octavia and marrying Cleopatra, but he timed it at the precise moment when he needed Egypt's treasure and navy to confront the belligerent Octavius.

III

Queen Bees

On European Queens

"I know I have the body of a weak and feeble woman, but I have the heart and stomach of a king."

•

Elizabeth I

1. Villages of Illusion

Myth! Catherine's Prime Minister Grigori Potemkin built model communities and housing developments that changed the Russian landscape almost overnight.

Many of the achievements that both history and legend have attributed to Catherine the Great, whether rightly or wrongly, she apparently owed to one man, Prince Grigori Alexandrovich Potemkin. The one-eyed Potemkin, who was the Queen's lover during his first two years, would go to any extent to execute her plans and feed her appetite for action. Once, during Catherine's tour of the Russian provinces in 1787, Potemkin as the then prime minister ordered the people to clean the streets, paint the fronts of their houses, wear their best clothes, and smile. The resulting ensemble became the centerpiece of a non-existent housing project, and the Queen, failing to notice the real misery and poverty behind the nifty facade, was impressed. Critics of the couple called the whitewashed communities 'Potemkin villages' in sarcasm.

Her byname notwithstanding, Catherine's greatness has no doubt been exaggerated, as she was only a reformer in ambition. Her numerous attempts at social and political reorganization all came to naught, and the assembly that she called to draft a constitution and a code of laws was a failure. Before her accession to power, she had planned to emancipate the serfs, but when confronted later with the realities of the situation, she not only tolerated the system but even strengthened it. She imposed serfdom on new territories like the Ukraine, which had until then been free, and, while pretending to help settle the Jews, she confined them to a zone, called 'the Pale', beyond which they were not permitted to travel. By distributing the so-called crown lands to her favorites and ministers, she worsened the lot of the peasants, who had enjoyed a certain autonomy. According to the Britannica, "At the end of her reign, there was scarcely a free peasant left in Russia, and because of more systematized control, the condition of the serf was worse than it had been before Catherine's rule."

226

Ninety-five percent of the Russian people, far from benefiting in any way from the achievements of her reign, were forced to provide the labor to finance the immense expenditures required for her ever-growing economic, military, and cultural projects. Although she managed to be called an enlightened ruler because of her love of art and culture, in other respects she was a cruel and unscrupulous despot.

2. Just Horsing Around

Myth! Catherine the Great was called 'The Semiramis of the North' for her aberrant ways, the most remarkable of which was her dallying with a horse.

Catherine II the Great is sometimes called 'the Messalina of the North' and at other times 'the Semiramis of the North'; this tends to confuse Messalina, the deviant wife of Emperor Claudius, with Semiramis, the deified founder of Babylon. Semiramis, far from being a profligate, was a completely asexual figure of Assyrian legend that was known for her beauty, intelligence and great administrative skills. Catherine's legendary sexual propensities have given her the reputation of a modern Messalina, but she is also likened to Semiramis because of her extraordinary mental gifts and executive prowess.

It is said that on her last night on earth, Catherine was preparing herself to be taken by a real stallion, but was crushed to death when attendants lost their grip on the ropes supporting the animal that was slowly being lowered on her. This is one of the stories about Catherine's alleged debauchery, which have their roots in the belief among historians that she pursued an inordinately active sex life in reaction to a repressed childhood. There is evidence that she had numerous lovers throughout her thirty-four year reign, particularly after her husband Peter was deposed and killed. Sympathetic biographers claim she had no more than 15 lovers over a 30-year period, but French historians writing with a clear anti-Russian bias insist she had many more. The latter originated the gossip that Catherine's lovers, numbering in the hundreds, were procured by her favorite minister and former

227

lover Grigori Potemkin, with two women of her court as *les eprouveuses* to test and approve her choices.

We can be sure, in any case, that no animal, much less a horse, figured in Catherine's death. Some sources claim Catherine was so grossly fat that she either died of a stroke while sitting on a commode at St. Petersburg, or broke the commode and died of blood loss from resultant injuries. This is not too far from the official report that the Empress, at age 67, suffered an attack of apoplexy while sitting on her commode, and died in her bed two days later.

3. The Cakes that Ate Paris

Myth! Marie Antoinette made the callous remark, "Let them eat cake."

From the time French revolutionaries attributed the statement to Marie Antoinette to dramatize her decadence and discredit her, it has been repeated to symbolize the insensitivity of Louis XVI's reign to the problems of the masses, which was an underlying factor in the French Revolution. There is evidence that Marie Antoinette's close friend Duchesse de Polignac once asked her, "How is it that these silly people are so clamorous for bread when they can buy such nice *brioches* for a few sous?" *Brioche* is a kind of cake that in those days was an inexpensive alternative to bread, and would have justified as normal the reply "Let them eat cake." But there is absolutely nothing to suggest that Marie Antoinette said words to that effect on this or any other occasion.

Rousseau did mention in his *Confessions* that a "great princess" had made the remark upon being informed that the country people had no bread during the Grenoble Bread Riots of 1739. But the incident had occurred fifteen years before Marie Antoinette was born, and Rousseau himself had written about it two years before she arrived in France and six years before she became queen. The line may have originated with the duchess of Tuscany in 1760, according to a French book published that year, although the restored Bourbon Louis XVIII would later write that the real source was Marie Thérèse, wife of Louis XIV.

228

4. Queen Bitch

Myth! **Marie Antoinette was the first Frenchwoman of royal blood to be brought before the guillotine.**

The French populace devised all sorts of derogatory nicknames for Marie Antoinette, who became unpopular with her constituents from the day she married Louis XVI. One that's especially intriguing was *L'autrichienne*, or 'The Austrian', ostensibly in reference to her Austrian origin. What the French really meant was precisely what the words sounded to their ears—*L' autru chienne*, or 'the ostrich bitch'.

Being Austrian, Marie Antoinette was not the first Frenchwoman of royal blood to be brought before the guillotine, as some believe. She was the first royal person after her own Louis to be beheaded by guillotine, but the first royal Frenchwoman to die in this manner would be one of the countless ladies of noble blood who were frequently seen in Louis' court. The guillotine, a notorious trademark of the Reign of Terror, was already more than a year old when Marie Antoinette met her fate on October 16, 1793.

Though not legally a French citizen, the expatriate queen was convicted of conspiring with foreign and internal enemies of the republic. The verdict was made doubly anomalous because the only indictment that was specified and for which some evidence was offered had little to do with treason. To prove she had tried to corrupt the monarchy, her prosecutors presented a signed deposition from her 11-year old son accusing her of sexual abuse. Her biographers say the son was probably drugged and beaten, and even if he had not cooperated, she would have been beheaded anyway.

5. The Prince who was a Prig

Myth! **Queen Victoria set the sexual tone in Victorian England.**

'Victorian', which describes Queen Victoria's long reign and its sexually repressive standards, ideals and styles, means, in a general sense, anything of a prudish or conventional bent of mind. One would have thought it was Victoria herself who set the trend, but social commentators say she was really sexually liberated and it was her Prince Consort, Albert, who was "extremely straitlaced and a great stickler for morality." An attractive man in his early years, the fat, bald and prematurely middle-aged prince died at the young age of forty-two after siring nine children with Victoria. His dissipation was not caused by extra-marital affairs, but by spending himself entirely on the frumpish queen. He was, according to some sources, rather effeminate and definitely a virgin when he married Victoria. When asked why he never looked at other women, he replied, "That species of vice disgusts me"—leading many to wonder why such an unhealthy regard for sex should come to be called Victorian instead of Albertian.

Victoria's own character, unlike Albert's, was totally incompatible with the rigid morés of her times, no matter what her 387 million subjects may have thought. For one, she was outspoken about her sexual feelings, as when, in her diary, she commended Albert for his "heavenly lovemaking." She liked to drink, and had no reservations about others drinking in her presence, sometimes even to excess. She wasn't reserved, and enjoyed dishing out reparteés that made, or would have made, her prince consort blush. During her widowhood, Victoria is suspected of having taken on several lovers, the best known of whom was her Scottish attendant, John Brown.

Part of the myth about the queen's prudishness is the advice she supposedly gave on how to endure sexual intercourse: "When I hear his (Prince Albert's) steps outside my door I lie down on my bed, close my eyes, open my legs and think of England." According to wordsmiths, the statement may sound Victorian (based on Albert's, not Victoria's, standards), but it actually is not. The real originator was one Lady Alice Hillingdon, who, in 1912, reportedly wrote in her journal, "I am happy now that Charles [her husband] calls on my bedchamber less frequently than of old. As it is, I now endure but two calls a week." The much-relieved lady capped the entry with the famously patriotic line popularly but erroneously attributed to Victoria.

6. Bloody Legacy

Myth! Queen Victoria suffered from hemophilia.

Hemophilia, a disease characterized by profuse bleeding from the slightest injury due to an inborn deficiency of a substance necessary for blood clotting, acts on the sexes in different ways. Only the hemophilic male is the real sufferer and may die from it, but the female, though not personally affected by the disease, is the only one who can transmit it to an offspring. Sons of a hemophilic male are normal, but half of the sons of a hemophilic female are sufferers. Daughters of a hemophilic male or female, although outwardly normal too, may transmit the trait as an overt defect to half their sons and as a hidden trait to half their daughters.

Hemophilia is known to have ravaged certain lines of European royalty, including King Alfonso XIII of Spain and Czar Nicholas of Russia. Queen Victoria, who was positive for the trait, bore a son who became a sufferer, and the disorder appeared among the male descendants of three of her daughters. For sure, Victoria inherited the bad gene from her ascendants, but just as certain is that she was not a sufferer, only a carrier and a passer.

7. No Sense of Rumor

Myth! Queen Victoria's favorite expression was, "We are not amused."

Victorian media pictured the Queen as a solemn figure who uttered the stock expression "We are not amused" when reacting to any jocular attempts by her courtiers. Considering that this response has done more than any other to stereotype Victoria as a frigid sovereign, it is rather unfortunate that only a few people know it is not true. According to a granddaughter, Princess Alice, the Countess of Athlone, the Queen was in fact "a very cheerful person" who categorically denied having ever used the phrase.

The mythical incident that started it all involved Alexander

Yorke, the frequent life of the party at the court of Queen Victoria at Windsor Castle, particularly after the death of the prince consort. This courtier was a short, plump man with greased brown hair, his dress habitually crusted with precious stones and his whole person heavily scented. As the son of the 4th Earl of Hardwicke, he had started hanging out with Queen Victoria's youngest son at Oxford, and eventually graduated to spinning green yarns at Victoria's court. On the evening in question, Yorke found himself seated beside a visiting German prince at dinner, listening to what apparently was an off-color joke. When Yorke exploded with laughter, the Queen, who was just across the table, looked up from her plate and asked what was so funny. Yorke, who thought the Queen might be sporting enough to share in the fun, confidently repeated the joke. Both the joke and the German prince have gone into anonymity, but Her Royal Highness' curt remark, "We are not amused," has remained an indelible part of the Victorian legend.

| 8. Cloak and Swagger |

Myth! Sir Walter Raleigh threw his cloak over a mud puddle to protect the feet of Queen Elizabeth I.

The talented English adventurer and legalized pirate, Sir Walter Raleigh, used his wiles to easily become the favorite courtier of Queen Elizabeth I. Schoolbooks depict him as a fawning Queen's gallant who liked to perform small acts of chivalry to demonstrate his loyalty. She adored his attentions so much that she showered him with many rewards, knighting him and granting him land in Ireland and charters to colonize the Americas. It is claimed he was the Queen's lover for many years, but fell out of favor when she caught him dawdling with Bessy Throckmorton, one of her ladies-in-waiting, and was eventually beheaded on Elizabeth's orders.

The anecdote of the cloak, undoubtedly part of this pseudo-history, was first recounted in Raleigh's own writings, then repeated years after Raleigh's death in *The Worthies of England* by Thomas Fuller, an overly imaginative historian who often elaborated on historical fact. Later, Sir Walter Scott picked it up and fictionalized it in *Kenilworth*. Others, like Victorian biographer Patric Fraser Tytler in his 1844 *Life of Sir Walter Raleigh* and Charles Kingsley in *Sir Walter Raleigh and His Times*, gave full faith and credit to Fuller's version.

According to the legend, Sir Walter stepped forth from a crowd, gallantly doffed his cloak and threw it over a mud puddle to protect the feet of the passing queen. Fraser's account is only slightly different: the dandy "found the Queen walking, till, meeting with a splashy place," she hesitated to go on. Raleigh thereupon "cast and spread his new plush coat on the ground, whereon the Queen trod gently, rewarding him afterwards with many suits." Critics take a cynical view of the incident, adjudging certain details—e.g., the casual encounter in a public place between commoner and queen, and both confronting a potentially hazardous mud puddle without weighing other alternatives—as too fanciful to be believed.

---

9. Blood Lust

Myth! Mary I was the bloodiest queen Europe ever had.

The first English queen to rule in her own right was not Elizabeth but her half-sister Mary I, also known as 'Bloody Mary', the fanatical Catholic who preceded her to the throne. It may be unfair to call Mary 'bloody', considering that the 288 executions she ordered were few by contemporary standards and not many more than those attributed to Elizabeth herself. A few of her victims were famous and powerful, and the rest, about 250, were of the working classes, mostly those who rebelled after she restored papal authority in England following the Protestant reign of her half-brother Edward VI. Her five-year reign produced not more than sixty executions per year, prompting one biographer to note that, "for a monarch of that era embarked upon a programme of religious suppression, this would indicate a considerable degree of self-restraint rather than blood lust."

According to most historians, Mary's real fault lay in her proving herself extremely unpleasant to her court and subjects, marrying Philip II of Spain against everybody's wishes, and losing Calais, England's last foothold on the mainland, to France. Mary

233

died a natural death, although she is sometimes confused with the Catholic Mary Stewart or Mary Queen of Scots, who ruled Scotland from 1542 until 1567, when Elizabeth I had her beheaded.

10. Out of the Closet and Off the Throne

Myth! Queen Christina abdicated her throne in favor of her lover Charles Gustavus.

In the 1933 film *Queen Christina*, Greta Garbo portrays Sweden's beloved but controversial queen in a celebrated performance that popularized the romantic aspects of the progressive monarch's tempestuous life. Garbo made her love scenes even more memorable because her real-life lover John Gilbert played Gustavus.

Christina, the Catholic daughter of King Gustav II Adolf, is one of only a handful of monarchs to abdicate freely, and on the presumption that her reason for abdicating was love, the only other European sovereign to do it with this fairy tale twist was Edward the Duke of Windsor. We are told, however, that the love expressed so hauntingly by Garbo in the movie was misplaced in real life. Christina could not love Gustavus, or any man for that matter, because she was a lesbian. Some biographers have even gone so far as to say she was a pseudohermaphrodite, with superficial male genitals and a masculine voice and appearance. Speculation about Christina's sexuality had been present from the very day of her birth when she was mistaken for a boy. Christina reputedly had a number of male lovers, but they were apparently all for show because her real love was Ebba Sparre, her lady-in-waiting.

Pressed by the Swedish Parliament to marry and produce an heir to the throne, she promised to wed Charles Gustavus, but her reaction to his expression of love was to accuse him of having 'romantic fantasies'. No one knew that her game plan, which eventually succeeded, was to name him her successor and repay his loyalty but not his love.

Within days after attending her cousin's coronation on June 6, 1654, the 28-year-old Christina left Sweden. Before her departure

234

she had her hair cut short and assumed masculine attire. She then journeyed to Denmark under the name of Count Dohna. Later, her sexual preference became even more manifest in her political ambitions. She negotiated with French minister Cardinal Jules Mazarin to be named King of Naples, but the plan came to naught due to an uproar after she ordered Giovan Rinaldo Monaldeschi, a member of her retinue, executed for treason. When the throne of Poland became vacant in 1668, Christina made a half-hearted and unsuccessful attempt to vie for the elective post of king at the urging of Cardinal Decio Azzolino, a powerful churchman whom she had befriended in Rome.

11. Stranger in the House

Myth! Wallis Simpson acquired the title Her Royal Highness Princess Edward upon her marriage to Prince Edward.

An underlying cause of the enmity between the Duke of Windsor and the British royals was the latter's obstinate refusal to call Wallis Simpson Her Royal Highness Princess Edward. Experts believe the Duke, who was himself called His Royal Highness Prince Edward when he was the heir to the throne, should have just gone ahead and given her the title. They contend that the Duke's title extended to the Duchess without further need of consent from the throne, an issue that the royal family ignored by avoiding every opportunity of having to address her themselves. When Wallis died in 1986, her body was allowed to be buried alongside her husband in the royal burial ground at Frogmore, as was her right. But during the twenty-eight-minute funeral service conducted by the dean of Windsor and attended by seventeen members of the royal family, her name was not mentioned once.

Royal apologists claim that a title of address, as differentiated from a title of nobility, is a mere convention that must be recognized by the throne to be effective. Thus, "His Majesty," "His Excellent Grace," and "His Royal Highness" are established by agreement between the monarch and his subjects and maintained as a custom until revised, unlike King, Prince, or

Duke, which are hereditary or conferred and consequently owned by the holder. On this basis, Wallis would have been justified to use the title Duchess or Princess by right of marriage, but not "Her Royal Highness" without the consent of the Queen.

12. Miss Liz Loveless

Myth! Elizabeth I was called the Virgin Queen because she was chaste.

Historians suspect Elizabeth herself devised the nickname 'The Virgin Queen' to advertise her alleged sexual purity. She reminded everyone of this by wearing pure white gowns, and ordering her court painters to pose her in a "virginal" manner. She had announced upon her crowning that she would remain a virgin all her life because she wished only to be "married" to her devoted subjects.

However, it is not quite certain that she kept her promise, unlike the modern Elizabeth II, who was at least a virgin bride. At what point of time Bess lost her virginity we do not know, but she had a spate of lovers that included Robert Devereux, a twenty-year old lad with whom the fifty-four-year old Elizabeth conducted a twelve-year affair. The affair ended tragically when Robert was beheaded for attempting to dethrone the queen, the same fate Sir Walter Raleigh met for allegedly abusing the Queen's confidence.

13. Designing Woman

Myth! Queen Anne originated the Queen Anne style of architecture.

Queen Anne, the last queen of England and Scotland, is popularly believed to have influenced the Queen Anne style of furniture as well as architecture popular in the eighteenth century. The furniture was marked by plain curves, walnut veneer, and cabriole-legged chairs, while the architecture was dominated by plain red brickwork in a restrained classical form.

In fact, Queen Anne had nothing to do with the furniture style bearing her name, as this evolved even before her reign. It was the socially active Sarah Jennings, first duchess of Marlborough and a forebear of Winston Churchill, who greatly influenced its development. Sarah herself probably thought of appropriating the queen's name to honor her close association with the monarch while working on her projects.

Queen Anne was even more remote from the architectural style called the Queen Anne, which was originated in the 1870s by the Englishman Richard Norman Shaw. Shaw needed a modernized eighteenth-century style for English country houses to show off at the British Pavilion of the 1876 Philadelphia Centennial Exposition. What came out—an eclectic combination of elements from Elizabethan cottages, Romanesque and Flemish renaissance—may be seen today in the row houses of New York City dating from the 1880s and 1890s.

IV

High-Heeled Treason

On Femmes Fatales

"I am a woman who enjoys
herself very much; sometimes I lose,
sometimes I win."

•

Mata Hari

1. The Woman with One False Leg

Myth! The great female spies operating for the Allies in World War II were mostly European, none being American.

Virginia Hall, America's greatest female spy, was the antithetical Jane Fonda in the sense that, unlike Jane, she failed to make it to Barbara Walter's list despite her sterling wartime qualifications. Because of the clandestine nature of her activities, Hall's life would have been relegated to history's dust bin were it not for Judith L. Pearson, who wrote her recent biography—*The Wolves at the Door: The True Story of America's Greatest Female Spy.* From its pages we learn that the British made Hall a Member of the British Empire and the US awarded her the Distinguished Service Cross 'for extraordinary heroism in connection with military operations against the enemy', the only civilian woman in World War II to have been so honored.

What many would have found most extraordinary about this Maryland woman was that she pursued her life-threatening career on only one leg, having lost the other from shooting herself in a hunting accident. Until Pearson's definitive work on her came out, Hall's peculiar circumstance had led many to speculate, including British historian M. R. D. Foot, who called her an 'indomitable agent with a brass foot'; French author Marcel Ruby, who said that she lost her leg in 'a riding accident'; others, who had her losing a limb after 'falling under a tram'; and former CIA officer Harry Mahoney, who describes an OSS mission in which she 'parachuted behind enemy lines with her wooden leg in her knapsack'. Actually, she landed in France by boat, with her wooden leg firmly attached to her upper limb from above the knee.

Virginia Hall's landing in Brittany from a British MTB did not make her the first woman to be infiltrated into Nazi-occupied France; this honor rightly belongs to another non-European, the Indian heroine Noor Inayat Khan, who spent most of World War II as a radio operator and an undercover agent in Paris helping the French Resistance. Betrayed and captured, she proved impenitent and uncontrollable, dying a horrific death on the stone floors of Dachau's notorious concentration camp. For her incomparable bravery, she was posthumously awarded the George Cross, which is the counterpart of the Victoria Cross and the highest civil decoration of the Commonwealth of Nations. A major international film on Khan's life and exploits, based on the book *The Spy Princess* by Shrabani Basu, is underway.

Britain is probably the best-known source of World War II female spies, thanks to Hollywood and British films of the genre. Still, Virginia Hall's counterpart in Britain did her gig in World War I and not World War II, and she was not as lucky. This was nurse Edith Cavell, who helped hundreds of soldiers in the Allied forces to escape from occupied Belgium to the neutral Netherlands, for which she was arrested and court-martialed by the Germans in 1915. She made no defense, admitting her actions, and was executed by firing squad on October 12, becoming a popular martyr and entering British history as a heroine. Some believe that she stood proudly before her executioners and said, "Patriotism is not enough, I must have no hatred or bitterness towards anyone." Actually, she did make the parting shot, but it was on the night before her execution, her sole audience being the Anglican chaplain, Rev. Gahan, who had been allowed to give her Holy Communion. The stirring words are inscribed on her statue in St. Martin's Place, near Trafalgar Square in London.

2. Dutch Treatment

Myth! Mata Hari was a beautiful young Asian who danced naked to obtain military secrets.

In the popular mind, Mata Hari was a beautiful young Asian who performed exotic dances, often in the nude, in various capitals of Europe, and while thus entertaining German and French officers, extracted military secrets from them. But this legendary image of the spy is a far cry from her real identity as Margaretha Geertruida Zelle, a Dutch officer's wife and former Java housekeeper. The historical Zelle was always properly clad in the tradition of Hindu temple artists when going through her routine as a fake Indian dancer.

Mata Hari (from the Malay phrase 'eye of the king') was arrested at her hotel in Paris, charged with espionage and executed in February 1917 after a short trial. To this day, there is no certainty that Zelle passed any military secrets to the enemy or that she was a spy at all. Some believe she was convicted primarily on the basis of her own fantasy stories, one of which—that she was a French agent—the French readily denied.

Contrary to her Mata Hari persona, Zelle wasn't young, Oriental or beautiful. Of Dutch parentage, she had returned to her homeland with her husband from his service in the Dutch East Indies, after which she had split from him to become an exotic danseuse in Europe consorting with military officers on both sides. According to some reports, Zelle—'her lower jaw aggressive, her brow simian and her breasts flabby'—was a plump, middle-aged divorcee of 42 when shot by the French. She probably didn't really look this bad, but chances are she didn't look a bit like Greta Garbo's Mata Hari either.

---

3. Fashion for Execution

Myth! Mata Hari dressed elegantly for the firing squad.

Mata Hari was awakened at 5 a.m. on October 15, 1917 and informed that she would be shot that morning. The reports all agree that she refused to be tied to the pole or blindfolded, and was composed in every respect when she faced the twelve soldiers—her firing squad—at the Chateau de Vincennes, the military compound outside Paris to which she had been taken.

A popular account says she was wearing a specially tailored suit she had ordered for the execution, a pair of new white gloves, a straw hat and a white veil. As the soldiers raised their rifles, she smiled and winked at them (how she could have done this behind her veil is not explained). In one truly ludicrous version, she wore nothing but a black velvet robe, and, at the last minute, accepted a glass of champagne. When the firing squad raised their rifles, she boldly threw off the robe, and standing before the riflemen stark naked, screamed, "Would you destroy one as beautiful as I?"

The simplest description of what happened may well be the only credible one: she stood straight before her executioners, dressed in drab prison clothes, and after she collapsed an army surgeon walked over, checked her briefly, then fired a final shot—the coup de grace—into her head to make sure she was dead. Her

241

body was taken to a city hospital in Paris where it was dissected for medical research.

4. Voices of Treason

Myth! There was only one Axis Sally broadcasting from Germany, as there was only one Tokyo Rose broadcasting from Japan.

Her listeners knew Mildred E. Gillars, born in 1900, only as Axis Sally, a female broadcaster working out of several Nazi-controlled radio stations in Europe. She was the most popular name in a company of cacklers that included Berlin Betty, whose voice became familiar to Anglo-American troops in North Africa, and Helen Sensburg, who called herself Mary of Arnhem in her Nazi propaganda broadcasts to British troops in Northwestern Europe in 1944-45. Gillars was less reverently known as the Berlin Bitch by Allied troops in Europe, but it was as Axis Sally that she became the epitome of treasonous womanhood.

Some question the fairness of Gillars' conviction in 1949 and her imprisonment for twelve years for broadcasting Nazi propaganda during the war, in the light of subsequent evidence tending to mitigate if not excuse her offense. As the Allies would later discover, there were several other women who took turns airing the Nazi cause and damning the Allies, all signing off as Axis Sally. It was not clear that Gillars hosted the most notorious broadcasts, since these were not recorded and her voice was not distinctively recognizable. Gillars undoubtedly did her part to spread the presence of Axis Sally over most of Europe, but this was relatively minor and she should not have taken all the blame.

Iva Toguri D'Aquino was convicted after the Second World War for broadcasting Japanese propaganda to American servicemen, first under the name 'Ann' (short for Announcer), then as 'Tokyo Rose'. She would probably have avoided her fate if she had been a Japanese national, but she was an American citizen born in 1916 of Japanese parents. Iva was a UCLA graduate (with a degree in zoology) who was caught by the war in Tokyo while visiting a sick aunt in July 1941. Unable to return to the US, she

242

was constrained to find work with the Japanese Broadcasting Company to avoid being sent to the factories.

Although Iva insisted she was not Tokyo Rose, she received a ten-year term for treason plus a $10,000 fine in 1949, serving her sentence until paroled in 1956. Her pardon by President Ford in 1977 may have been encouraged by reports that Tokyo Rose never existed, or that, as in Axis Sally's case, there were several 'Tokyo Roses' and Iva was only one of them. The sole evidence at Iva's trial was testimony about a woman's voice telling American servicemen, between familiar selections of American music, that their wives and girlfriends were being taken over by the civilians who remained behind, and that there was no reason to fight because the Japanese were going to win anyway. In her defense, many GIs mused that, while they had thoroughly enjoyed the music they heard on the air, they had laughed off the accompanying remarks as being silly.

| **5. Ringing Out the Dead** |

Myth! Broadcasters Seoul City Sue and Hanoi Hanna disappeared after the war and have managed to remain anonymous.

Axis Sally and Tokyo Rose have drawn a picture of the treasonable female spy as one who voluntarily manages a propaganda campaign for an enemy or hostile nation to the prejudice of her own country's interests. Women propagandists abounded in wartime, but many didn't quite fit the treasonable mold. Some owed little or no allegiance to the country they were dishonoring, while others were able to prove their hosts unduly influenced their actions through force or intimidation.

Seoul City Sue, a play on the popular 1940s song 'Sioux City Sue', was the nickname given by American GIs to the female announcer of a series of North Korean propaganda radio broadcasts during the Korean War. Members of the US Army 588th Military Police Company first heard her in August 1950 reading the names off the dog tags of killed American soldiers to the accompaniment of music. According to the *Time* issue of August 21, 1950, "Sue pronounces her r's better than most East

243

Asians, but her voice, unlike California-born Tokyo Rose's, is 'strictly un-American'. One U.S. officer thought she sounded like a Korean who might have lived in England. And she was nowhere near so effective as either Sally or Rose."

Later that same month, the Methodist Missionary Organization (MMO) identified Seoul City Sue as American-born Mrs. Anna Wallace Suhr, wife of a Korean newsman. Suhr, then in her mid-forties, had tutored American diplomats' children in Seoul as a former missionary schoolteacher in Korea. Many of her sympathizers claim the dull tone of her broadcasts proved she was under intense pressure when she made them. A Korean War Project newsletter dated September 1, 2006, essentially confirms the findings of the MMO but clarifies Seoul City Sue was an American woman from Arkansas whose maiden name was Ann Wallis (not Wallace). She was caught up in the Korean War with her husband, a Korean educator (not newsman) named Suhr or Suh, and was forced to broadcast for the North Koreans after her capture in 1950. The same newsletter expresses the fear that the North Koreans may have executed the couple as later broadcasts under her name sounded distinctly different. However, other reports have raised the possibility that Ms. Wallis is still in North Korea and may even have been featured in a North Korean film.

Lingering impressions from the Vietnam War would suggest that Trinh Thi Ngo, born in Vietnam in September 1931, was one of the more effective weapons of psychological warfare unleashed by North Vietnam on US troops during that war. This champion propagandist of the Viet Minh was popularly known as Hanoi Hannah but called herself Thu Houng, 'the fragrance of autumn'. At the height of the war, she went on the air three times a day to broadcast in stilted but still recognizable English, encouraging U.S. soldiers to abandon their units and go AWOL, reading the list of newly killed or imprisoned Americans, perorating on the unjust and immoral nature of America's involvement in Vietnam, and playing popular American anti-war songs to incite feelings of nostalgia and homesickness among GIs. She made extensive use of American idioms and hip expressions although she was noticeably awkward with it, and connected with her American audience mainly because "she was female and had a nice soft voice."

Appearing once for a post-war interview with Don North ("The Search for Hanoi Hannah"), she was perceived as a "pleasant

244

looking woman, slim, well groomed and attractive," and not looking at all like a "dragon lady." Because of her uncanny ability to obtain information about American military presence in certain areas (which she attributed to "proper research") and the temerity with which she announced Viet Cong attacks even before they happened (which she denied), she became popular enough on both sides to make her an iconic figure of the war.

6. Sisters Under the Skin

Myth! Most of the accusations hurled at Hanoi Jane by former American POWs had a factual basis.

Not to be confused with Hanoi Hannah is the American Hanoi Jane, a rebellious young spirit who, in her zealous pursuit of world peace in the 1960s and early 1970s, propagandized the interests of North Vietnam while it was technically at war with the United States. The former POWs and soldiers familiar with the way both Hanoi Hannah and Hanoi Jane 'consorted' with the enemy insist Hannah's sin is quite forgivable because she was an enemy national and therefore committed no treason. But Jane's is beyond reprieve because she happens to be Jane Fonda, one of Barbara Walters' '100 Most Important Women of the Century', who committed her indiscretions at the height of her popularity as a beloved Hollywood screen figure.

The white paper on Jane Fonda states that in 1972, she toured North Vietnam and, ostensibly in the name of peace, defended the cause of communism, insulted and defamed American POWs by whitewashing the Viet Cong's treatment of them, and later called them liars when they spoke out. Seven years later, Fonda won an Oscar for her portrayal of a caregiver who devotes herself body and spirit to a paraplegic Vietnam War veteran. Some say her intense acting was a way of expressing remorse for her conduct during the war; if so, she made it official in 1988 when she offered a formal apology on national television to Vietnam veterans and their families. The gesture, writes David Emery in "Urban Legends and Folklore", "didn't mollify everyone but established some distance between the new Fonda and old Fonda, whose actions, she finally admitted, had been 'thoughtless and careless'."

245

Sifting through the hate mail that flooded the Internet after Barbara Walters announced Fonda's inclusion in her list, Emery found that two of the three basic accusations against the actress were complete fabrications. The first—that Fonda betrayed POWs by turning over slips of paper they gave her to their captors, and POWs were beaten and died as a result—was branded by Retired Col. Larry Carrigan as 'a figment of somebody's imagination'. Carrigan, who had been previously tagged as the source of the claim, insisted he never met Jane Fonda. The second—that a POW spat at Fonda, for which he was brutally beaten—did not happen either, according to Air Force pilot Jerry Driscoll, the purported author of the story. Only the third accusation—that a POW was beaten for refusing to cooperate or meet with Fonda during her visit—proved to be true, although Jane's defenders were quick to point out that their idol could hardly be held responsible for something she did not know, much less acquiesce to. She would not have agreed to such treatment, they said, recalling Hanoi Hannah's statement that when she once asked Jane Fonda if she would like to meet American pilots in Hanoi, 'she refused, she didn't want to'.

Explorers,
Discoverers
&
Pioneers

I

A Traveler's Tale

On Marco Polo and Ancient China

"I have not told half
of what I saw."

•

Marco Polo

1. The Man who Played Polo

Myth! Marco Polo wrote about his travels in a book he titled 'Il milione'.

Popular history tells us it was Marco Polo who wrote the most durable, comprehensive and perceptive travel book on Asia. Originally titled *Il milione* and also called *The Travels of Marco Polo*, this geographical classic has made an impact on exploration, trading and diplomacy worldwide.

Serious historians find it odd, however, that Marco Polo did not keep any journals or diaries of his experiences while he was traveling. Practically all that is known about this rover before he finally retired from his wanderings derives from the text of *Il milione*, which was prepared long after his return to Italy. The same historians say this is most disturbing in the light of the fact that Marco didn't write the book. He only related the contents to one Rustico (or Rustichello) da Pisa, his cellmate when he was in prison for having taken part in a Mediterranean clash against the Genoese. Apparently, like several other famous travelers of his time, Marco had an aversion to the use of pen and ink or else did not have sufficient literacy for writing.

Unfortunately, what Rustico wrote no longer exists. The original, cast in Franco-Italian, a language not familiar to Marco, has undergone some 140 different manuscript transcriptions as well as translations in a dozen different languages and dialects. This has caused confusion regarding which districts Marco traversed during his travels and which he only heard about from information gathered en route. Researchers have found it exceedingly difficult to ascertain the places the Polos visited and what they did during their long years in the Mongol empire. Heightening the ambiguity of geographical information is the paucity of personal details. According to the Britannica, this "has left a void that has eagerly been filled in by romantic hero-worshippers, who see (Marco) as a brilliant young courtier enamouring princesses and governing provinces."

Some critics opine that Rustico, a popular writer of romances and a specialist in chivalry and its lore, may have contributed some bias, if not his own fiction, in the writing of the original. This could explain why the 'Travels' tends to portray its hero as "a braggart, who made too much of himself; a drifter ready to believe the gossip of ports and bazaars." Others love to point out that the book's original title, *Il milione*, derives uncomfortably from the phrase 'tall story', and may have been intended by either Marco or Rustico as an inside joke. While many are apparently not bothered by the extent to which the author and his ghost-writer turned the account into a fable, a few, following the tack of Marco's famous contemporary Dante Alighieri, consider the entire book an invention and have begun to ask the question, "Did Marco Polo really visit China?"

2. Touring on a Persian Carpet

Myth! The book 'Il milione' is a reasonably faithful account of Marco Polo's travels.

That Marco Polo's book was entirely ghost written, and much of its contents either fabricated or embellished, seem no longer in contention, but critics say there are indications for an even worse scenario, which is that Marco Polo never visited China. Dr. Frances Wood, head of the Chinese, Manchu and Mongolian Collections at the British Library, in her own book, *Did Marco Polo Go To China?* (1995), brands Marco as a plagiarist of the first order who pilfered his work from Arab and Persian sources and mixed in it a dash of his wild imaginings. Dr. Wood suggests that Marco Polo probably never got further than his family's trading posts on the Black Sea, from where he had access to the Persian and Arabic guidebooks to China that he used as the basis for his account.

Dr. Wood's conclusion is an almost total abrogation of Marco Polo's position as the first major Western source of information about ancient China, and as founder of the commercial and social link between East and West that subsequent explorers and traders from both sides would later exploit to their advantage. Her major arguments focus mainly on Marco's travel itinerary, which she says (1) lacks coherence, is impersonal, and is incorrect as to some dates, distances and events; (2) cites geographical and proper names in Persian in lieu of Mongolian or Chinese; (3) omits many important aspects of Chinese life and material culture, including a) the Chinese writing system, b) books and printing, c) tea and tea drinking, d) the Chinese custom of foot binding, and e) cormorant fishing; (4) is incorrect as to its description of some major city landmarks, such as the Marco Polo Bridge; and, most importantly, (5) ignores the existence of the Great Wall.

Adding weight to Dr. Wood's charges is the finding that Marco Polo lied outright about certain of his accomplishments in China. For instance, he was purportedly present at the siege of Hsiang-yang, where he taught the Mongols how to use the catapult, even though this particular siege ended in January 1273, at least a year before the three Polos reached north China in 1274 or 1275. Marco said he was for three years governor of Yang-chou in Chiang-su, yet no gazetteer of Yang-chou mentions him in their records; in fact, Marco, his father and uncle are not mentioned in any Chinese source of the period. Finally, he claimed that his father and uncle were the first 'Latins', i.e., Western Europeans, ever seen by Kublai Khan, despite the known fact that they had been preceded in the kingdom by at least one Frankish embassy.

---

3. One for the Road

Myth! **Marco Polo was Italian.**

Not even the Britannica knows for sure whether Marco Polo was born in Venice, Italy, or in Korcula in Croatia. Most Croats, along with one British historian (James A. Gilman, who founded 'The Institute of Marco Polo'), believe that Marco first saw the light of day in Korcula; consequently they have given him the Slavic name Marko Pilich as well as a coat of arms with distinct Croatian elements. Their claim rests on nothing more than the presence on the island of families with surnames similar to Polo, and Marco's supposed participation—and capture—at the Battle of Korcula (Curzola) between the Republic of Genoa and the Republic of Venice. However, many doubt Marco was ever involved in the fighting at Korcula because of proof that he had already been taken prisoner by the Genoese at a previous minor engagement near Laiazzo.

Those who don't cater to the Croatian view are not without reason for putting Marco's birthplace in Venice: Korcula island was, in Polo's time, part of the Republic of Venice, although today it is a component of Croatia, Italy's neighbor across the Adriatic Sea. Venice is clearly indicated as Polo's birthplace in the book *Il milione*, an indication that Polo himself may have believed he was Venetian.

A middle solution to the issue of Marco's nationality would be that he was Venetian either because he was born in Korcula when it was still part of Venice, or because he was born in Venice although descended from Croatian parents.

4. In Xanadu did Kubla Khan

Myth! **Marco Polo was the first European to visit the court of Kublai Khan and the one that gave the name Cathay to China.**

Marco Polo is not, as is supposed, the first *known* European to penetrate the Mongol court of Kublai Khan. That distinction belongs to his father Niccolo, who had gone to visit the Asian king even before Marco was born. However, this is not to say that Niccolo was the first European to foray into ancient China, since there were others from the continent, mainly traders, who had arrived before him. Marco was already 15 years old and orphaned by his mother when Niccolo returned. Two years later, Marco joined his father's entourage on their second trip, and at the age of 20 arrived in Cathay to begin a 17-year sojourn in Kublai Khan's dominions.

The poetic name of China is Cathay, a name that some say Marco Polo gave to the country and which all Chinese rulers, starting with Kublai Khan, accepted. Marco may have popularized the name Cathay for China, but he did not originate it. Long before Kublai Khan received the Polos, Cathay was the traditional name of China north of the Yangtze River (the south was called Mangi); more precisely, it referred to that part of China that the 16th-century navigators sought to discover via a northeast or northwest passage. The word comes from Khitai, a southern Manchurian Tartar kingdom of the 10th century whose semi-nomadic people came under the rule of the Liao dynasty of northern China.

5. Every Which Way but East

Myth! The errors and inconsistencies in 'Il Milione' are indefensible proof that Marco Polo never visited China.

Since the case against Marco Polo feeds to a large extent on internal and non-positive evidence consisting of the errors, omissions, discrepancies and fabrications found in his book, the refutation of Dr. Wood's arguments has relied mainly on the plea that, as Marco did not write *Il milione* himself, he should not be made entirely responsible for its failings. With that in mind, his defenders say, those for which he can be held accountable would not be sufficient to carry the proposition that Marco lied about his China venture and that he never visited that kingdom.

Moreover, there are extenuating factors to lessen Marco's accountability, e.g., his relative lack of education, his seeming ignorance of (or lack of interest for) the written language, his lack of imagination (despite being a keen observer), and social limitations that prevented him, during his seventeen years in Mongol-ruled China, to 'mix' properly with the Chinese, learn their language, and show interest in their ancient culture and family customs. Marco's incorrect description of the famous bridge in Peking may have been due to a faulty recollection on his part or an early scribal error. Finally, the Great Wall was a fortification built or re-built by the Ming government in the 16th and 17th centuries, and, as it is seen today, did not exist in Marco's time. "Before the Ming there were only a series of ramparts, erected in different periods and at no stage was there a continuous 'line', only discontinuous walls, differently placed and shifting position from dynasty to dynasty." Besides, there is no mention of the Great Wall as a material reality in the Chinese sources of the 13th century.

Incidentally, though Marco is popularly believed to have introduced spaghetti, ravioli and ice cream to the West, he did not do so and never claimed to.

To strengthen their position, Marco's supporters offer confirmation of certain discoveries that their hero made during his travels, i.e., the Mingsha Dune and a river on the Silk Road; paper money, which the Chinese had used for centuries; and a substance Europeans would come to know as coal. Dang Baohai, a history professor at Beijing University, proved that certain of Marco's unique assertions—viz., (a) a legend about the birth of a Khan of Ouigour, an ancient nationality in northwest China; (b) Mongolian authorities being forced to pull down ramparts built by the Han Nationality during the Yuan Dynasty (1271-1368); and (c) Kublai Khan ordering the planting of trees along roads—were in accord with Chinese and Persian historical documents, local chronicles and laws issued during the Yuan Dynasty

For their own conclusion, Dr. Wood's critics ask: Could one so incoherent and lacking in imagination weave such a lavish and exotic adventure simply from reading foreign guidebooks? In short, could Marco Polo have told the truth? Says one commentator: "Ask his 13th-century contemporaries, and the answer would be a resounding no. And yet, in 1324, as Polo lay on his deathbed, a priest beseeched him to retract his 'fables'. His reply: 'I have not told half of what I saw'."

6. Monster from Outer Space?

Myth! The Great Wall of China, built 2,000 years ago to protect against marauding Huns, is the only man-made structure visible from outer space.

Despite tourist guides proclaiming that it's about 2,000 years old, most of what can be seen of the Great Wall of China has only been there for 600 years. The original construction initiated by Shih-Huang Ti of the Ch'in (qin) dynasty in the third century BC has been almost completely replaced by a smaller one built about AD 1420 by the Ming dynasty.

The present wall stretches for 3,890 miles, from the yellow Sea to the Gobi Desert, or 5,500 miles if trenches and certain natural extensions were included. It was obviously conceived only as a local fortification along with the other unconnected walls and fortresses that sprouted over time in the Chinese mainland. Several centuries later "the dots were connected and the (great) wall took its ultimate form." The word 'great' is often regarded as gratuitous because the wall is not an integrated product and has proved largely ineffective. It is said that thousands of slaves who died of exhaustion from building it were buried in or near the structure, prompting wags to claim that it should perhaps be listed as a wonder for being the longest graveyard in the world.

Some writers say that if the purpose of the Wall were to protect the border from attack by the Huns, this was just an ostensible reason, since it was apparent that the fortification would only hold against certain types of intrusions. As the founders of the Manchu dynasty would later prove, invading hordes could always overwhelm the guards on the ramparts and let their horses in.

One other reason cited is that the emperor wanted to contain the population in order to prevent them from fraternizing with outside barbarians. But again, this seems only incidental. According to Owen Lattimore, "The true purpose had to do with stabilizing the conquests that had been made in China itself, and with setting to rights a new order of society." Over a period of eighty years, the Ch'in Empire had gradually conquered the smaller feudal kingdoms, which built walls to protect their own borders. To assimilate these conquests into the whole, there was a need to interconnect the walls and consolidate them with the main wall. There were two other reasons to be subserved: first, the conquerors had a huge standing army with nothing to do, and the danger inherent in an idle band of armed men was a cause for concern; and second, agriculture was giving way to a nomadic society, and it was apparent the cultural change would make the expanded territory less homogeneous and possibly even more decentralized, weakening the government's control. This "led to the decision to employ the army towards consolidating a wall that would keep China's size manageable by limiting westward migration, thereby making it easier to rule centrally."

We have all heard the unsolicited observation that the only visible thing on earth from outer space is the Great Wall of China. According to NASA, the earth as seen from that distance, much less from the moon, takes up only two degrees of arc in the sky and basically looks like a big blue marble. Alan Bean states that "(n)o man-made object is visible on this scale. In fact, when first leaving earth's orbit and only a few thousand miles away, no man-made object is visible at that point either." Some astronauts who have orbited the earth may have reported seeing the Great Wall of China as a hair-thin line meandering across the mainland from 180 miles up. But this is from nearer in space, where one may discern any number of man-made structures that look like long, straight lines, such as highways, railroads, canals, and, of course, walls. Still, contrary to the almost Confucian belief that arose after Apollo 11's historic mission, there is no location in space where the only man-made thing visible on earth is the Wall.

II

The Sailor Who Fell From Grace With The Seers

On Columbus and Vespucci

"Gold is a treasure, and he who possesses it
does all he wishes to in this world, and
succeeds in helping souls into paradise."

•

Christopher Columbus

1. A Continental Op

Myth! Columbus was Italian but looked French.

The only documentary proof of Columbus' place of nativity is a will written in 1498, which introduces its purported author with the telltale phrase "I, being born in Genoa..." Most historians doubt the veracity of the will, however, and to this day the testament is not given much importance. According to his son Fernando, Columbus never really revealed where he was born, preferring to call himself "a man of the sea." Several countries claiming to be his birthplace include Corsica, where Columbus has a tombstone (the town of Calvi claims both his birth and his remains); France, where in 1687 a French lawyer named Jean Colomb insisted he was a descendant; England, the Colombian birthplace a book published in London in 1682 pointed to; Norway, where Norwegians say his real name was Christopher Bonde; Portugal, where he settled to become a successful merchant seaman; and Spain, whose government sponsored his most famous explorations. Other nationalities attributed to him are Greek and Armenian. He did live for quite a time in Genoa, where a statue is erected in his honor, but so did he in Spain, Portugal and the other lands to which he voyaged.

If none of Columbus' names offers a clue to his identity, neither does any of his physical features. Gerard Depardieu, the popular French star, was hired for the lavish Hollywood movie *1492: The Conquest of Paradise,* supposedly on the strength of the actor's striking similarity to a portrait of Columbus. The question which of several portraits is accurate remains, however, as in practically every one, Columbus' appearance is different from the others. As far as is known, none was posed for or depended on the artist's first-hand knowledge of the mariner; all were based on written or spoken descriptions made mostly after Columbus' death, or copied from other works. Since no drawing, sketch, or painting in existence is known to have been made of Columbus while he was alive, we cannot be sure what he really looked like. His pictures are currently quite common, but there is no evidence to corroborate that any one of these has a resemblance to the great navigator.

2. Asking for a Wide Berth

Myth! Columbus tried to convince the sages of the University of Salamanca that the earth was round.

As late as 1961, the Encyclopedia Britannica had suggested, albeit in a self-advertisement, that Columbus was the first to see the world as round. Fortunately, the venerable tome reversed itself in the main text. Although Columbus did meet with the professors of Salamanca to try to obtain backing for his trip, the shape of the globe was not the real issue. Both Columbus and his critics, like most others at the time, knew the earth was curved, and that a direct westward passage to the Orient was not only possible but would be easier and faster.

The ancient Greeks were already toying around with the idea of a round world two thousand years before the Age of Exploration began, with Plato being practically the first to theorize about it. Later, Aristotle, who lived in 384-322 BC, was able to deduce the proof from the spherical shadow of the earth on the moon during an eclipse. Before Plato, Anaximander had rejected the earth's flatness, but missed his chance for greatness when he also proposed that the earth's shape was cylindrical. Pythagoras would later develop the spherical concept in the sixth century BC, and this would persist throughout the medieval period.

At some point, theologians who had spurned the idea because it was contrary to the Biblical interpretations of the Christian Church began to accept it on the ground that a round shape was perfect and God-given. By the time Columbus left on his voyage, there were already globes depicting that the earth was round.

The real point of contention between Columbus and his would-be sponsors was the width of the ocean, which the latter believed the explorer was grievously underestimating and would prevent him from reaching the Orient if he went due west. The sages were right, of course, and Columbus, who perceived the distance between the Canaries and Japan as 2,400 miles, compared to the actual distance of about 12,000 miles, was wrong. Had he not stumbled upon America along the way, his erroneous calculations would have sent him to oblivion and certain death. The explorer was apparently influenced by Ptolemy's concept of a considerably

259

smaller earth, which the ancient astronomer derived from faulty equivalents of Moslem estimates of a degree of longitude.

Columbus may not have been the first to say that the world was round, but he was the first to say it was not really round but pear-shaped. He gave this description of the earth upon reaching the mouth of the Orinoco River in modern Venezuela. A hundred years later, Newton predicted the same shape as something the earth would assume in the future from the centrifugal forces caused by its rotation, which would make it bulge at the equator. Both Columbus and Newton were proved right when the Vanguard satellite saw the earth's shape in March 1958 as it went into orbit.

3. Alias Colombo

Myth! Columbus had the same name since birth.

It is not entirely clear that English historians gave Christopher Columbus his Latinized name, but one of its earliest appearances was in 1553, long after his death, in a book by Petrus Martyr. What is certain is that he never signed the name Columbus, nor did he ever use it in his lifetime. Still, he might have been called Columbus, since it was close enough to Cristoforo Colombo, the name most historians believe he was born with.

It is said the explorer took up residency in at least three countries, where he changed his name each time to fit the local culture—Cristoforo Colombo in Italy; Cristovao (also Christovam and Christobal) Colom in Portugal, where he lived as a young man; and Cristobal (also occasionally Christoual) Colon (sometimes Colamo) in Spain, where he died after spending his most productive years. He used the last appellation during his famous voyages, ignoring his son Fernando's preference for Christoporus Colonus. There were other variations, like Christoferus Colom, Cristoferi Colom, and Christofferus de Columbo. He was called Xpoual de Colon in his agreement with the King and Queen of Spain before his first venture across the Atlantic. After 1493, his signature consisted of ".s.," ".S.A.S.," "X M Y," and ":Xpo FERENS"—a strange combination of letters and punctuation marks that no one has been able to decipher to this day.

4. The Christic in Christopher

Myth! Columbus was Roman Catholic.

Because his patrons were Spain's Ferdinand II and Isabella, the most Catholic of monarchs, Columbus gave the impression of being Catholic himself. It also helped that when he asked for their support, his proposal was to undertake the project for Christianization first before colonization.

However, Columbus was not Catholic, much as the Italian faithful would want him to be. If he had a religion, it was probably Jewish, because his father was a Jew and had immersed him in Jewish traditions. As a lad, Columbus could quote the Jewish prophets and mystics, and his early exercise books, as well as his later letters, displayed a style of writing much influenced by the Old Testament. In his last letters to his son, he used *beit-hay*, the Hebrew symbol for "Praised be the Lord," and his purported will adhered to Jewish customs in disposing of worldly goods.

It is generally inferred that when Columbus first arrived in Spain, he became a *converso*, or a convert to Christianity, as were so many Jews in that anti-Semitic land. Still, some historians believe that if he had been converted, it was only for show, not so much to avoid being expelled as a *nonconverso* following Spanish policy, but to please his patrons. In Spain, his actions remained consistent with Jewish practice, as in 1492, when he postponed setting sail from Palos in Andalusia for a whole day because it was Tishah B'ab, the Jewish holy day of fasting and mourning.

5. The Sainted and the Painted

Myth! The ships Columbus used in his voyage of discovery were officially named Pinta, Niña and Santa Maria.

261

One of the famous Columbus ships was called *Pinta*, or Lovely Lady, because she floated gracefully. *Niña*, or Baby, was given to another because she was small. *Santa Maria*, of course, was for the Blessed Virgin Mary.

It appears this wasn't wholly the case, however. In Columbus' time, ships had no official names, and "Pinta," "Nina" and "Santa Maria" were only nicknames. Moreover, Columbus' voyagers had previously been known by other names, all of them more sedate than the ones later given by his men. *Pinta*, whose original name is lost in history, was a reference to the Pinto family in Palos, where the ships were readied for their ventures, but it also meant "Painted Lady," or prostitute. *Niña*, formerly called the *Santa Clara*, was redubbed "Little Girl," sailor slang for an easy woman. Columbus' flagship, the *Santa Maria*, was for a long time nicknamed *La Gallega* or *La Gallicia* ("The Lady from Galicia") because it was built in that region of Spain. A newer nickname, one with a femme fatale connotation, was *La Galante* or *Marigalante* ("Dirty Mary"), but Columbus' sponsors demanded that it be changed to the more dignified *Santa Maria* in honor of Jesus' mother.

6. Romancing her Stones

Myth! Queen Isabella used her jewelry to finance the first of Columbus' voyages of exploration.

It is said that after some hesitation, Isabella, prompted by one of her ministers, finally agreed to sponsor Columbus' voyage. Lacking state resources, she put up her own jewels to underwrite the project. Columbus' son Fernando and another biographer, Bartolome de las Casas, told this tale decades after the explorer's death.

The story could not have been true, since there was hardly a venture at that time that Spain's vast treasury could not have supported. Moreover, it is highly unlikely that Isabella would have been generous with her personal assets for a project beset by too many unknowns.

In fact, the first time Columbus requested for help from the Queen, he was turned down for the reason that the crown's funds were tied up in a holy war against the Islamic Moors in southern Spain. She finally acceded when Granada, the last Islamic stronghold, fell in January 1492. She used funds from her government coffers, fattened by confiscating property from Jews, Moslems and infidels, and required one town—Palos—to supply ships and provisions for Columbus' journey as a punishment for tolerating smuggling. Other sources say Isabella offered the pledge of her crown jewels against the expenses, but Luis de Santangel, a confidante of the queen and keeper of King Ferdinand's privy purse, told her it was not necessary.

---

7. New World Revisited

Myth! Columbus was the first European to sight the New World and the first to land in the North American continent, and Colombia, the only country named after him, was the first he visited in South America.

Some history textbooks notwithstanding, Columbus did not make the first land sighting in the New World himself. At 2:00 a.m. on October 12, 1492 (October 21 under the current Gregorian calendar), just as the crew was threatening to mutiny and force a return to Spain, a lookout aboard the *Pinta* named Rodrigo de Triana sighted moonlight shimmering on land. He was thrilled to report the finding to Columbus, but to his consternation, Columbus claimed that he had seen the light the night before—on October 11—and that, as proof, he had put this down in his journal. If he had indeed made the sighting, they asked, why had he kept the discovery to himself during all the time that trouble was simmering among his crew? Wasn't it possible that he had imagined the whole thing? It later came to light that the Spanish monarchs had authorized Columbus to offer a reward of an annuity of 10,000 *maravedis* to the first person who sighted land, and Columbus was just petty enough to pay the amount to himself.

The fact is, Columbus never even saw the North American continent. During his four expeditions to the New World, all of his explorations were of islands in the Caribbean or on the coast of South America. He first landed in a place he named El Salvador (not the same as modern El Salvador), the exact location of which was termed by the natives *Guanahani* but is unclear. Sometimes held to be Watling Island (officially renamed San Salvador in 1926), at other times Great Turk Island, a landspit not far from San Salvador, it is likelier to be Samana Cay, according to recent computer-assisted investigations. Columbus also discovered Cuba and Hispaniola (Haiti and the Dominican Republic) on this initial trip. Incidentally, not even the name Haiti was a Columbian legacy, as it was what the Arawak called their island before Columbus named it Hispaniola. From Hispaniola, the name changed to St. Domingue under the French. The island was later split into two parts, the western reverting to the name Haiti and the eastern becoming the Dominican Republic.

On his second trip Columbus found Puerto Rico and Jamaica and visited the Virgin Islands, Antigua and Santa Cruz. Only on his third attempt, in 1498, did he land on continental America— South America, to be exact—where he sighted Venezuela. Colombia, the only South American country on the Caribbean coast that Columbus *did not* visit, is also the only country in the world that carries his name. Before the end of August of the same year, the intrepid discoverer sighted Tobago, Grenada, and Margarita. He made a fourth voyage, landing in Honduras and Jamaica. To the day of his death in 1506, Columbus refused to take credit for the discovery of a new continent, persisting in his belief that he had reached his intended destination of India.

8. The Logic of the Log

Myth! Columbus kept a second log understating the distances traveled to falsely assure the crew that they were not far from land.

On September 9, 1492, the first time he ventured out on his campaign of discovery, Columbus began keeping two logs. One, a true reckoning of his course and distance, he kept secret. The other was a false account of the ship's location understating the distances traveled so the crew would not be frightened by sailing so far from land.

The irony of it is that, according to recent findings, Columbus' false entries are actually nearer the truth than his supposedly

264

accurate ones. The explorer overestimated his distance by nine percent in his private log, placing his discovery much farther west than it actually is. The false log contained no such error, which meant that Columbus had given his sailors a record that was, for all practical purposes, virtually correct.

Incidentally, none of the logs is written in Italian, as many suppose. Nothing extant of what Columbus wrote, including his journals and even his letters to his Genoese correspondents, is in a language other than Castilian. Neither are the logs those that legend claims were recovered from the sea. According to a story that most students of Columbian history accept, Columbus was on his way home on February 14, 1493 in the *Nina* when a terrible storm overtook his ships. Thinking there was no chance of survival, he sat at his desk and scrawled desperately an account of the voyage, wrapped the parchment in a waxed cloth, tied it, and sealed it in a tight cask that he threw into the sea. All this may well have happened, but none of the documents purportedly retrieved from the sea proved genuine.

9. Colonial Mentality

Myth! Columbus as colonizer was a compassionate libertarian and dedicated evangelizer.

For centuries, the trend has been to idealize Columbus as the man who brought the Christian faith to the naked savages of the New World. One historian, begging to differ, says that if Vespucci was a liar and a thief, Columbus was a mass murderer, probably the greatest practitioner of genocide who ever lived.

Columbus never actually gave himself a chance to Christianize Haiti because of greed. When he reached the island, he found it peopled by friendly Arawak Indians. Instead of reciprocating the Indians' kindness, Columbus, under pressure to bring back riches to Spain, required Indians over fourteen years old to make regular contributions of gold. Indians who did not comply had their hands cut off and bled to death, or were enslaved and shipped to Spain. It is estimated that no single Arawak Indian survived after Columbus' fourth voyage to the New World. Far from feeling guilty about the practice of slavery, Columbus boasted he was doing it "in the name of the Holy Trinity." Within two years of Columbus's arrival, half of the 250,000 Indians on Haiti had died through murder, mutilation or suicide. In 1515 there were just 50,000 Indians left, in 1550 only 500, and by 1650 none.

10. An Italian Job

Myth! Columbus, whose remains lie buried in Seville, died penniless, disgraced and in chains.

The once respected explorer was incarcerated for failing to fulfill his promise of gold, silk and spices from the New World. After his release, he shadowed King Ferdinand in the hope that he would be given some reward for the wealth he succeeded in bringing in from the expeditions. He saw the King once, but nothing happened, so when the royal court moved to the town of Valladolid in 1506, the white-haired Columbus, only in his early fifties, followed painfully on the back of a mule. A sailor gave him a room to stay and cared for him as his condition worsened. Columbus suffered from heart disease and his legs and belly grew swollen, until, on May 1, he died dejected.

This version, which paints a bleak picture of the last few years of Columbus' life, has gained credence on the basis of some of his personal writings. But serious historians lean towards what is apparently an opposite version, which is that Columbus, though slightly humiliated by his short incarceration, was restored to his former station in life after leaving prison. His will and other documents provided by his son and former associates indicated that he possessed considerable wealth at the time of his death in Valladolid on May 20, 1506. Although he persistently complained that he had been neglected by the court of Ferdinand and Isabella and had not been properly rewarded for his work, this did not mean that he was destitute and abandoned. It is widely known that when he died, he died a reasonably popular and respected man.

Several years after his death, Columbus' remains were disinterred and removed to a convent in Seville, Spain. However, in his will Columbus had asked to be buried in Santo Domingo, the Dominican Republic. Accordingly, sometime between 1536 and 154I, his body was transferred to the cathedral in that city. Just before ceding the island to France in I795, the Spanish authorities ordered the remains exhumed and taken to Havana in order to keep them under the Spanish flag. When Spain lost Cuba in the Spanish-American War, Columbus' bones were again dug up and transferred to the cathedral in Seville, where they rest to this day.

Many investigators maintain that Columbus' remains were never really removed from Santo Domingo. When that island was threatened with British invasion in I655, the archbishop had ordered every external trace of Columbus's tomb effaced, lest the enemy should desecrate it. In I877, while the city cathedral was being repaired, excavations made under the direction of Father Francisco Bellini revealed a lead casket containing inscriptions and other evidence tending to prove that it contained Columbus. This casket had not been disturbed in I796, bolstering the theory that the bones previously removed were those of Columbus's son Diego or some other member of the family.

---

11. Dreamland Chronicles

Myth! Vespucci beat Columbus by a year to become the first European to touch the American mainland.

Based on his account of the voyage that landed him in South America in 1497, Vespucci reached the mainland of the Americas shortly before Cabot, and at least 14 months before Columbus, did. The records of that trip have since been impugned, which means Vespucci never actually saw North America. This makes Juan Ponce de Leon, the Spanish explorer who came to Florida in 1513 in search of the elusive 'fountain of youth', the first known European to touch US soil.

Amerigo's hard-core fans insist Vespucci should at least be recognized as the first to realize that America was a new continent and not a part of Asia. They claim Vespucci's exploration along the eastern coastline of South America had convinced him that he was looking at a new continent, 'a bold contention in his day when everyone, including Christopher Columbus, thought the seafaring trailblazers setting out from European docks were traveling to East Asia'. Historians dispute even this, however, stating that, as

Vespucci's own writings implied, he only perceived America as a new land, and did not comprehend it as a new world any more than Columbus did.

12. Bluffing with Four of a Kind

Myth! Vespucchi made four voyages to the New World to Columbus' one.

Vespucci's published letters described four sailings to South America, one each in 1497, 1499, 1501 and 1503. Columbus did not realize that he himself had reached the Western Hemisphere in 1492, and so did not bother to dispute Vespucchi, particularly the claim that the voyages established the existence of a new continent.

The consensus now is that Vespucchi made no more than two of the four trips that he mentioned, and faked the rest. His 1497 trip, on which he claimed to have discovered South America, was completely fabricated, while his third voyage was put in doubt when he gave two accounts that differed markedly in important details. And on the voyages he did make, he did not take the leading role, being only an astronomer and not a captain as he had maintained. The commander in 1499 was Alonso de Ojeda, who had sailed with Columbus on his second voyage, and the one in 1501 was Gonocalo Coelho, another of Spain's' explorers. When two of the letters in which Vespucci made his assertions—the 'Mundus Novus' (New World) and the 'Lettera' (or 'The Four Voyages')—failed the authentication test, Vespucci's supporters argued that, while the subject documents may have indeed been forgeries, they were in all likelihood written by others of the same period and therefore true to the facts.

Vespucchi's adventures—partly simulated as they were—tried to follow the Columbian pattern, except that Columbus was the master of all his sorties and he was more honest with his account. After his 'discovery' of America, Columbus made three more trips to the New World, of which only the first seems to have been as nearly successful as the original one he made in 1492. The second ended up with his fleet being shipwrecked and his crew marooned in Jamaica for a year. On the third and last trip, Columbus was so old and infirm that it turned out to be more a sentimental journey than one of exploration.

While a clear majority believe the Waldseemüller-Mercator intervention did occur, many still wonder why Amerigo Vespucci, if he has such an exalted place in conventional history, has not merited a single statue in his honor in the New World. He has a portrait engraved on the pedestal of Columbus' statue in Grant Park, Chicago, and is one of the background figures in a scene depicted on the Columbus Doors of the Capitol in Washington, DC. But the only known statue of Vespucci anywhere in the world is at the Uffizi in his hometown of Florence, Italy. The answer obviously is that Vespucci's purported accomplishments are mostly offshoots of his imagined sailings to the New World and have lost all credibility.

There is one place in the American continent where a statue of Vespucci can stand confidently, and that is Brazil. History tells us that upon reaching the northern coast of South America, Vespucci split from the voyage master Ojeda and headed south to become the first European to see Brazil and to explore the mouth of the Amazon River.

---

13. Land's Sake

Myth! Amerigo Vespucci gave America its name.

The name Amerigo Vespucci began to assume historical significance only when its owner thought of putting a label on the map he had constructed of the new continent that he claimed to have visited on several occasions between 1497 and 1503. Contrary to popular belief, however, the label he devised was not America but *Mundus Novus*, or New World.

According to the most favored apocrypha, the real mapmaker responsible for calling the new land America was Martin Waldseemüller, who had come upon what looked like one of Vespucci's correspondences in Lorraine's Academy of the Vosges in 1507. Without knowing that the letter was a forgery and that most of the exploits it described never happened, the young German cartographer included it in his book, *Cosmographiae introductio,* and there suggested that the name America be adopted

269

for the new land in Vespucci's honor. The story goes on to say that 'America' was first applied to Brazil alone, but later, Mercator extended it to the entire Western Hemisphere, including North America. Ironically, Vespucci never even saw North America, and he died in 1512 totally unaware that he had been accorded the undeserved honor.

To repeat, the Waldseemüller story is, at this time, apocryphal, as not everybody is sold on the idea that Vespucci is the etymological source for America's name. Various others have been cited, the two most popular being Richard Ameryke and Leif Ericsson. Ameryke (*ap* Maryk, or 'son of Merrick' in Welsh) was a merchant and real estate speculator who later became sheriff of Bristol, England. He reportedly agreed to be a principal backer of John Cabot's expedition to the New World in exchange for, among other things, the promise that the new land would be named after him. Leif Ericsson's name has been put forward mainly because, in the Scandinavian languages, *amt* means 'land of', and 'Land of Eric' translates into 'Amteric', an old form of America. Another promising origin is the Spanish word *Amerique*, from the American Indian word *Americ*, the name of a Nicaraguan mountain range not far from where the first white man to approach the New World sailed.

14. Moonlighting on the Main

Myth! Vespucci invented a method of measuring the distance between the moon and the earth.

Vespucci's ignominy seems to have been made complete with the debunking of his only scientific achievement by the respected historian Samuel Morrison. Vespucci has, for a long time, been credited with inventing a new lunar astronomy, but according to Morrison, the technique was already known during Vespucci's time. He is, says Morrison, "to be praised for having heard about it. But he is merely pulling his reader's leg in implying that he was able to use it." This is because "to turn a primitive plumb-line quadrant or a mariner's astrolabe on its side to measure the angular distance between the moon and a planet...is impossible, especially at moonrise, with the instruments at his disposal."

270

III

From Columbus Circle To The Strait Of Magellan

On Famous World Explorers

"The church says the earth is flat, but I know
that it is round, for I have seen the shadow on
the moon, and I have more faith in a shadow
than in the church."

•

Ferdinand Magellan

1. Coming Full Circle

Myth! After Magellan's death in the Philippines, his shipmate Sebastian del Cano brought the expedition back to its point of origin in Spain to complete the first circumnavigation of the world.

For a time, Ferdinand Magellan held the distinction of being the first circumnavigator of the world—until someone pointed out that in the 1519 expedition he undertook for Spain, he reached only halfway around the globe. In 1521, the second year of his Pacific voyage, the Portuguese explorer landed on Mactan Island in what is now the Philippines, and there died at the hands of the natives, led by an indomitable chieftain named Lapulapu. The one who later turned around to complete the voyage was the leader of Magellan's mutinous crew, Sebastian del Cano. Leaving behind Magellan's body on the hostile beach, del Cano, along with thirty-one survivors of the ill-fated expedition, brought the remainder of the fleet back to Spain in 1522.

There was little doubt the Spaniards could have conquered the indigenous Filipinos by force of arms. Instead, the treacherous del Cano became one of history's dubious achievers by abandoning Magellan and completing what is popularly regarded as the first circumnavigation of the world. Fortunately, because of the belief that the underrated Magellan was unjustly deprived of his rewards, researchers endeavored to find a way to restore the glory to the Portuguese. One of the little-known facts their efforts turned up is that, while del Cano circumnavigated the world in a single voyage, Magellan did it ahead of him in a combination of two voyages. In 1512, Magellan sailed east as far as Banda Island, which was about 130° longitude east. On his star-crossed voyage to the Philippines nearly a decade later, he completed the circle by sailing west to a point 124° longitude east.

Del Cano sailed halfway around the world to the Philippines, then returned to Seville essentially on the same route but in a reverse direction. Purists say this was not a real circumnavigation. But neither was Magellan's, which was accomplished in two entirely separate voyages albeit the routes completed a circle. In 1577 the Englishman Sir Francis Drake went around the globe in

272

only one direction in a single voyage, making him in the truest sense the first circumnavigator of the world.

2. By the Time they Got to Phoenicia

Myth! The Phoenicians are the greatest explorers the world has ever known.

Many of the great explorers of the past whom we honor today came from Italy, Spain, Portugal, or elsewhere in Renaissance Europe. Yet we can't really say that the people from any of these places were, generally speaking, the greatest in the naval art of exploration. Before the Golden Age, there were the Vikings, who made some of the most significant discoveries in the world, but on the whole the achievement of this group was limited in time and scope. Whenever history treats of how the conquest of the sea began, the focus is neither on the Vikings nor on the Renaissance navigators but on the ancient Phoenicians. Recoveries from the earliest known shipwreck showed to the world the pioneering nature of this people as bold seafarers.

Actually, hard-nosed historians have not been fully convinced about the Phoenicians either, saying that, while these ancients may have been the world's greatest seafaring traders, the experience did not necessarily turn them into the world's greatest explorers. According to the first Europeans to enter the Pacific, the honor belongs to those navigators whose nautical skills rivaled their own and who had already mastered the great ocean long before them. These were the Polynesians, whose presence throughout the ocean's constellation of isles showed an extraordinary seafaring heritage dating back to 2500 BC or earlier. Driven from one island to another by overpopulation, famine or defeat in battle, Polynesians always planned their voyages well in advance, during which they built massive double-hulled canoes from large tree trunks with primitive tools of stone, shell and bone. Their navigators, skilled in both theory and practice, were taught from early childhood to read nautical information in many types of ocean environment. This culture produced prodigious feats of migration that, by the eighth century, brought Polynesians to all of Micronesia and virtually every habitable speck in a vast triangle

273

bound by Hawaii on the north, New Zealand in the southwest, and Easter Island to the east.

---

3. The Hazards of Ocean Racing

Myth! The Spanish conquistador Hernando Cortez was the first European to sight the Pacific Ocean.

John Keats in his poem 'On First Looking at Chapman's Homer' describes "stout Cortez when, with eagle eyes, / He stared at the Pacific.../ Silent, upon a peak in Darien." But according to most history books, it was Vasco Nuñez de Balboa, not Cortez, who fixed the first European eyes on that magnificent ocean. Joining the expedition of Fernando de Encisco for the Gulf of Urba in 1510, Balboa hid himself in a barrel, then deposed Encisco to take command of the fleet. On 25 September 1513, upon first sighting the ocean from a peak in Darien (the Isthmus of Panama), he dispatched a scouting party that landed on the shore. He himself joined the party on the 29th, but it was allegedly a companion, Alonzo Martin, who became the first European to sail on its waters when he launched a small boat on the Gulf of St. Michael.

By inciting mutiny and seizing control of Enciso's vessel, Balboa acted dishonorably preparatory to accomplishing his feat. It serves justice somewhat that the Spaniard is recognized only for having discovered the Pacific from the American side. By the time he reached the Isthmus, somebody had already seen the ocean from the Asian side. In 1511, the Portuguese under Antonio d'Abreu had sailed into the Pacific from the other direction by way of the Indian Ocean. Scholars consider Abreu the real discoverer of the Pacific because his voyages to the Spice Islands led to Ferdinand Magellan's exploration of the waters. Magellan called the blue expanse the Pacific in 1520, after he had sailed through the strait carrying his name.

Strictly speaking, neither Balboa nor Abreu was the first, nor even the second or the third, to sight the ocean. And Alonzo Martin was probably not the first European to sail on its waters either. Other Europeans like Marco Polo, who is believed to have sailed on the Pacific on his way to Java in the thirteenth century,

274

had long ago explored the Asian side. In 1315 a European mapmaker was already featuring the western side of the Pacific in a crude drawing of China.

4. First to Go Down Under

Myth! **Captain James Cook discovered Australia.**

James Cook is arguably the greatest seagoing explorer of all time, but he is way down the list of actual explorers who came to Australia. It's a long list, with the earliest dates going as far back as the 13th century, when the Chinese told Marco Polo they had seen the continent and he mentioned as much in his writings. The sea-faring Malays who explored the northern coast during that period may have been ahead even of the Chinese. The first Europeans to set foot on the continent were the Dutch, led by Captain Jansz of the Dutch ship Duyfken, which landed at Cape Keerweer in 1606. This was a year after a Portuguese vessel captained by one De Torres had sighted Australia but did not touch shore.

During the next fifty years, the Dutch proceeded to explore inland and called the place New Holland. It was only in 1688 that an Englishman—the pirate William Dampier—saw Australia for the first time. After returning to England to report his findings, Dampier was sent back in 1699 to investigate further. In 1768 Cook made his third and final voyage across the Pacific, and two years later Cook made a claim for England, earning for him the dubious award of being the discoverer of Australia.

5. John Juan Giovanni

Myth! **Giovanni da Verrazano was the first Italian to touch the North American mainland.**

Although Verrazano reached the Carolinas, New York Bay and Newfoundland in 1524, John Cabot, who touched Newfoundland in 1496 while sailing for the English, beat him to the punch. Some say this proves the Anglo-Saxons have as genuine a claim to be the discoverers of America as their more publicized Latin rivals. Unfortunately for the English, the merit of this view is dimmed by the fact that Cabot was as Italian as Verrazano was.

Born Giovanni Caboto probably in Genoa, Cabot was, from the middle 1470s, a citizen of Venice, where he married, had two sons, and busied himself as a merchant. Around 1490 he moved to Valencia, Spain, and became known there as Juan Caboto Montecalunya. In Spain, he tried to convince officials that a westward journey to the Indies was possible, but when Columbus preempted the idea, he moved his family to Bristol. The British, jealous of Columbus, were persuaded by the man now called Cabot that a northern Atlantic route, following the English fishing routes, would be cheaper and therefore more profitable than the Genoese's southern path.

6. Sir cum Navigator

Myth! Prince Henry of Portugal was called the Navigator because he loved the sea and sailing and personally led voyages of exploration.

It is often asked whether Prince Henry, the fourth son of King John I of Portugal and known as the Great Navigator, deserves every bit the sobriquet accorded him by his subjects and validated by history.

The answer as often given is, yes he does, but only in the sense that he founded and ran an institute in Sagres, Cape St. Vincent, dedicated to the development of the science of navigation and the training of explorers and navigators. He paid for the erection of an observatory to augment the facilities of the school, and personally financed ships and seamen destined to traverse the deep and unknown waters comprising more than half of the world in the fifteenth century. If Henry accomplished anything in the field of exploration, it was indirectly through the efforts of his students and protégés, some of whom were eventually responsible for the discovery of the Madeiras in 1418 and the start of systematic exploration of the Guinea coast in 1430, while others embarked on voyages that culminated in the rounding of Cape Verde in 1446 and the discovery of the Azores in 1448. Prince Henry is thus regarded as the inaugurator of the Age of Discovery, being the first high-ranking official to arouse widespread interest in navigation not only in Portugal but also in other European countries.

But as a practical matter, Prince Henry was the personal antithesis of navigation, for he hated the sea and never sailed himself. His phobia prevented him from participating directly in any voyage of exploration. The only time he was known to have sailed for a distance was in 1415, when he took part in the capture of the port of Ceuta in Morocco from the Moors.

---

7. California Suite

Myth! Sir Francis Drake established the first British settlement on the California coast, where he put up a brass plate claiming the territory in the name of the Queen.

The famous ship that made its voyage of circumnavigation (1577-1580) under the command of Sir Francis Drake is recorded in history books as *The Golden Hind*. What is not mentioned is that when the ship first set sail in 1577, it was called *The Pelican*, and was renamed *The Golden Hind* only at Port St. Julian, near the entrance to the Straits of Magellan, in 1578.

It was apparently during this voyage that Drake, having anchored off the California coast in 1579, set up a brass plate naming the territory New Albion (or New England) and claiming it in the name of Elizabeth. In 1936 what looked like Drake's plate was found near San Francisco with the inscription appearing to be reasonably authentic. A replica was in due time presented to Elizabeth II and kept in Buckland Abbey, Drake's Devonshire property and now a museum. But in 1977 a reported analysis of the composition of the brass by the Lawrence Berkeley Institute of the University of California and the Research Laboratory for Archaeology at Oxford found that it was of late 19th- or early 20th-century manufacture. What would have been the only proof that the first British settlement was in the western United States rather than in the east turned out to be fake.

This attempt at historical duplicity has not cast much of a shadow on the fact that Sir Francis Drake successfully circumnavigated the world, and did almost all of it using just the Golden Hind. This, along with the treasures he pirated from the Spanish and brought home, so enthused Queen Elizabeth I that she boarded his vessel upon its arrival and knighted him on the spot! The truth, of course, is that the French ambassador Monsieur de Marchaumont knighted Drake, on 4 April 1581, on orders of the Queen, who excused herself from the task so as not to displease the Spanish.

8. Polar Wandering

Myth! **Robert Peary, with his black comrade Matthew Henson and four Eskimos, reached the North Pole ahead of everyone.**

Robert Peary's claim that he was the first to reach the northernmost point on Earth was supported by the press and, among several scientific bodies, the National Geographic Society. The US Congress, despite some doubts, recognized Peary's assertion in 1911.

Shortly thereafter, evidence was offered to prove that New Yorker Dr. Frederick Cook, in the company of two Eskimos, preceded Peary to the Pole by almost a year. Cook had actually reported his claim several days before Peary made his own announcement, and had shown the journal for his expedition to the Norwegian discoverer of the South Pole Roald Amundsen, who deemed it genuine

Both claimants gave convincing accounts, but both also seemed to have burdened their stories with contradictions that could not readily be explained. Their journals contained wrong calculations, erroneous descriptions, and identifications of landmarks that later proved nonexistent. In light of these dubious claims, another name, that of American Richard Byrd, has been proposed for the honors. Byrd claimed to have flown over the North Pole in 1926, although this has equally been disputed for lack of witnesses. As

278

expected, the Russians have their own candidate for the feat, one Otto Schmidt, who may have set foot there in 1936. The first uncontested surface attainment of the North Pole was by American Ralph Plaisted in 1968.

Matthew Alexander Henson, a black, worked with Peary as his personal assistant for half of his forty-two years. But Henson's claim to fame is more than just being a valet to the famous explorer. It is said that he, not Peary, was the first American to reach the North Pole in 1909.

Peary's record of his adventure cited Henson for being indispensable in dealing with the Inuit and overseeing the sleds and dog teams. The two were in the company of only four Eskimos on the final 132-mile leg of the trip, with Peary, who had lost eight of his toes in a previous adventure, riding most of the time in a dog sled. On the last day, Peary sent Henson and the Eskimos ahead to break a trail, telling them to stop short of the goal. What Peary's report didn't mention was that, instead of stopping, the advance party proceeded until, on April 6, Henson and the Eskimos reached the North Pole and gave a cheer. Peary arrived later, and hardly able to hide his anger, went through the ceremony of establishing his presence by putting a strip of flag in a container with a note that he had taken the North Pole for the United States. To make sure he would be the first one to announce the feat, Peary left Henson and the Eskimos in a temporary camp and negotiated the trail back alone.

Henson was never recognized for his contributions to Peary's achievement, much less for his controversial role (which he never revealed) as the first human being on the North Pole.

9. The Englishman who Went Dutch

Myth! **The Dutchman Hendrik Hudson discovered the river, the straits and the bay that bear his name today.**

There was no famous Dutch explorer named Hendrik Hudson during the Age of Discovery. There was an explorer named Henry Hudson, whose early life is obscure, but historians agree that he was born an Englishman and he lived and died as one.

Hudson made four voyages of exploration, of which the first two and the last were made under the auspices of the British. The impression that he was Dutch was probably because the Dutch East India Company sponsored his third and most notable voyage aboard the Half Moon in 1609. It was the Half Moon that sailed up the river named for him, and on the strength of this voyage, the Dutch laid claim to New York and started to call him Hendrik. The English felt so strongly about his working for the Dutch that when the Half Moon put in at Dartmouth in 1609, it was seized and Hudson, along with the other Englishmen of the crew, was commanded to stay home and serve England.

On his fourth voyage, Hudson sailed to the New World in the Discovery, but in the spring of 1611 most of the crew mutinied and placed him with several companions in a small boat that they set adrift. The Discovery returned safely to England, while Henry Hudson was never heard of again.

Contrary to popular belief, Henry Hudson did not discover the river, the straits and the bay bearing his name. They were all first seen by other Europeans decades before Hudson's first voyage. Esteban Gomez, a Portuguese working for Spain, preceded Hudson to the river by eighty-four years, which is why the New York waterway became known for that length of time in Spain as the Rio de Gomez. Possibly even ahead of Gomez was the Florentine Giovanni da Verrazano, who had written that he was there in March 1524, and was in fact the first to sight the land that would be New York City. Hudson did not reach the river until 1609, when it was referred to as the North River to distinguish it from the South (Delaware) River. Hudson's exploration was only partial because when he realized the river was not part of the fabled Northwest Passage, he promptly turned around at Albany and abandoned the task.

Like the river, both the strait and the bay were known long before Hudson's time. The Portuguese found both bodies of water in the mid 16th century, although some historians speculate that John Cabot, the Genoan who sailed for the English, may have reached the strait as early as 1498. Hudson saw the bay (actually an inland sea) only in 1610, when his crew revolted against him on the *Discovery*. Nonetheless, it was named after him because he was left there to die by the mutineers.

10. Green Fields of Ice

Myth! Greenland has more greenery and less ice than Iceland.

Iceland and Greenland have names that connote climatic and environmental conditions. Obviously, one is a place warmed by lush foliage and flower-ringed mountains, and the other is a vast extent of ice and cold.

The obvious is correct only if the meanings of the names are reversed. As modern-day visitors to these two destinations can attest, Greenland has considerably less greenery and more ice than Iceland. Located in the Arctic Circle, the island, regarded (somewhat inaccurately) as the largest in the world at 840,000 square miles, is four-fifths covered by an enormous, permanent ice sheet 1,000 feet thick on the average. The other one-fifth is almost barren tundra with sparse vegetation and few trees. The coast is practically the only place that turns green during its very brief summer. The main livelihood is fishing augmented by sheep raising, and agriculture is virtually nonexistent.

It is said that Erik the Red invented the name Greenland in the hope of giving prospective settlers the false impression that the desolate island was full of greenery and life. Of late, the legend has been undermined by evidence that Greenland was actually warmer and much greener than Iceland during Erik's time. According to scientists, Greenland has, for some yet unexplained reason, experienced a sudden shift in climate since its discovery. However, any controversy about Greenland's etymology has become largely irrelevant because on May 1, 1979, this former Danish territory came under home rule and changed its name to the native-sounding Kalaallit Nunaat.

If the story about the Vikings naming Greenland to attract settlers is false, it is likely that the story about the same Vikings naming Iceland to discourage settlers, hoping they could keep the place to themselves, is also false. The 'Ice' in Iceland is a contradiction that fortunately has not dampened the flow of tourists to that country. Although located at latitude 66 degrees North, with its northern border abutting the Arctic Circle, Iceland is 25 percent green vegetation and only 10 percent ice. It has lush forests, flower-ringed mountains and hot springs. Warmed by the Gulf

Stream, the temperature even in midwinter rarely falls below freezing, exhibiting not much more than a 10-degree Centigrade variance with England throughout the year. Reykjavik itself has almost the same weather pattern as New York, and even outdoor pools are heated by geothermal methods to allow Reykjavik's residents to swim comfortably in the dead of winter.

Coincidentally, it is not just Iceland but also Reykjavik that is a misnomer. The latter means 'smoky bay', but there is no smoke or smog to bother the inhabitant or visitor—the smoke refers to the clean and healthy steam that rises from the hot springs. Reykjavik and most of Iceland are on top of the list of the pollution-freest places on earth.

Because of their proximity to the Northern European region, Iceland and, to a lesser degree, Greenland are sometimes regarded as parts of the Scandinavian group. Technically, however, Scandinavia consists only of Norway, Sweden, and Denmark.

IV

A Rock Bound Pilgrimage

On Settlers of the New World

"...those who do not wish to know ask
questions of those who cannot tell."

•

Sir Walter Raleigh

1. Plymouth-to-Plymouth Resuscitation

Myth! A single ship carrying mostly religious persons called Pilgrims left Plymouth, England, in 1620 bound for the New World.

Those who left Plymouth in Southampton, England, in 1620 were aboard not one but two ships, the Mayflower and the Speedwell, which sailed only a month apart with the same destination in mind. On her first 300 nautical miles, the Speedwell developed engine trouble twice. The first breakdown required it to dock at Dartmouth for repairs, but the second forced it to sail back to Southampton, where it was abandoned. The Mayflower, with its 102 passengers and crew, made it to North America.

Contrary to the popular belief that the Mayflower group was mostly religious, only thirty-five were members of the English Separatist Church. About two-thirds were non-Separatists, most of them service people, such as the crew, the servants and paid military personnel (the latter including Miles Standish and John Alden). A few were the so-called 'strangers', who differed from the 'saints' in that their purpose for voyaging was adventure or to find a better life in the New World.

None of those aboard the Mayflower was originally called a Pilgrim, while at Plymouth, they were briefly referred to as the Old Comers and, later, the Forefathers. The word 'Pilgrim' was completely unknown until it was found in a work written by William Bradford some years after the landing. Bradford's manuscript got lost, but the name resurfaced in 1820 when, at a commemorative bicentennial celebration, the phrase 'Pilgrim Fathers' was used by Daniel Webster, and the term has stuck since then.

2. Soil Kissing

Myth! Plymouth was the first English settlement in New England, but the earlier Jamestown was the first English settlement in America.

284

The Mayflower landing at Plymouth is often regarded as the prelude to the establishment of the first English colony in New England. This is not correct. The first such colony was the one formed at Popham Beach, Maine, at the mouth of the Kennebec River in 1607, predating the coming of the Pilgrims to Plymouth by thirteen years. Sir John Popham, Chief Justice of England, funded its founding and had his brother George lead it. One hundred and twenty people journeyed with George to the site and organized what eventually became a short-lived community. Within a few months, George died and his second-in-command named Gilbert returned to England to assume a large family fortune. These two events, aggravated by a hard winter, left the colony without leadership and short of supplies. As Popham Beach was also the first English settlement in America, its rapid disintegration ending with its abandonment in 1608 promoted Jamestown, Virginia, which came in its heels in 1607, as the first *permanent* English settlement in the New World.

It is said, though without much proof, that the first British settlement in 'New England' as well as in America was really California, not Maine. This apparent geographical inconsistency arises from the claim that Sir Francis Drake settled a slice of California in behalf of Queen Elizabeth I and dubbed it 'New England' (Nova Albion) in the 1570s. Drake's early use of the name calls to mind that the British had explored some parts of the southwest even before they began to set their sights on the east. Unfortunately, the queen declared that all matters and records relating to Drake's adventure be kept secret to avoid threats of Spanish intervention in the eastern colonies.

3. Welcome as the Flowers in May

Myth! **Upon reaching the New World on December 21, 1620, the Mayflower dislodged its 102 passengers in the presence of welcoming Indians.**

To say that 102 left England with the Mayflower and 102 reached Plymouth, Massachusetts, on the same vessel is correct but misleading. Not the entire original 102 saw the new continent, since one from the crew and another from the passengers died before the Mayflower could land. However, two children who were born on board during the long voyage across the Atlantic eventually replenished the number.

The date the Pilgrims landed in Plymouth became confused when the Old Style calendar in vogue during the Pilgrims' era was converted to the New Style calendar in the 1700s. During most of the nineteenth century, the arrival was celebrated annually on dates that alternated between December 21 and December 22. Massachusetts finally ended the controversy in 1895 by declaring December 21 a legal holiday. However, this has not changed the fact that the first landing was actually done elsewhere than at Plymouth: a scouting party on a shallop came ashore while the Mayflower was still moored at Provincetown, and it was only days later that the ship moved anchor to Plymouth and the passengers began to disembark.

As depicted in paintings and drawings, the first to touch Plymouth soil was a motley group that included women and children, and these are often shown landing directly from a beached Mayflower with a visible Rock and some friendly Indians welcoming them. There is obviously some misrepresentation here, since history doubts there was a Rock and is sure there were no Indians. Also, logic dictates that the Pilgrims could only have landed in small groups by one or more shallops conveying them from the Mayflower to the shore.

4. Fellow Travelers on the Mayflower?

Myth! The Mayflower Compact forged on the high seas was the first democratic instrument to establish a representative government in America.

Contrary to popular accounts, the Mayflower Compact was not forged on board the vessel while it sailed the high seas. It was a full two days after the historic landing at Plymouth, when the 'strangers' declared they would be free from any commands, that the instrument was signed and became effective.

The document has since been held as the first truly democratic instrument in America—according to some historians, the first constitution even—because it established a representative government by the agreement of the governed. But according to those who reject this view, only 41 signed the Compact, and their true intention was to draw up a church covenant to bind the group together. A secular objective at most was to provide a modus vivendi for mutual defense and preserve peace and order in the light of threatened mutiny, desertion and violence. It did not establish any government or the shape of a future government among the settlers, but even if it did, it was a year too late. The first in the New World to achieve this end was the House of Burgesses, an elected legislative assembly put up by the original settlers of Jamestown, Virginia, in 1619.

Neither did the Mayflower Compact, as claimed, encourage the first stirrings of democracy in the New World. Initially imbued with an innovative sense of justice and equality, the Pilgrims actually experimented first with rudimentary concepts of communism, such as working with and sharing in community-owned resources. It was only when they realized the system was inefficient that they shifted to competitive enterprise and capitalism.

---

5. Lost in America

Myth! The New World's first lost colony was Roanoke, where all the settlers disappeared and were never heard from again.

The Roanoke colony that thrived briefly in the 1580s was not the first European settlement in the New World to disappear without a trace. Nearly a century before this North Carolina (not Virginia) disaster, a colony of Europeans was established by Columbus—more out of necessity than by choice—somewhere in the Caribbean. For three months following his first landfall on October 12, 1492, the Genoan had moved his little fleet through the uncharted and often dangerous waters around the Bahamas, Cuba and Hispaniola. One dark night toward the end of the cruise, as he was preparing to return to Spain, his flagship, the Santa Maria, foundered on a coral reef in Caracol Bay near Cap Haitien. When it became apparent that it would not be able to make the return voyage, Columbus had the ship dismantled, and out of its timbers constructed what should rightfully be regarded as the first European fort in the New World. He called it La Navidad, for the day of its founding, and left a garrison of forty volunteers while he took the rest of his crew back to Spain. A year later, when he returned to the Caribbean on his second voyage, he found the settlement totally deserted. Apparently, the Europeans had abused the hospitality of the natives by committing numerous robberies and rapes, and the Indians retaliated by killing all of them.

Two groups of settlers—not one, as we have been led to believe—put up the colony on Roanoke, an island inside North Carolina's Outer Banks, in the 1580s. The first group was sponsored by Sir Walter Raleigh, and settled in 1585 under the leadership of Sir Richard Grenville, but unable to cope with the hardships, all returned to England the following year. A second group was again sponsored by Raleigh, arriving in Roanoke in 1587 under the command of Governor John White. This was the famous 'lost colony', which vanished and was never found, although contrary to some accounts, not all of its members disappeared. The leader, John White, went back to England for supplies, was delayed by the British war with Spain, and returned to the colony three years later to discover the disappearance.

6. Secret of the Trunk

Myth! The lost colonists of Roanoke left the message 'CROATAN' carved on a living tree.

Except for its vanished members and the strange word 'CROATAN' found inscribed on a tree near the gate of the fort, the New World's 'lost colony' was physically preserved, with no sign of anything gone wrong. This is the description of the riddle of Roanoke that we often read in history books without being aware that it is shot full of holes.

First, the mystery word was not CROATAN but CROATOAN, and it was not the signal of distress that the colonists had agreed to leave in case they were required to quit in haste. The pre-arranged signal, a cross, was nowhere to be found. Second, CROATOAN was not carved on a living tree but on a tree that had been made into a doorpost for the gate of a small fort-like structure. It was CRO that was found carved on a living tree stripped of bark. Third, with no clue as to who was responsible, all buildings in the colony had been dismantled and all supplies taken, leaving only some small fortifications here and there. Fourth, 40 stone tablets that were discovered more than three centuries later, allegedly describing the death of many colonists from disease and Indian attacks, were revealed to be a hoax.

Many historians believe much of the enigma surrounding CROATOAN is pure fancy and a mere attempt to glamorize the disappearance of the colony's inhabitants. They see the word as an indication—though not a message—that the settlers had tried to move to the nearby Croatoan Islands, site of present-day Cape Hatteras, but had perished at sea or were killed by the Indians in the process. It is said that later generations of Croatoan Indians looked and spoke like Europeans, suggesting that some of the colonists had survived and were assimilated by them.

7. Dated Artifact

Myth! The Pilgrims saw a big rock on the beach, and promptly carved the date '1620' on it.

The date '1620' is indeed carved into Plymouth Rock, the large stone that can be seen in Plymouth today, but there is absolutely no written account or other reliable proof of the Pilgrims landing near a rock and carving a date on it. The myth started in 1741, a hundred twenty-one years after the supposed event, when 95-year-old Elder John Faunce identified the boulder as the original landing site. Faunce claimed he had heard about the landing as a boy from his father, a settler who didn't arrive with the Pilgrims but reached America only three years after the Mayflower.

The Rock was removed from its original site near the shore in 1774, when it accidentally split in half. The two pieces were separated for over one hundred years, and one was used as a step for a building entrance. They were rejoined in 1880 at what was believed to be the rock's original location. Some civic-spirited or tourism-oriented citizen in Plymouth probably carved the date only at this time. The legend started by Elder Faunce did not

289

receive great popularity until it was revived eighty years later during the 1820 bicentennial celebration of the Pilgrims' landing, when the story suddenly became widely believed.

8. Leif in Minnesota

Myth! **The Mayflower passengers were the earliest Europeans to settle in America.**

The nobility of the Mayflower pedigree lies in the belief of claimants that their forebears were the first European settlers in the New World. This, of course, is false. The Jamestown colonists from England made their home in the Americas ahead of the Plymouth Pilgrims. And even earlier were some of Columbus' men and the Spanish, who dominated the New World for almost a century before the arrival of the English.

We have to go well beyond the Columbian time frame to look for the first European settlers—the Vikings, who founded Vinland (believed to be a part of North America) at the beginning of the 11th century. Recorded in extant Scandinavian sagas was an expedition of three ships carrying some 250 men and women from Greenland, who arrived in Vinland and settled there. After a year the natives, probably Indians or Eskimos, drove them out.

Interestingly, some historians, while readily conceding that the Vikings were the first European settlers in the New World, are unwilling to acknowledge that they were its discoverers. Daniel Boorstin leads with the argument that to settle does not necessarily mean to discover; the latter is an encounter, a "coming up against, a meeting that conflicts with the familiar or the already known." For the Norsemen, the Vinland experiences were almost passing ones—in less than two years they would be driven back to Greenland by the natives. No discovery or encounter occurred, because "(w)hat they did in America did not change their own or anybody else's view of the world." The places they touched— Vinland, Bergen, Greenland and Iceland—were all in the same climatic zone and were not much different from each other. The Viking settlements in Greenland were on the same latitude as Bergen, from Bergen to Iceland was just a few degrees of latitude

290

to the north, and from Bergen to Vinland was a mere 10 degrees to the south.

9. English Daughters and Dutch Uncles

Myth! The Pilgrims named their new home in America after Plymouth, England, where they hailed from.

Not many people realize that the Pilgrim saints who sailed from Plymouth, England to the New World in 1620 actually hailed from Leyden, Holland. They remained English, and used to be a congregation from Nottinghamshire, but their reformist ideas and religious views had forced them to flee to Leyden. James I had been appalled by their rebellious spirit and had wanted them to conform to the Church of England on pain of being punished or driven out. Calling themselves Separatists, they found Holland a liberal haven, until a dozen years later, they decided they had had enough of Dutch culture and hoped the virgin territories of the New World would offer more space for their beliefs.

Most everybody assumes the Pilgrims gave Plymouth, Massachusetts, its name to honor the English port from which they had sailed. This is false. It was Prince Charles who gave the name—six years before the Pilgrims landed. In 1614, when Captain John Smith of Jamestown asked him to rename the Indian villages he had located on a map, the Prince promptly replaced the Indian name 'Accomack' with 'Plymouth'. The royal act is today considered one of the few historically authenticated displays of precognition.

10. Born on the Fourth of July

Myth! Virginia Dare was the first American-born child of European settlers.

Not a few Mayflower descendants will insist the first American-born child of European settlers was Peregrine White, who was delivered on board the vessel as it lay at anchor in Cape Cod Bay, Massachusetts, in 1620. Actually, White was only the first English baby born in New England, and was preceded by Virginia Dare, the first English baby born in America. Dare's birthplace was not Roanoke, Virginia, as her name would suggest, but the lost colony of Roanoke in North Carolina. Her grandfather, Governor John White, survived the colony and left a diary confirming Virginia's birth in 1587, but no one knows if she ever grew up, and if she did, whether as a white or an Indian.

Dare was the first American born of English settlers—but not of European settlers. If the Greenland sagas are to be believed, the first European-American was Snorro Karlsefni, who was born at the beginning of the 11th century to Viking parents in Vinland somewhere in North America. A well-to-do Icelander named Thorfinn Karlsefni had sailed to Greenland and there married Gudrid, the widow of Leif Ericsson's brother. From Greenland, the couple joined the short-lived expedition that founded Vinland, and it was during their brief sojourn in the latter settlement that Gudrid bore the child Snorro.

---

11. Meeting Bob & Carol & Ted & Alice

Myth! The New England town meeting was a regular assemblage of ordinary men and women discussing and voting on issues.

Hollywood's interpretation of local politics as it worked in colonial America is through scenes of ordinary men and women gathered at town meetings to openly discuss and vote on issues. Based on this cinematic treatment, most people regard the New England town meeting as a venerable embodiment of the American democratic ideal. But historians believe it is more a mainstay of democratic mythology. First, it created the presumption that everybody was allowed to vote, when in fact only male white men with property could vote. Second, the votes were not on issues but on who should be the town representatives in the provincial assemblies. And third, the meeting was held only twice a year on the average.

Popular media has largely missed the fact that most political power in America by the mid-18th century was in the hands of provincial officials, the select few who could levy and collect taxes, pass laws, settle disputes, and generally dispense justice and administer government. According to the *Britannica*, these leaders "undoubtedly represented the interests of their constituents more faithfully than any royal official could, but it is clear that the politics of provincial America were hardly democratic by modern standards." In Virginia and Maryland, landlords and a few prominent merchants and lawyers dominated the provincial assemblies, while in New York, these were manor lords who often displayed genuinely feudal behavior. "In general," continues the *Britannica*, "both social prestige and political power tended to be determined by economic standing; and the economic resources of colonial America, though not as unevenly distributed as in Europe, were nevertheless controlled by relatively few men."

---

12. An Undeserved Boone

Myth! Boone, famous wearer of the coonskin cap, discovered Kentucky and had it set up as the 14th American colony.

Daniel Boone, the legendary Kentuckian, was not from Kentucky at all. He was born in Philadelphia, died in Missouri, settled in North Carolina, and hunted in Virginia, Nebraska and Tennessee. While he is acclaimed in words and song as the discoverer of Kentucky, this needs qualification, according to the *Britannica*, because many white men had traversed Kentucky before Boone ever set foot on it.

In the beginning, he made incursions into Kentucky merely to trap and hunt; later, he tried to settle his family there, but was always repelled by hostile Indians. Under the employ of the Transylvania Company, he was finally able to blaze a trail into the wilderness and establish the first permanent white settlement in Kentucky territory. However, his plan of establishing Kentucky as a 14th colony never materialized, and, instead, Kentucky was made a county of Virginia.

Boone, like most frontiersmen, is often seen in pop art and film

293

media wearing a coonskin cap, and he is sometimes confused with Davy Crockett for exhibiting this idiosyncrasy. In reality, Boone didn't like coonskin caps—he thought them uncivilized—and would not be caught wearing one.

13. Along Tobacco Road

Myth! Sir Walter Raleigh returned from Virginia in 1586 to introduce tobacco to Europe.

Mythmakers claim that Sir Walter spent some time in Virginia in 1586 and took a shipload of tobacco with him back to Europe, which "sold for its weight in silver." This, of course, never happened. For one, Raleigh liked tobacco and was probably responsible for its popularity in England, but he did not introduce it there or to any other part of the continent. For another, Raleigh, it appears, never even set foot in Virginia or any part of North America.

No one is sure who brought tobacco to Europe, although the theories are not found wanting. One of the favorites is that Columbus' men returning from Cuba introduced it into Spain. But this may have been superseded by the story that in 1558, a Spanish physician named Francisco Fernandez returned with the weed after he had been sent out by King Philip II of Spain to investigate products of Mexico. From the Iberian Peninsula the item was supposed to have traveled to France in 1559 through the auspices of the diplomat Jean Nicot, but others say it was Thevat who brought it to France in 1556. How it got into England is even more controversial. A couple of sea captains, one of whom could have been Sir Francis Drake, were believed to have introduced it there from France in 1586. There is a record of how Drake and Sir Ralph Lane, returning in 1586 from the first unsuccessful attempt to colonize Roanoke Island, North Carolina, presented Raleigh, the organizer of the expedition, with pipes and tobacco. Earlier, in the log of his 1565 visit to Florida, Sir John Hawkins, a privateer, mentioned the smoking of tobacco, but did not state whether or not samples were brought back.

Assuming it was Raleigh who had procured England's initial supply of the tobacco, it must have been from somewhere other

294

than Virginia. While it is true this gallant was commissioned by Elizabeth I to administer the settlements in that part of the New World, he never set foot on the US mainland, much less Virginia. Being the queen's favorite, he was forbidden most of the time to leave England, and although the capital of North Carolina is named in his honor, his adventures in the new continent took him only to South America and Newfoundland. The three settlements that earned for him his reputation as the foremost English colonizer in North America during his time were nowhere in Virginia, but on offshore islands near the North Carolina coast.

Incidentally, there's a famous anecdote that's designed to suggest Raleigh's involvement in the introduction of tobacco into civilized society. It is said a servant who was alarmed by the tobacco smoke coming out of Sir Walter Raleigh's mouth doused the queen's knight with ale. However, no matter how much the cigarette makers of Virginia cherish the story, there's not the least bit of substance to it. Historian Jerome Brooks says the story did not even appear until the eighteenth century, long after Raleigh had died.

---

14. Landing a Delicate Craft

Myth! Plymouth, Massachusetts, was the first landing point of the Pilgrims in the New World.

Some if not most history texts don't bother to quibble about the difference between *to land* and *to settle*, not realizing that the first is a single act whereas the latter is a continuing series of acts. Hence, when they say Plymouth was the first landing point of the Pilgrims in the New World, what they actually mean is that Plymouth was where the Pilgrims first settled in the American continent after their long trans-Atlantic journey.

No doubt the Mayflower was originally bound for Virginia, where there were other Englanders, but how or why it got diverted and landed in Massachusetts instead is the question. Some say that on learning they were not welcome in Virginia, the Pilgrims changed their heading for 'Hudson's River', the future site of New York. Because of poor navigation and unexpected strong winds, the ship went off-course and landed by mistake in Massachusetts. Others believe the crew was forced to cut the trip short when provisions—"victuals and beer," according to the Mayflower's journal—ran low.

However it may have happened, the Pilgrims reached Plymouth—but not before making two other landings elsewhere in Massachusetts. The first ever was four days after the seafarers had pulled into Cape Cod bay on November 21, 1620, when an exploring party disembarked on the site of what is now Provincetown. This group returned to the ship and was replaced by a second team, which confirmed the initial findings that the Provincetown harbor was not suitable for the Mayflower. The second landing occurred when yet another scouting party was dispatched in a shallop (a small open boat) to the south, arriving near present-day Eastham, where the immigrants had their first encounter with Indians. The skirmish prompted them to head back to the ship, and a group of scouts was once more dispatched to circle Cape Cod bay. On December 19 first mate Clark stepped ashore, giving his name to Clark's Island, and two days later the colonists decided to land on Plymouth proper and *settle* there.

V

Pilgrims' Progress

On Pilgrims and Puritans

"God has brought us where we are, to
consider the work we may do in the world,
as well as at home."

•

Oliver Cromwell

1. A Thanksgiving Story

Myth! The earliest model for Thanksgiving Day is the Pilgrims' first harvest festival in Plymouth in 1621.

Thanksgiving as we know it today is only remotely related to the Pilgrims' celebration in 1621 and to the various similar festivities that were held afterwards in the colonies. The 1621 event was the first harvest festival held in America, and was a weeklong, public reenactment of the institution called Harvest Home in the England the Pilgrims had left behind. Inherent in the rejoicing, and the nearest thing to a thanksgiving, was its recognition of a God-given bounty, one that ended a period of want. But outwardly, the Pilgrims were also paying homage to an earthly benefactor, the Patuxet (not Wampanoag) brave Squanto, who taught them how to catch eel and grow corn, and who, having learned English as a slave in Europe, served as an interpreter with the Native American community. It was widely accepted that without Squanto's help the Pilgrims might not have survived the New World.

Never becoming regular, subsequent celebrations depended on whether the year had a bountiful harvest or was prosperous; it could be held at any time of the year, even in July, and not just in the fall. On each of these occasions, there was no pious sobriety, solemnity, or heaven-directed gratitude to mark the Pilgrim holiday, only revelry, sports and feasts. The Pilgrims, despite their religiosity, did not intend it to be a day to formalize their thanks to God, but to celebrate the gathering of the harvest and generally to have fun. It must have been for this reason that the earliest writers on the subject—Edward Winslow in *Mourt's Relation* and William Bradford in *Of Plymouth Plantation*—described the event in full detail but never mentioned the word 'thanksgiving'.

Closer to our concept of a national thanksgiving holiday was the one set by the Continental Congress for Thursday, December 18, 1777, to celebrate the defeat of General Burgoyne at Saratoga. But it was a one-time affair, like the day of thanks George Washington proclaimed on Thursday, November 26, 1789 to celebrate the new Constitution. The idea of having a *regular* and *official* day of gratitude for the blessings of nationhood originated with Mrs. Sarah Joseph Hale, the editor of a popular women's magazine, whose tireless lobbying beginning in 1827 finally resulted in making it official under a Lincoln proclamation in 1863 and an act of Congress in 1941.

2. Fish is our Dish, but Dig that Pig

Myth! The first real Thanksgiving on American soil was a celebration a shipload of English settlers held in Virginia in 1619.

An earlier Thanksgiving celebration in America, one with a definite religious flavor, was not a harvest festival and neither was it Protestant-led. It was a Catholic mass that took place in San Elizario, a small New Mexican community near El Paso, in 1598—twenty-three years before the Pilgrims' festival. Don Juan de Oñate, a Spanish nobleman born in Mexico (and sometimes called 'the last conquistador'), had brought an expedition of 500 colonists and 7,000 heads of livestock from southern Chihuahua to their new settlement on the banks of the Rio Grande—nearly 350 miles of desert terrain—incidentally forging a trail now known to Americans and foreign tourists as El Camino Real. To celebrate the end of their exhausting journey, Señor Oñate sponsored a Thanksgiving Mass in a chapel that he had ordered constructed, capped by a public feast of fish, fowl and deer. Oñate also performed the ceremony of *La Toma* (Taking Possession), by which he claimed the new province for King Philip II of Spain.

Most lay and religious members of the Church regard the Oñate celebration as the first true Thanksgiving in what is now the US. Being Catholic, they are understandably pleased that it was not 'grimly Protestant', as is believed, and that the main dish it featured was not turkey but a Catholic staple—fish. But others of the US faithful don't share the same view, saying that no less than the Library of Congress has already given recognition to a similarly Catholic celebration held 57 years earlier in Texas at the behest of another Spanish conquistador. On Ascension Thursday in May 1541, after marching north from Mexico City in search of gold, Spanish explorer Francisco Vasquez de Coronado, with 1500 men and surrounded by friendly Teya Indians, heard an early morning Eucharistic mass at Palo Duro Canyon in the Texas panhandle. Although it was only in 1959 that the Texas Society

Daughters of the American Colonists began commemorating the event, there is no record of any other Thanksgiving celebration in US territory predating it. Devoid of all political and religious considerations, this was undoubtedly the first Thanksgiving held on American soil.

It would have been expected of John F. Kennedy, as the US' only Catholic president, to give the 1541 event the recognition it deserved. Instead, JFK gave the nod to a much later celebration that certain English (and presumably Protestant) settlers held in Virginia in 1619. In that year, 38 people on board the Margaret landed at the Berkeley Plantation on the James River under the patronage of a London company, which ordered them to commemorate the occasion with an annual day of Thanksgiving. The ship's captain, John Woodlief, offered a collective prayer and ordained that the day be "yearly and perpetually kept holy as a day of Thanksgiving to Almighty God."

Virginians had paid little attention to this occurrence until 1958, when they started an annual reenactment. More recently, they initiated a campaign for President George W. Bush to affirm Kennedy's imprimatur by granting a 'Presidential Pig Pardon', which would recognize Virginia as the venue of the first Thanksgiving and declare that ham, not turkey, was the main dish served on that occasion. Bush's term ended before he could act on the request, although many opine that he would have declined it anyway if he had a chance to do so. For one, Texas, site of the 1541 celebration, is Bush's home state, and for another, what occurred there happens to have the historical advantage over any other pretender. Also, by choosing a Catholic event over a Protestant one, Bush, a Methodist, would prove he was devoid of political and religious influence, in contrast to the 'injudiciousness' of fellow Republican Abe Lincoln, who revealed a certain Northern bias when he made the Pilgrim version official.

---

3. Food for the Gods

Myth! The Pilgrims had stuffed turkey and pumpkin pie for their first Thanksgiving dinner.

Mrs. Sarah Hale's first novel, *Northwood*, published in 1827, had an entire chapter devoted to a detailed description of a Thanksgiving dinner complete with stuffed turkey and pumpkin pie. As a result, these two items have become the traditional Thanksgiving fare of every American home.

There is no proof, however, that the intrepid crusader obtained her ideas for a Thanksgiving menu from a Pilgrim source. The Pilgrims' journals mentioned 'fowl' and 'deer', and contemporary writings included leeks, watercress, wild plums and dried berries. From these have been deduced ducks, geese, venison, seafood, vegetables, and dried fruits, as well as hasty pudding and popcorn. But turkey and pumpkin pie are nowhere indicated, and the consensus is that they were probably not served.

Researchers claim to have encountered the word 'wild Turkies' in early colonial writings, presuming this was in reference to the wild type of turkey that used to abound in the New World. But it could also have meant ducks, geese and members of the pheasant family. In the language of the seventeenth-century Pilgrims, a 'turkey' was any guinea fowl, that is, any bird with a featherless head, rounded body and dark feathers speckled white.

While stuffed turkey may still have been a possibility, it seems certain that no pumpkin pie, or any pie for that matter, was in the menu. The record showed that the Mayflower had by then run out of flour, and it was still many years before wheat would be successfully cultivated in New England. Without flour for a piecrust, there could be no pumpkin pie, although there could be pumpkin served as, say, a vegetable in boiled form.

4. Cabin Fever

Myth! The Pilgrims were the first to build log cabins in America.

The idea that the first colonists lived in log cabins or houses is firmly enshrined in American tradition, but it is fallacious. The earliest English colonists, including the New Amsterdam Dutch, the Pilgrims, the Puritans and the Founding Fathers, did not utilize this type of dwelling and probably didn't even know what it looked like. At the outset, they built temporary shelters, such as tents, Indian wigwams, and huts or cottages covered with bark, turf, or clay, after which they proceeded to construct the kind of habitation they had been used to in the home country—framed houses with thatched roofs.

Although perfectly suited to the American wilderness, the log cabin was never a part of American nascent history, which means that paintings of Pilgrims with muskets on shoulders, returning to these abodes after Thanksgiving dinner with the Indians, are bunk. It was only a century later, during the Revolutionary War, that log cabins became popular, spreading south and west. With the expansion and settling of the western lands, the crude but strong structure proved to be viable for frontier America. It could be built by only one man with nothing more than an axe, and provided good protection against the weather and Indian attack. Even then, it was not an original American creation nor was it used in the colonies for the first time. Virtually unknown in England, it was brought to Delaware in 1638 by Swedish settlers who claimed no kinship with the Pilgrims. The log cabin remained in the Delaware Valley until German immigrants introduced it independently into their own settlements in the latter half of the century.

---

5. Down the Primrose Path

Myth! The Puritans were notorious for their 'Sabatarian, antiliquor, and anti-sex attitudes'.

The Puritans were known in earlier times for their 'Sabatarian, antiliquor, and anti-sex attitudes', but the more open-minded assessment today is that they were really moderate. As one writer puts it, they were prone to 'enjoy life's many delights' yet quick to 'guard against its excessive pleasures'.

Puritan prudishness was a fabrication of 19th century historians, who showed Cromwell as old-maidish when in fact he was a patron of the arts and of athletic games, music and fast horses. Contrary to the myth, Puritans smoked, ate and drank heartily, and some of the most conservative ones owned extensive wine cellars and large collections of pipes and tobacco.

Puritanism considered intercourse within marriage a positive good, and even tolerated extra-marital relations to an extent, as in the practice of bundling. Sex was a public concern and was regularly discussed during meetings. In some ways Puritan families may have been even more open about sex than American families today. Children got plenty of sexual education because they slept in close proximity with their parents.

The strongest charge leveled against the Puritans—that they punished sex offenders brutally—is exaggerated. Most adulterers got off with just a whipping and a fine, and in all of 17th-century Massachusetts only three adulterers were ever put to death. Sodomy was usually punished with death, but rape, adultery, and fornication were pardonable. Although sexual offenders were more often than not ostracized, transgressors were generally allowed to continue to play a role in the community.

6. 'Zion in the Wilderness'

Myth! Pilgrims and Puritans alike joined in celebrating the 1621 harvest festival in Plymouth.

The colonists who came with the Arabella and settled in Salem in 1630 were Puritans, not Pilgrims. Most Americans today—including President Ronald Reagan—seem hard put to distinguish the Puritans from the Pilgrims, who arrived ten years earlier on the Mayflower to found Plymouth. Encyclopedias, artists and journalists don't make it easier and mix the two up all the time. One has only to see Thanksgiving posters showing Puritans instead of Pilgrims to realize that the confusion is quite real.

In fact, the Puritan John Winthrop, commander of the Arabella and the first governor of Massachusetts—but whom Reagan described as a Pilgrim Father—was a known Pilgrim-hater. Most Puritans didn't appreciate the Pilgrims (and vice-versa), much as the leftists and the rightists or the liberals and the conservatives today don't appreciate each other. Both the Puritans and the Pilgrims sailed to America principally to free themselves from religious restraints, but unlike the Pilgrims, the Puritans hoped by their example to reform the Church of England without having to

303

'separate' from it. Puritans who later espoused separatist causes were either corrected or expelled from the colony. According to the Britannica, the Puritan leaders never wanted their colony to be an outpost of tolerance in the New World; "rather, they intended it to be a 'Zion in the wilderness,' a model of purity and orthodoxy, with all backsliders subject to immediate correction."

7. Democrats, Autocrats and Other Crazies

Myth! The democratic ideal originated with the Puritans, who fled to the New World in pursuit of it.

That the democratic ideal originated with the Puritans is one of the mainsprings of American political thought, but it is terribly flawed. The Puritans may have shown themselves as democrats when they fled religious intolerance in England, but they just as readily proved unworthy of the brand upon landing in the New World. Says one historian: "The religious freedom they sought in the New World was for themselves only; it did not extend to those who disagreed with them."

Governor John Winthrop derided democracy as 'the meanest and worst of all forms of government', and put this belief into action by causing the expulsion of anyone who dared to challenge Puritan thinking. This highly influential Puritan leader is the best proof for the view that the American concept of democracy did not derive from the 17th-century Puritan doctrines of the New England fathers, but from the 18th-century Anglo-European climate of resistance to monarchy and the divine right of kings. Locke, Berkeley and Hume rather than Calvin and Knox provided the philosophical foundation for democracy, and its dynamic source was the American Revolution, not the landing at Massachusetts Bay. As aptly put: "It is quite impossible to imagine that the Declaration of Independence or the Constitution of the United States could ever have emerged from the royalist, theocratic, and authoritarian climate in which lived the actual Puritans ostensibly depicted in those Thanksgiving Day advertisements."

304

8. Any Color provided it's Black

Myth! The typical Pilgrim dressed conservatively in black, topped by a black conical hat for the male and a dainty white cap for the female.

Besides the log cabin, the other items most often identified with the Pilgrims' lifestyle are the black conical hat, the women's white caps, and the silver-buckled belts. But it seems the conical hat never existed in American culture, while the Pilgrims as a rule did not wear big silver buckles on their belts and the women were not always bonneted with dainty white caps. The one surviving portrait of a Pilgrim shows an Elizabethan gentleman who would no doubt have felt uneasy wearing silver buckles or a conical hat.

Like the Pilgrims, the Puritans have been painted as a somber group of self-effacing fundamentalists, and as a result the image of people dressed conservatively in black lingers in the public mind. But in truth, they liked bright colors. Nathaniel Hawthorne hinted as much when he bedecked many of his characters in rich garb, and even depicted Hester Prynne, his heroine in *The Scarlet Letter*, as one highly skilled in elaborate needlework. Some of the Puritans may have dressed habitually in black, but so too did a lot of non-Puritans, more for a social than a religious reason.

9. Pure as Snow but Cold as Ice

Myth! The American Puritan was more repressive and vicious than his English counterpart, particularly in the advocacy of Anglicanism.

False impressions about the Puritans abound. One is that, having come from England, they belonged to the Anglican Church and established an extension of it in the New World. Actually, the Puritans had no single church; each town in which they settled had its own church independently of the others. The Anglican Church became an established church in the southern colonies, but not in the northern ones dominated by the Puritans. These émigrés came in many shades of belief and did not represent a party or creed in the strictest sense, becoming identifiable as a group only out of their common desire to 'purify' their respective churches of their 'papist' or 'Romish' practices.

The belief that the American Puritan was more repressive and vicious than his English counterpart is also highly disputable. Only 20 persons were hanged in Salem in 1692, whereas one English witch-hunter alone notched 300 hangings in two years (1645-47). And while four Quakers were executed in Boston, 3,000 dissidents died in prison under Elizabeth I.

Finally, there is the myth that the Puritans chose to settle exclusively in New England because they liked the cold weather, which gave them pleasure to endure it. This is controverted by the simple fact that of the 75,000 Puritans who migrated between 1629 and 1640, most established themselves in warm-weather communities: 35,000 to the West Indies, 3,000 to Bermuda, and 8,000 to Virginia. Only 14,000 decided to stay in Massachusetts.

VI

Bucks To Bucks

On Peter Minuit and New York City

"Hoeveel van
deze God verzaakt plaats?"

•

Peter Minuit

1. Island in the Stream

Myth! Manhattan is the only island borough of New York City that's entirely cut off from the mainland.

Non-Americans who have only a vague impression of New York City's geography think Manhattan is an island borough that's *entirely* cut off from the mainland. Actually, Richmond, which is co-extensive with Staten Island, is the only one that can be called that. Surprisingly, Manhattan does not qualify as an island, and neither do two other boroughs, Queens and Brooklyn, though both are on Long Island and are not part of the mainland.

Those who maintain that Manhattan is entirely separated by water from the North American continent do not readily notice that a piece of it, called Marble Hill, sits on the U.S. mainland. Marble Hill is a quiet fifty-two-acre neighborhood that's geographically part of the Bronx and whose only connection to Manhattan Island is a bridge over the Harlem River. It was, until 1895, physically integrated with Manhattan and separated from the Bronx by a shallow stream called Spuyten Duyvil Creek. When the Harlem Ship Canal was dug that year—a 400' x 15' channel blasted out of solid rock—Marble Hill was entirely severed from the rest of Manhattan. Later the creek was filled in, welding the neighborhood to the Bronx and forever to the U.S. mainland.

2. Baghdad Underground

Myth! The foreign city most likened to Manhattan is Baghdad.

Manhattan is the setting of several famous short stories written by O. Henry, whose hallmarks are the ironic coincidence and the surprise ending.

In these stories, the author, whose real name is William Sydney Porter (1862-1910), often referred to Manhattan as 'Baghdad-on-the-Subway' and to everyday New Yorkers as 'the four million' (the city's population at the time). There was never any physical resemblance between the two cities, but Baghdad (or Bagdad), the capital of Iraq, was once the home of eminent scholars and artists, as Manhattan reputedly was in O. Henry's day. Also, like the ironic coincidence that usually caps a O. Henry story, recent events have made apparent the strong geopolitical connection between New York and Baghdad: Manhattan's symbolic Twin Towers became a prime target for terrorists from Baghdad's part of the world (reportedly in retaliation for the First Gulf War), and Iraq was forcibly occupied by American forces (possibly in retaliation for the Twin Towers attack).

With the emergence of China as the second largest economy after the US, the Baghdad comparison has been discarded in favor of a China link that gives Manhattan the new soubriquet 'Shanghai-on-the-Hudson.' The rather unromantic and casual reason is that NYC and Shanghai are the most populous cities in their respective hemispheres. At other times, New York suffers the nickname 'the Calcutta of the West' because the extremes of poverty and wealth on the island—'from ghastly slum to tycoon luxury'—are claimed to be on an almost equal scale with those of India's tatterdemalion metropolis. A rather unfair metaphor, perhaps, considering the greater number of homeless in San Francisco and the more expansive poverty in Chicago or Washington, DC.

---

3. Cheap Town, New York Is

Myth! The Dutch purchased Manhattan from the Indians for $24 worth of beads and cash.

The dollar was not in use in 1624, and wouldn't be for another one hundred fifty years; in fact, money in general was not yet in vogue. But that year, Peter Minuit executed a deed of purchase for Manhattan island that many history books say cost him less than today's hourly rate for most casino workers in Native American reservations—a meager $24 for the entire length and breadth of the famous New York City borough!

If you want to find out the true worth of those $24 today, consider that on August 21, 1625, the daily wage of a special clerk in Southampton, England, was 13 pence. Applying some fancy arithmetic involving cost indices and currency conversions, you should be getting a figure ranging from Cecil Adam's $72 to James W. Loewen's $4,800. In between is Russell Bailyn's estimate of $600. It's still a niggardly amount by any standard.

The acquisition was from local Indians, who accepted payment in the form of two boxes containing an unknown quantity of cloth, trinkets, metal pots and hatchets. According to writings since the mid-1840s and famous paintings of the event (see, e.g., Alfred Douglas' *Purchase of Manhattan Island by Peter Minuit*, 1626), the assortment included beads as well. However, although certain beads called 'wampum' were a favored medium of exchange by the colonists, experts argue that there's absolutely no evidence to prove that New York's first documented real estate deal was financed with beads.

Beads or no beads, nobody really knew the dollar worth of the goodies, for it was only in the 1840s that a New York newspaper writer began to make an effort at calculation. The amount of $24 was arrived at notwithstanding that the transaction occurred two hundred years earlier and no list was ever made by the Dutch of the specific items traded. Coincidentally, the estimate fell in line with the earlier tradition that valued the whole lot at roughly 60 Dutch guilders, or 2,400 English cents.

---

4. Indian Giver

Myth! The purchase price for Manhattan was paid to the Canarsee Indian Tribe as the traditional owner of the island.

The price estimate of $24 has been readily assimilated in popular history and has persisted to this day as the value of the greatest real estate bargain ever. But, as it turned out, it wasn't really a bargain. Minuit would learn too late that he had paid the wrong tribe of Indians, the Canarsees, who were native to Brooklyn and did not own a single square inch of Manhattan. Most of the island belonged to the Weckquaesgeeks, who continued to live on parts of it and were so angered at being left out of the deal that they warred sporadically with the Dutch for years.

We are told that, in the interests of peace, the Dutch finally agreed to pay for Manhattan again, at a price that, though still unstated, was probably more realistic than the value of the trifles paid the first time. Other historians dispute this, however, saying that from the very start, the Weckquaesgeeks refused to negotiate away their birthright. Instead of making an offer, the Dutch "waited as a series of inter-Indian wars, some instigated by (them), and a series of epidemics weakened the Weckquaesgeeks...(t)hen in the 1640s, with the aid of the Canarsees and other Native Americans on Long Island, the Dutch eliminated most of the Weckquaesgeeks." That is to say, far from legitimizing the Minuit deal, the Dutch simply reinforced their presence on Manhattan Island through the usual mode of colonization—conquest.

Assuming a new deed was forced on the losing Weckquaesgeeks and a tribute paid to them to salve their wounds, this would have meant little to either side. The Indians had no real understanding of the concept of private land ownership, much less of the legal nature of possession and the negotiability of real estate. The Dutch, on the other hand, couldn't care less if their acquisition of Manhattan was valid or not as long as they were able to put up stakes in the New World—and show off their colonizing prowess to their European neighbors—in the quietest possible way.

For his efforts, Peter Minuit's countrymen honored him with a monument that they donated to the City of New York in 1926. Located inside Battery Park in lower Manhattan, it consists of a huge flagpole at the base of which is a bas-relief depicting Minuit's meeting with the Canarsees. The caption reads as follows: "The purchase of the island of Manhattan was accomplished in 1626. Thus was laid the foundation of the City of New York."

5. Queens' Bureau

Myth! Queens is the only New York City borough named for a group of persons.

While the common impression is that the name Queens refers to a group of queens, in fact it refers to only one, Catherine of

Braganza, consort of Charles II.

Another borough of New York City—the Bronx—is just the opposite: the name is popularly believed to be singular, but in reality it is plural. It refers to the Broncks (or Bronks), a wealthy clan headed by Jonas Bronck, who settled in that area of New York in the 19th century. Jonas claimed 500 acres north of the Harlem River in 1639, and promptly affixed his surname to various features of the local geography, notably the Aquahung River, which became the Bronx River. Later on, that part of Westchester County bordered on the east by the Bronx River was appended to New York City, and became known as the Borough of the Bronx. The intention was probably to call these places Bronck's river and the Borough of Bronck's, but as with Queens (which used to be the Queen's Borough), the Dutch removed the apostrophe to show their dislike for the progressive case. They then fused the 'k' and 's' together and transformed the result into their phonetic equivalent 'x'. The article 'the' became convenient when Bronx, no longer a possessive name, remained appended to 'river' and other place nouns, and began to allude to the whole clan instead of just their founder.

6. We'll Take Manhattan

Myth! **After purchasing Manhattan, the Dutch gave it the name Gotham.**

Batman's beloved Gotham City, a cartoon rendition of a US crime-ridden metropolis, is not as fictitious as most people think it is. Even the least informed of Bob Kane's fans realize that the real-life model is New York City, and that it wasn't Kane who invented it. Because the word has a decidedly Dutch ring to it, some people think Minuit might have coined the word and used it as a veiled reference to Manhattan.

In fact, it was the American writer Washington Irving, of British-Dutch descent, who first applied the word Gotham to New York City in a letter of February 13, 1807 to the *Salmagundi Papers*. According to some of his biographers, Irving gave the name because he thought New Yorkers were pretentious and silly, and deserved to be called "Gothamites," after the legendary Three

312

Wise Men of Gotham who went to sea in a tub. In another version, the name meant 'the hamlet of the Goths', to satirize New York as a haven of barbarians.

What is most likely is that Irving borrowed the name from another Gotham of history, a village in southern England dating back to the reign of King John in the 12th century. Irving was evidently impressed by the legend of this village and saw an allegorical relevance to New York and its inhabitants. As the story goes, the villagers were faced with the prospect of a visit from the king, who was planning to establish a hunting lodge near their Nottinghamshire site. Fearing this would mean higher taxes and other stringent measures, and to avoid the heavy expense of entertaining John and his court on their sojourns, they all feigned lunacy according to a preconceived plan. It is said that the king's messengers, on seeing the residents, reported the spot unsuitable for sane people to inhabit.

What could have been a Minuit coinage was the name Manhattan itself. Both Encarta and Wikipedia believe Manhattan is Dutch patois for 'hilly Island' (*manah* 'island' and *atin* 'hill'). On the other hand, the American Heritage Dictionary of the English Language (4th edition) traces the word to Manna-hatta, the name of the American Indian tribe from which 'Peter Minuit of the Dutch West Indies Company bought the island in 1626'. Quite possibly, Minuit christened what he saw was a 'hilly island,' then attached the name Manhattan to the place as well as to one of the Indian tribes living there. This doesn't change the fact, however, that Minuit transacted his business with the Canarsees and the Weckquaesgeeks, neither of which seemed to be related to the Indian tribe called Manhattans (or Manna-hattas).

7. Gators in the Gutters

Myth! New York City's sewers are infested with alligators.

Misconceptions about Manhattan would be unadventurous reading without mentioning the now famous whopper about alligators thriving in the city's sewers. The matter has become a serious talking point ever since the staid New York *Times* reported a sighting of the reptiles at the unlikely location in February of 1935. In that occurrence, several boys shoveling snow into an open manhole saw an alligator and pulled it out of the sewer below.

In fairness to the Times, of their many reports about alligator sightings in and around New York City, this has been the only one that places the occurrence in a sewer. Unfortunately, the report was given more credence than it deserved when long-time NY maintenance supervisor (not Commissioner) of sewers Teddy May recounted that in the same year, he and his men hunted and killed 73 alligators ranging in size from 2 ft. to 5 ft. over a period of several weeks.

Writing about May's 'achievement' in his book *The World Beneath the City* (1959), sports reporter Robert Daley readily assumed that the saurians were introduced into the system by returning New York residents who brought the pets from Florida and, becoming wary of their continued presence in their houses, dumped them down the lavatory. Thomas Pynchon's 1963 novel *V* embellished the legend further with the detail that the creatures turned blind and albino from their life of darkness in the sewers, and grew to monstrous size on their diet of rats.

There has never been any official confirmation of the 1935 sightings, and even Teddy May's role as superintendent of New York City sewers appears to have been hyped. May has been described as a long-time hands-on worker for the New York sewer system, but the real story is that he rose no higher than foreman. As his own fans admit, the only things that made up for his limited education and unlikeable personality were his colorful grammar and a highly fertile imagination. Anent the latter, May claimed to have salvaged a $25,000 ring lost by General Grant's daughter, as well as incriminating evidence against notorious gang lords, from the murky underground waters of New York City.

Blog gossip (e.g., on October 12, 2008, "an 8 ft. alligator that had been reported for months was finally caught and removed from the New York Sewer System near Central Park") is now part of the stuff that keeps the urban legend going. Like others of its kind, the legend is likely to persist in spite of assurances by responsible NYC officials that neither tail nor snout of the animal has ever been spotted (officially, that is) in the sewers, and of expert findings that alligators can only survive and reproduce in a warm environment such as Florida's.

314

❄○❄

LIST OF TOPICS IN THIS VOLUME

KINGS, EMPERORS & DICTATORS

Roman Scandals
Persecution Complex
Days of the Living Dead
Beastly Behavior
Fiddling with Fire
The Winter before the Fall
Phantom Empire
They ate Horses, didn't They?
City on the Edge of Forever
Naying in a Hoarse Voice
Bloody Mama

Cut Out To Be Somebody
Unnatural Born Roman
After July Comes August
Latin 101 ca 47 BC
Caesar's Place was no Caesar's Palace
A Roman Head with no Heir?
Triangle with an Angle
Killing Time in the Capitol
You too, you Brute?
The Day his Number Came Up
Guilty by Suspicion
Bang the War Drums Softly
Tripping in Africa

Lion Heart Or Lying Heart?
Trading Places
Looking for Richard
Mismanagement by Proxy
Brother John hates Brother Hood
The King had a Weak Constitution

Kings' Row

Post-marital Syndrome
Humpty Dumpty Sat on a Throne
The Spider's Stratagem
Oxford Don Alfredo
These Kings' English was German
A Not so Great Dane
Presumptuous Air
By Love Dispossessed
His Own King's Counsel
King Leer
Wales in the Knight

Louie Louie, Louie Louie

Marie Quite Contrarie
The Red and the Gray
Stealing a March
State Deportment
Apocalypse Now!
End of the Line
Masked Marvel
Louis-Philippe's Fillip
A Mass to Win the Masses

Personality Complex Or Complex Personality?

Mens Sana in Corporal Sano
The Corsican Father
A Political Stunt?
The Emperor's Old Groove
Not Feeling Nappy Tonight
The Taste is Napoleon, But...
Ants in his Pants or Pest in his Vest?
Cold Napoleon
Short Nap not Agreeable to Pope
Sneezing the Life out of his Prisoners?
Ruling with an Iron Duke
Who Else was in the 'Loo?
Killing Room
The Knight who Hated Black Mail
Club Wellington 1, Team Napoleon 0
Carved with Pride

317

Queen Creole
'Able was I ere I Saw Elba'
French Spirit
Only the Sphinx Knows

The Hand That Rocked The World

Self-made German
Portrait of the Nazi as a Painter
Heil Schicklgruber!
The Fuehrer had a Ball
Like Kissing Hitler
Chief Execution Officer
Morpheus Ascending
From Hynkel to Hister
Ice in his Veins and Malice in his Heart
Fahrenheit 1938
New Twist on an Old Symbol
A Reich Staged Fire
Heil to the Dark Chief
No Fences Tempt Bad Neighbors
Black God, White Devil
Mutant Ideology
Christian Heart
One-Step Victory
Child of the Damned
Nutsy Nazi

Majorities Of One

Alexander's Wartime Bent
The Last Days of Shahdom
Wise as an Owl, Poor as a Dormouse
The Bad, the Good and the Bohemian
Buttons and Bows
Gay Warriors
Straddler on a Horse
The Man from Five Corners
The Iron Giant
Mummy's Boy
Frankly Franco
The Duke of Railroads

318

FOUNDING FATHERS, US PRESIDENTS & BRITISH PMS

By George He Did It!?
The Lost Days of Youth
The Politician in Washington
George Makes a Pitch
Two Rivers Ran Through It
A Lot of Weemsy
Washington Confidential
Dollar Economy
When Push comes to Pull
This Washington Bridge was all Wood
When Washington was in New York
Plain Ole George
Unfounded Fatherhood
Between Washington and Cleveland
The Ninth Configuration
Surrender by Proxy
Goodbye, Columbia
Putting on a Cold Front
Pater Primus
What'd You do During the War, Mr. President?

All About Abe
Harps and Mauls
Man of the Prairie
His Old Kentucky Home
Would You Buy a Lincoln from this Man?
Lincoln's Lost Love Letters
Honest to God
Northern Mind, Southern Heart
Abecedarian Abe
What Counts is Winning What Counts
Addressing an Envelope
Debatable Results
By, For and Of the Majority
Nobody's Fool
More Lincolnesque than Lincoln

A Double's Jeopardy
Multiplier Effect
Letter to an Unknown Woman
Obits and Hearses
Bearded in his Den
The Second Guest was Second Guessed
Against all Flogs
John: 1838
The Army Saves Face—and a Life
Mine, Yours and Ours

The Life And Times Of Hardy Andy
Born in the USA
Taming the Great Beast
Politics is Division
A Degree of Literacy
Presidential 'Seel of Aproval'
Cabin on the Sea
Rachel Getting Married—Again
Cotton Wall Jackson

Tommy Knocking Tales
Uncle Tom in the White House
Slave to his Affection
Only on Paper
The Autocrat as a Liberal
Incredibly Edible
The Elephant that Morphed into an Ass
Granite Mountain Men
Security Counsel
Jeffersonian Economics
Draftsman's Contract

Some Founded, Others Foundered
The Trouble with Harry
Pass Before you Kick
Not Worth a Guinness
The General gets Brassed off
Big Trouble in Little Rock
Good Night, Vietnam
The Little Boat that Couldn't

The Eagle Spreads its Wings
Still Voices, Distant Lives
President for a Day
When Jack went Hog Wild
The Great Silence

Buttling For The State
Winnie the Pooh-Poohed
Unrequited Toll
A Few Good Men
No Peace in Appeasement
Better Diseased than Deceased?
Lord of his Peers
No Picnic for a Peacenik
Curtain Call
Sign of Five
The Lie about the Lie
Altered Echo
Three-Headed Dog of War
Sounds Good like Winston Should

QUEENS, GRAND DAMES & HEROINES

In Praise Of Famous Women
Maid of Honor
Minute Maid
A Total Lack of Sense
Born to Kill
Night Walker with a Lamp
In Pursuit of a Foggy Notion
Freedom Rides the Rails
People Movers
The President's (a) Lady
Flawed Gam
Women Under the Influence
Angel of Mercy
I am Siam

Queen's Gambit Declined
Suicide Redux

Banged-up Nile Blonde
Death at First Bite?
A Nose for Intrigue
Fabulously Stoned
Egyptian Needlework
Angles and Incest
Mistress of Foreign Affairs

Queen Bees
Villages of Illusion
Just Horsing Around
The Cakes that Ate Paris
Queen Bitch
The Prince who was a Prig
Bloody Legacy
No Sense of Rumor
Cloak and Swagger
Blood Lust
Out of the Closet and Off the Throne
Stranger in the House
Miss Liz Loveless
Designing Woman

High-Heeled Treason
The Woman with One False Leg
Dutch Treatment
Fashion for Execution
Voices of Treason
Ringing Out the Dead
Sisters Under the Skin

EXPLORERS, DISCOVERERS & PIONEERS

A Traveler's Tale
The Man who Played Polo
Touring on a Persian Carpet
One for the Road
In Xanadu did Kubla Khan
Every Which Way but East
Monster from Outer Space?

The Sailor Who Fell From Grace With The Seers
A Continental Op
Asking for a Wide Berth
Alias Colombo
The Christ in Christopher
The Sainted and the Painted
Romancing her Stones
New World Revisited
The Logic of the Log
Colonial Mentality
An Italian Job
Dreamland Chronicles
Bluffing with Four of a Kind
Land's Sake
Moonlighting on the Main

From Columbus Circle To The Strait Of Magellan
Coming Full Circle
By the Time they Got to Phoenicia
The Hazards of Ocean Racing
First to Go Down Under
John Juan Giovanni
Sir cum Navigator
California Suite
Polar Wandering
The Englishman who Went Dutch
Green Fields of Ice

A Rock Bound Pilgrimage
Plymouth-to-Plymouth Resuscitation
Landing a Delicate Craft
Soil Kissing
Welcome as the Flowers in May
Fellow Travelers on the Mayflower?
Lost in America
Secret of the Trunk
Dated Artifact
Leif in Minnesota
Born on the Fourth of July
Meeting Bob & Carol & Ted & Alice

An Undeserved Boone
Along Tobacco Road
English Daughters and Dutch Uncles

Pilgrims' Progress
A Thanksgiving Story
Fish is our Dish, but Dig that Pig
Food for the Gods
Cabin Fever
Down the Primrose Path
'Zion in the Wilderness'
Democrats, Autocrats and other Crazies
Any Color provided it's Black
Pure as Snow and Cold as Ice

Bucks To Bucks
Island in the Stream
Baghdad Underground
Cheap Town, New York is
Indian Giver
Queens' Bureau
We'll Take Manhattan
Gators in the Gutters

SELECTED READINGS

Adams, Cecil, *The Straight Dope*, New York: Ballantine Books, 1986

Adams, Cecil, *More on the Straight Dope*, New York: Ballantine Books, 1988

Agel, Jerome and Glanze, Walter D., *Cleopatra's Nose, The Twinkie Defense, & 1500 Other Verbal Shortcuts in Popular Parlance*, New York: Prentice Hall Press, 1990

Alterman, Eric, *When Presidents Lie*, London: Penguin Books, 2004

Aron, Paul, *Unsolved Mysteries of History*, New York: Barnes & Noble Books, 2000

Aron, Paul, *More Unsolved Mysteries of History*, New York: Barnes & Noble, 2004

Aron, Paul, *Did Babe Ruth Call His Shot?*, New Jersey: John Wiley & Sons, 2005

Barham, Andrea, *The Pedant's Return*, New York: Bantam Books, 2006

Barthel, Manfred (translated by Howson, Mark), *What the Bible Really Says*, New York: Wings Books, 1992

Battle, Kemp P., *Great American Folklore*, New York: Barnes and Noble, 1992

Boardman, Barrington, *Flappers, Bootleggers, "Typhoid Mary" & the Bomb*, New York: Harper & Row, 1968

Boller, Jr., Paul F., *Presidential Anecdotes*, New York: Penguin Books, 1981

Boller, Jr., Paul F. and Davis, Ronald L., *Hollywood Anecdotes*, New York: William Morrow, 1987

Boller, Jr., Paul F. and George, John, *They Never Said It*, New York: Oxford University Press, 1990

Boller, Jr., Paul F., *Not So!*, New York: Oxford University Press, 1995

Boorstin, Daniel J., *The Discoverers*, New York: Random House, 1983

Boorstin, Daniel J., *The Creators*, New York: Random House, 1992

Breuer, William B., *Daring Missions of World War II*, New Jersey: Castle Books, 2001

Breuer, William B., *Deceptions of World War II*, New Jersey: Castle Books, 2001

Brokaw, Tom, *The Greatest Generation*, New York: Random House, 1998

Brown, Anthony Cave, *Bodyguard of Lies*, London: W. H. Allen & Co. Ltd., 1977

Brown, Peter H. and Pinkston, Jim, *Oscar Dearest*, New York: Harper & Row, 1987

Botting, Douglas & the Editors of Time-Life Books, *The Pirates*,

Virginia: Time-Life Books, 1978

Bullis, Don, *The Old West Trivia Book*, California: Gem Guides Book Company, 1993

Carnes, Mark C. (ed.), *Past Imperfect*, New York: Henry Holt and Company, 1996

Cole, Sylvia & Lass, Abraham H., *The Dictionary of 20th-Century Allusions*, New York: Ballantine Books, 1991

Cowley, Robert (ed.), *What Ifs? Of American History*, New York: G.P. Putnam's Sons, 2003

Craughwell, Thomas J., *Urban Legends*, New York: Barnes & Noble, 2000

Crofton, Ian, *Brewer's Cabinet Of Curiosities*, London: Weidenfeld & Nicolson, 2006

Davis, Kenneth C., *Don't Know Much About History*, New York: Avon Books, 1992

Davis, Kenneth C., *Don't Know Much About Geography*, New York: Avon Books, 1993

Davis, Kenneth C., *Don't Know Much About Mythology*, New York: Harper, 2005

Davis, Kenneth C., *Don't Know Much About World Myths*, New York: HarperCollins, 2005

Davis, Kenneth C., *Don't Know Much About Anything*, New York: Harper, 2007

Del Re, Gerard & Patricia, *History's Last Stand*, New York: Avon Books, 1993

Dickson, Paul & Goulden, Joseph C., *Myth-Informed*, New York: Putnam Publishing, 1993

Diefendorf, David, *Amazing...But False!*, New York: Sterling, 2007

Donald, David Herbert, *Lincoln*, London: Jonathan Cape, 1995

Durant, Will, *Caesar and Christ*, New York: Simon and Schuster, 1944

Durant, Will, *The Age of Faith*, New York: Simon and Schuster, 1950

Durschmied, Erik, *How Chance And Stupidity Have Changed History*, New York: MJF Books, 1999

Eastman, John, *Retakes*, New York: Ballantine Books, 1989

Editors of Time-Life Books, The, *Visions and Prophecies*, Virginia: Time-Life Books, 1988

Editors of Time-Life Books, The, *Feats and Wisdom of the Ancients*, Virginia: Time-Life Books, 1990

Evans, Harold, *They Made America*, New York: Back Bay Books, 2004

Evans, Ivor H., *Brewer's Dictionary of Phrase and Fable*, New York: HarperCollins, 1991

Farquhar, Michael, *A Treasury of Deception*, New York: Penguin, 2005

Farquhar, Michael, *A Treasury Of Foolishly Forgotten Americans*, New York: Penguin, 2008

Feldman, David, *Why Do Pirates Love Parrots*, New York: Collins,

2007

Filler, Louis, *The Muckrakers*, Chicago: Henry Regnery Company, 1968

Flexner, Stuart Berg, *Listening to America*, New York: Simon & Schuster, 1982

Flexner, Stuart and Doris, *The Pessimist's Guide to History*, New York: HarperCollins, 2000

Fox, Robin Lane, *The Unauthorized Version*, New York: Vintage Books, 1993

Funk, Charles Earle, *Thereby Hangs A Tale*, New York: Harper & Row, 1985

Gardner, Martin, *The Magic Numbers of Dr. Matrix*, New York: Dorset Press, 1990

Gardner, Martin, *Science Good, Bad and Bogus*, Buffalo: Prometheus Books, 1989

Garrison, Webb, *Behind the Headlines*, Harrisburg: Stackpole Books, 1983

Garrison, Webb, *A Treasury of White House Tales*, Nashville: Rutledge Hill Press, 1996

Gentry, Curt, *J. Edgar Hoover*, New York: W.W. Norton & Co., 1991

Goldberg, M. Hirsch, *The Book of Lies*, New York: Quill / William Morrow, 1990

Gore, Chris, *The 50 Greatest Movies Never Made*, New York: St. Martin's Griffin, 1999

Gottlieb, Agnes Hooper et al., *1000 Years, 1000 People,* New York: Barnes & Noble, 199

Graham, Lloyd M., *Deceptions and Myths of the Bible*, New York: Citadel Press, 1975

Greenberg, Gary, *101 Myths of the Bible,* New York: Barnes & Noble, 2000

Greig, Charlotte, *Conspiracy,* New York: Barnes & Noble, 2003

Gribbin, John, *The Scientists,* New York: Random House, 2002

Griffin, Lynne & McCann, Kelly, *The Book of Women*, Maine: Bob Adams, 1992

Haining, Peter, ed., *A Sherlock Holmes Companion*, New York: Barnes & Noble, 1994

Hamilton, Edith , *Mythology*, Boston: Little, Brown and Co., 1942

Handford, S.A. (transl.), *The Fables of Aesop*, London: Penguin Books, 1964

Hardwick, Michael, *The Complete Guide to Sherlock Holmes*, New York: St. Martin's Press, 1986

Hay, Peter, *Movie Anecdotes*, New York: Oxford University Press, 1990

Haycraft, Howard (ed.), *The Art of the Mystery Story*, New York: Grosset & Dunlap, 1946

Haycraft, Howard, *Murder for Pleasure*, New York: Carroll & Graf Publishers: 1984

Hayward, James, *Myths & Legends of the Second World War*, Stroud, Sutton Publishing, 2003

Hendrickson, Robert, *World Literary Anecdotes*, New York: Facts on File, 1990

Hendrickson, Robert, *American Literary Anecdotes*, New York: Facts on File, 1990

Hendrickson, Robert, *British Literary Anecdotes*, New York: Facts on File, 1990

Herbert, A. P., *Uncommon Law*, London: Methuen & Co., 1964

Hersch, Hank and Bechtel, Mark, *Classic Rivalries*, New York: Sports Illustrated Books, 2003

Holden, Anthony, *Behind the Oscar*, New York: Plume, 1993

Holland, Barbara, *Hail to the Chiefs*, New York: Ballantine Books, 1990

Holt, Patricia Lee, *George Washington Had No Middle Name*, New Jersey: Citadel Press, 1988

Innes, Brian, *Fakes & Forgeries*, New York: Reader's Digest, 2005

Isaacson, Walter, *Pro & Con*, New York: G. P. Putnam's Sons: 1983

Jackson, Robert, *Unexplained Mysteries of World War II*, New York: Gallery Books, 1991

Jeffers, H. Paul, *History's Greatest Conspiracies*, New York: Barnes & Noble, 2004

Jennings, Peter & Brewster, Todd, *In Search of America*, New York: Hyperion, 2002

Johnsen, Ferris, *The Encyclopedia of Popular Misconceptions*, New York: Carol Publishing, 1994

Johnson, Paul, *Modern Times*, New York: Harper Collins, 1991

Jones, Judy and Wilson, William, *An Incomplete Education*, New York: Ballantine Books, 1987

Kahn, David, *The Code-Breakers*, London: Weidenfeld and Nicolson, 1967

Kerr, Philip, ed., *The Penguin Book of Lies*, London: Viking Press, 1990

Keyes, Ralph, *"Nice Guys Finish Seventh,"* New York: Harper Perennial, 1993

Kick, Russ, *You Are Being Lied To*, New York: MJF Books, 2001

Kick, Russ, *Everything You Know Is Wrong*, New York: Barnes & Noble Books, 2002

Lane, Sheldon, ed., *For Bond Lovers Only*, New York: Dell Publishing, 1965

Lass, Abraham H., Kiremidjian, David & Goldstein, Ruth M., *Dictionary of Classical, Biblical, & Literary Allusions*, New York: Ballantine Books, 1988

Leighton, Isabel, ed., *The Aspirin Age, 1919-1941*, New York: Simon and Schuster, 1965

Lindskoog, Kathryn, *Fakes, Frauds & Other Malarkey*, Grand Rapids: Zondervan Publishing House, 1993

Llewellyn, Sam, *Small Parts In History*, New York: Barnes & Noble, 1992

Lloyd, John & Mitchinson, John, *The Book Of General Ignorance*, New York: Harmony Books, 2006

Loewen, James, *Lies My Teacher Told Me*, New York: Simon & Schuster, 1995

Loewen, James, *Lies Across America*, New York: Touchstone, 1999

Lorie, Peter, *Superstitions*, New York: Simon & Schuster, 1992

Macrone, Michael, *By Jove!*, New York: HarperCollins, 1992

Macrone, Michael, *Brush Up Your Shakespeare!*, New York: Harper Collins, 1990

Magee, Bryan, *The Story Of Philosophy*, New York: Barnes & Noble, 2006

Manser, Martin, *Melba Toast, Bowie's Knife & Caesar's Wife*, New York: Avon Books, 1990

Matthews, John, *Pirates*, London: Carlton Books, 2006

McCullough, David, *Truman*, New York: Simon & Schuster, 1992

Montagu, Ashley and Darling, Edward, *The Prevalence of Nonsense*, New York: Dell, 1969

Moore, Laurence, *Lightning Never Strikes Twice*, New York: Avon Books, 1994

Morrow, Ed, *The Grim Reaper's Book of Days*, New York: Carol Publishing Group, 1992

Most, Glenn W. and Stowe, William W. (eds.), *The Poetics of Murder*, New York: Harcourt Brace, 1983

Nash, J. Robert, *Darkest Hours*, New York: Simon & Schuster, 1977

National Insecurity Council, The, *It's A Conspiracy!*, Berkeley: Earth Works Press, 1992

Opie, Iona & Peter, *Classic Fairy Tales*, New York: Oxford University Press, 1980

Page, Michael & Ingpen, Robert, *The Time-Life Encyclopedia of Things That Never Were*, Virginia: Time-Life Books, 1988

Panati, Charles, *Panati's Extraordinary Origins of Everyday Things*, New York: Harper & Row, 1989

Panati, Charles, *Sacred Origins Of Profound Things*, New York: Penguin, 1996

Pappas, Theoni, *The Joy of Mathematics*, California: Wide World Publishing / Tetra, 1989

Pappas, Theoni, *Mathematical Scandals*, California: Wide World Publishing/Tetra, 1997

Pearson, John, *James Bond*, London: Colins Publishing, 1986

Perkes, Dan, *Eyewitness to Disaster*, New York: Gallery Books, 1985

Platnick, Kenneth B., *Great Mysteries of History*, New York: Dorset Press, 1987

Poirier, René (transl. by Crosland, Margaret), *Engineering Wonders of*

329

the World, New York: Barnes & Noble, 1993
Poundstone, William, *Big Secrets*, New York: Quill, 1983
Poundstone, William, *Bigger Secrets*, Boston: Houghton Mifflin
Company, 1986
Poundstone, William, *Biggest Secrets*, New York: William Morrow &
Co,. 1993
Powell, Michael, *Forbidden Knowledge*, Massachusetts: Adams Media,
2007
Randi, James, *Flim-Flam!*, New York: Prometheus, 1982
Rawson, Hugh, *Devious Derivations*, New York: Crown Publishers,
1994
Reader's Digest, The, *Great Cases of Interpol*, Hong Kong: Reader's
Digest, 1982
Reader's Digest, The, *Facts & Fallacies*, New York: The Reader's Digest
Association, 1988
Rees, Nigel, *The Nigel Rees Book of Slogans & Catchphrases*, London,
Unwin Paperbacks, 1984
Rees, Nigel, *A Word in your Shell-like, London: Trafalgar Square, 2007*
Roberts, Andrew (ed.), *What Might Have Been,* London: Phoenix, 2005
Robertson, Patrick, *The Guinness Book of Movie Facts & Feats,* New
York: Abbeville Press, 1991
Rogers, Tom, *Insultingly Stupid Movie Physics,* Naperville: Sourcebooks
Hysteria, 2007
Rosenbaum, Ron, *Travels with Dr. Death,* New York: Penguin Books,
1991
Rosenberg, Bernard & White, David Manning, eds., *Mass Culture: The
Popular Arts in America*, London: Collier-Macmillan, 1964
Rowan, Richard Wilmer, *33 Centuries of Espionage*, New York:
Hawthorn Books, 1967
Rowse, A. L., *William Shakespeare*, New York: Harper & Row, 1963
Sanders, Dennis & Lovallo, Len, *The Agatha Christie Companion*, New
York: Berkley Books, 1989
Sanello, Frank, *Reel v. Real,* New York: Taylor Trade Publishing, 2003
Shenkman, Richard & Reiger, Kurt, *One-Night Stands with American
History*, New York: Quill, 1982
Shenkman, Richard, *Legends, Lies & Cherished Myths of American
History*, New York: Harper & Row, 1988
Shenkman, Richard, *Legends, Lies & Cherished Myths of World History*,
New York: Harper Collins, 1993
Shirer, William L., *The Rise and Fall of the Third Reich*, New York:
Exeter Books, 1987
Stewart, Desmond and the Time-Life Editors, *Early Islam*, New York:
Time-Life Books, 1972
Tamarkin, Bob, *Rumor Has It,* New York: Prentice Hall, 1993
Thornton, Willis, *History: Fact & Fable*, New York: Dorset Press, 1992

Tiballs, Geof, *The Olympics' Strangest Moments,* London: Robson Books, 2004

Tuleja, Tad, *Fabulous Fallacies,* New York: Harmony Books, 1982

Vankin, Jonathan and Whalen, John, *Based On A True Story,* Chicago: Chicago Review Press, 2005

Walker, Barbara G., *Woman's Encyclopedia of Myths and Secrets,* San Francisco: Harper & Row, 1983

Wallace, Robert and the Editors of Time-Life Books, *World of Leonardo,* New York: Time, 1966

Wallace, Robert and the Editors of Time-Life Books, *World of Rembrandt,* New York: Time, 1968

Ward, Philip, *Panama Hats, Crocodile Tears and Other Common Fallacies,* New York: Barnes & Noble, 1993

Wecter, Dixon, *The Hero in America,* Michigan: The University of Michigan Press, 1963

Weir, Stephen, *History's Worst Decisions,* New York: Metro Books, 2009

West, Nigel, *A Thread of Deceit,* New York: Random House, 1985

Whitehouse, Arch, *Espionage and Counterespionage,* New York: Doubleday, 1964

Wiley, Mason and Bona, Damien, *Inside Oscar,* New York: Ballantine Books, 1988

Williams, Hywel, *Days That Changed The World,* London: Quercus, 2006

Wills, Gary, *What Jesus Meant,* New York: Penguin Books, 2007

Winter, Gordon and Kochman, Wendy, *Secrets of the Royals,* New York: St. Martin's Press: 1990

Wise, David and Ross, Thomas B., *The Invisible Government,* New York: Bantam Book, 1964

Wright, Mike, *What They Didn't Teach You About The 60s,* California: Presidio, 2001

Zich, Arthur, and the Time-Life eds., *The Rising Sun* (World War II), Alexandria: Time-Life Books, 1978

———*Mysteries of Mind, Space & Time,* Westport, Conn: H. S. Stuttman Inc., 1992

———*The New Encyclopedia Britannica,* 15th Ed., Chicago: Encyclopedia Britannica, 1994

———*The Truth About History,* New York: Barnes & Noble, 2007